School Leadership in the 21st Century
Second edition

Education reform continues to be a dominating feature of education in the UK and many other countries throughout the world. As a result of this, it is now more important than ever that headteachers and other schoolteachers develop the skills that will enable them to lead and manage their responsibilities effectively.

In *School Leadership in the 21st Century* all the major aspects of school leadership are discussed, including:

- Strategic and ethical dimensions of leadership
- Leading and managing change
- Leading and managing staff in high performance schools
- Information for student learning and organisational learning
- Transformation of schools in the 21st century

The authors of this completely updated and revised edition have addressed the new standards and competency frameworks, making this an essential read for all headteachers and aspiring headteachers on NPQH or LPSH courses and anyone else with an interest in school leadership.

Brent Davies is Professor of Leadership Development at the University of Hull.
Linda Ellison is Senior Lecturer in Educational Leadership at the University of Nottingham.
Christopher Bowring-Carr is a Lecturer and Consultant in Educational Leadership and Management at the University of Hull.

School Leadership in the 21st Century

Second edition

Developing a strategic approach

Brent Davies, Linda Ellison and
Christopher Bowring-Carr

RoutledgeFalmer
Taylor & Francis Group
LONDON AND NEW YORK

First published 1997
by Routledge
This edition published 2005
by RoutledgeFalmer
2 Park Square, Milton Park, Abingdon, Oxon OX14 4RN

Simultaneously published in the USA and Canada
by Routledge
270 Madison Ave, New York, NY 10016

RoutledgeFalmer is an imprint of the Taylor & Francis Group

Typeset in Palatino by
Keystroke, Jacaranda Lodge, Wolverhampton
Printed and bound in Great Britain by
TJ International Ltd, Padstow, Cornwall

British Library Cataloguing in Publication Data
A catalogue record for this book is available from the British Library

Library of Congress Cataloging in Publication Data
A catalog record for this book has been requested

ISBN 10: 0–415–27951–8 (hbk)
ISBN 10: 0–415–27952–6 (pbk)

ISBN 13: 978– 0–415–27951–2 (hbk)
ISBN 13: 978– 0–415–27952–9 (pbk)

This book is dedicated to
Mike Billingham and Max Sawatzki,
outstanding educationalists

Contents

Figures

Tables

Notes on contributors

Dr Brent Davies is Professor of Leadership Development at the University of Hull. He is also Special Professor at the University of Nottingham and a Faculty Member of the Centre on Educational Governance at the University of Southern California. Brent spent the first ten years of his career working as a teacher in South London. He then moved into higher education as an authority on leadership and management development programmes for senior and middle leaders in schools. He was Director of the International MBA in School Leadership at Leeds Metropolitan University, moving to the University of Lincolnshire and Humberside to establish the first Chair in Educational Leadership and create the International Educational Leadership Centre in Lincoln. He moved to the University of Hull in 2000 to establish the International Leadership Centre. In 2004 he moved within the University to become a research professor in leadership development at the University of Hull Business School. He has published extensively with 16 books and 60 articles on leadership and management, including 'The New Strategic Direction and Development of the School' (2003, RoutledgeFalmer), 'The Handbook of Educational Leadership and Management' (2003, Pearson), and 'The Essentials of School Leadership' (2005, Sage). He has two current research interests: strategy and strategic leadership, focusing on creating the strategically focused school; the emerging public/private sector in education in the USA and the UK.

Linda Ellison is a Senior Lecturer in Educational Leadership at the University of Nottingham where she leads programmes in educational leadership and management and is Director of the Postgraduate Studies International Summer School. She has worked with a great many UK LEAs, heads, teachers and schools and with school district staff, principals and teachers in a variety of countries such as Chile, Australia, Canada and Hong Kong. Linda has a number of national and international research projects in the area of school leadership, such as those on the strategically focused school, home–school links via the school office, and heads' lives. She has written a wide range of books and papers on school leadership and management and is joint series editor of Routledge's School Leadership and Management series.

Christopher Bowring-Carr taught English in England, Italy, Kuwait, and Turkey. He was an education officer in Leicester, a principal in the USA, and an HMI for 15 years. He then moved to Northern Ireland, was a research officer at the University of Ulster, and after that was a consultant, and a tutor on MA and MBA courses with the Open University, the University of Leicester and the University of Hull. He has now retired and lives in Madeira.

Mick Brookes is Headteacher of Sherwood Junior School in Nottinghamshire. Previously he was Head of a Primary School in Lincolnshire (1978–1985). Mick also worked on secondment with the LMS team in Nottinghamshire (1993/4) and was National President of the NAHT (2000/1). He is currently a national consultant for School Finance.

Professor Brian J. Caldwell is Managing Director of Educational Transformations Pty Ltd in Melbourne, Australia and Associate Director of iNet (Global) (International Networking for Educational Transformation) of the Specialist Schools Trust in England. From 1998 to 2004 he served as Dean of Education at the University of Melbourne. His previous appointments include Head of Education Policy and Management at the University of Melbourne and Head of Teacher Education and Dean of Education at the University of Tasmania. He has served as Wei Lun Visiting Professor at the Chinese University of Hong Kong, and Visiting Professor at the National College for School Leadership in England. His international work over the last decade includes presentations, projects and other professional assignments in or for 32 countries on six continents. He is co-author of books that have helped guide educational reform in a number of countries, most notably the trilogy on self-managing schools.

Dr Barbara J. Davies has extensive experience in primary school leadership and management. After graduating from Oxford University, Barbara taught in primary schools in Oxfordshire, West Germany and West Sussex. She took up her first headship in West Sussex followed by her second in North Yorkshire. She was a Senior Lecturer at Bishop Grosseteste College in Lincoln, working in initial teacher education before specialising in leadership and management in the primary sector at the University of Lincolnshire and Humberside, where she was a course leader for a Masters degree in leadership and learning. Subsequently she returned to primary headship in Nottinghamshire before taking up her current post as Headteacher of Washingborough Foundation Primary School in Lincolnshire. Barbara gained a Masters degree in Educational Management in 1994 and completed her Doctorate in Educational Leadership at the University of Hull in 2004. Her thesis is focused on developing the strategically focused primary school. She has published a number of books and articles in the field of educational leadership.

Viv Garrett is a consultant in educational leadership and was, until recently, Principal Lecturer in the Division of Education at Sheffield Hallam University. Her special areas of expertise are professional development for school leadership and the leadership and management of change. She has extensive experience in these fields both in the UK and overseas. She is a tutor on the National Professional Qualification for Headship and the Leading from the Middle Programmes for the National College for School Leadership, and is also working with the General Teaching Council on the development of the Teacher Learning Academy.

Max Sawatzki worked as a popular and successful international consultant on effective leadership until his sudden death in 1998.

Peter Smith taught in Nottinghamshire for 37 years, 19 as a primary school headteacher. Following extensive work with other schools through the school's Beacon role, Peter now works as an External Adviser and NPQH tutor in the East Midlands.

1 Introduction

Brent Davies

Since the publication seven years ago of *School Leadership for the 21st Century*, considerable change has enveloped the educational world. In the UK, the elections of the 'New' Labour Government have resulted in many policy initiatives and structural changes impacting on school leadership. Most significantly, the creation of the National College for School Leadership (NCSL) has given both a national focus and national resources to the development of leadership in schools. Linda Ellison and I have been pleased with the popularity of the book and gratified by the number of reprints. When the publishers Routledge (now RoutledgeFalmer) invited us to write a second edition we were delighted. However, the delight turned to apprehension with the realisation that it was not possible to rewrite the original edition but it was necessary to create a completely new book with different chapters and new insights. This we have done and we have renamed the book *School Leadership in the 21st Century*, engaging our good friend and colleague Christopher Bowring-Carr to assist us. Sadly, two of the contributors to the first edition have met untimely deaths through illness. Mike Billingham and Max Sawatzki were outstanding educators and in recognition of that we have dedicated this rewritten book to them. Max's outstanding chapter is the only one retained in full from the first book; it was, and remains, a classic.

'THE LEADERSHIP DEBATE' AND OTHER CHANGES

This new book is set against the backcloth of significant developments in the field. The NCSL has put forward 'Ten school leadership propositions' (National College for School Leadership 2001) which demonstrate a significant broadening of the government's previous views on effective leadership. The wider academic community, both in the UK and overseas, has produced an increasing number of volumes on every type of leadership. We do not intend to replicate every one of these many perspectives but to take some key issues both in the type of leadership that the twenty-first-century school leader needs to deploy and in the specific areas in which leadership is needed.

THE STRUCTURE OF THE BOOK

We have organised the book into four parts. Part I aims to provide readers with a framework to review their own leadership and the leadership necessary to develop their schools. It does not replicate the discussions about the different theories of leadership but seeks to explore three perspectives that leaders should have and that they need to develop with others in the school. The first perspective, which is explored in Chapter 2, is that strategic leadership, by most standard definitions, is forward-looking, seeking a new future for the school and, to achieve this, the leaders in the school need to develop a strategic view and strategic leadership skills. As well as taking a strategic view, leaders are faced with a very turbulent environment and have to make many decisions under pressure. In this environment it is vital that decision-making is based on our second perspective, a sound ethical basis. To this end the ethical dimension of leadership is examined in Chapter 3. Concluding this first part of the book, we draw on the competence and competency movements within leadership development in Chapter 4. While the competency framework has been a dominant theme over the past ten years with the adoption of that framework by many NCSL courses, it is not without its critics. Although we consider that it is not the only framework for effective leadership, it remains a core one. Of particular value is exploring the distinction between competence, competency and the much-used term 'standards'.

Part II considers some of the major leadership challenges that schools face and activities which must take place. The first challenge is that of leading the organisation in a sustainable way, not just in the short term but also over the medium to long term. In Chapter 5 the concepts of strategy and strategic thinking as well as traditional concepts of planning are reviewed in a completely new framework for establishing the strategic direction of the school. This chapter is focused on what should be done in order to establish a strategic process and approach which will enable strategic leadership to flourish. It is inevitable that any strategic process that takes the school from its present place to some future position will involve a considerable amount of change. How to lead and manage this change process is therefore the focus of Chapter 6. This is followed, in Chapter 7, by a key insight into how we can lead and manage staff to achieve the aims and objectives of the school.

Part III addresses the key issue of learning and the support for learning. Chapter 8 seeks ways to avoid the problem of seeing leadership and management as an end in itself and focuses on leadership in relation to the core purpose of schools, learning. The informational approach used by schools should promote deep fundamental learning rather than simple test results. The next two chapters look at using information to support learning in secondary and primary schools. The maxim 'assessment *for* learning' rather than 'assessment *of* learning' is critical in Chapter 9, while Chapter 10 focuses on information for organisational learning. Chapter 11 then addresses how learning and the school are resourced by considering school finance. While many school leaders may consider the 'fair funding' concept to be an oxymoron and may feel that there is little room for manoeuvre within current fiscal restraints, we do not consider that to be an accurate picture. The advent of multiple initiatives from central government has resulted in a bidding culture where resource management has become both more significant and more complex, requiring leadership as well as management dimensions.

The final section, as befits a book on leadership, is a profound and insightful chapter which considers the future of the education system by examining the need for transformation and the components of a blueprint for the future of schools.

In meeting the challenge of creating the new book we have kept true to the ambitions which we had for the first book. Those were to make it both useful and accessible to practitioners, to provide leaders in schools with insights and perspectives that would assist them in leading their schools in a positive and creative way, and to be futures-orientated, seeing leadership, like education, as a broadening and enlightening process and not a reductionist managerial agenda. The way the book has been received by leaders in schools has been very encouraging.

Part I

The dimensions of leadership

2 The strategic dimensions of leadership

Barbara J. Davies and Brent Davies

CHARACTERISTICS OF STRATEGIC LEADERS

Brent Davies, in Chapter 5 of this book, argues for the development of the strategically focused school. Key to that strategic focus is the quality of the strategic leadership in the school. If we are to support and enhance the development of strategic leadership in schools, we need to be able to build a framework of understanding of what strategic leadership might comprise. This chapter will consider what organisational abilities and individual characteristics can be associated with strategic leadership. The chapter does not purport to describe a new form of leadership, such as transformational or instructional leadership, but analyses the strategic element in the leadership repertoire. It identifies characteristics of individuals who are successfully undertaking a strategic leadership role or skill. However, there is a difficulty in isolating out the strategic element of good leadership as B. Davies (2003: 303) has identified:

> The difficulty in reviewing the literature, or interpreting the results of my current research, is that it is not always easy to distinguish the characteristics of 'good leadership' from those of 'strategic leadership'.

The second difficulty to consider is whether we are talking only about strategic leadership being associated with the formal leader of an organisation, or about a broader base of individuals who contribute leadership insights to the strategic process. In this chapter, we recognise that there may be a number of individuals in an organisation who demonstrate a strategic perspective or ability. Thus, we take the view of distributed leadership (Bennett *et al.* 2003) which involves several individuals within the organisation being involved with the strategy.

With these concerns in mind, the chapter attempts to draw out those distinctive strategic elements of leadership. Strategy, as defined in Chapter 5, encompasses direction-setting, broad aggregated agendas, a perspective to view the future and a template against which to evaluate current activities. Leadership is defined by Bush and Glover (2003: 10) as:

> a process of influence leading to the achievement of desired purposes. It involves inspiring and supporting others towards the achievement of a vision for the school which is based on clear personal and professional values.

What successful activities or behaviours do strategic leaders engage in? To facilitate discussion, we put forward nine factors associated with strategic leadership. These are, first, those abilities to undertake organisational activity and, second, individual abilities.

Strategic leaders have the organisational ability to:

- be strategically oriented;
- translate strategy into action;
- align people and organisations;
- determine effective strategic intervention points;
- develop strategic capabilities.

Strategic leaders have personal characteristics which display:

- dissatisfaction or restlessness with the present;
- absorptive capacity;
- adaptive capacity;
- leadership wisdom.

Each factor will be considered in turn.

Strategic leaders have the ability to be strategically oriented

This quality involves the ability to consider both the long-term future (Adair 2002, Beare 2001, Boisot 2003, Stacey 1992), seeing the bigger picture, as well as understanding the current contextual setting of the organisation. Strategic orientation is the ability to link long-range visions and concepts to daily work. Korac-Kakabadse and Kakabadse (1998: 9) suggest that 'visionary leadership is transformational by nature, and as such, quite different from planning, which is a managerial or a transactional process'. Javidon (1991), quoted in Korac-Kakabadse and Kakabadse (1998: 10), suggests that 'visioning depends on understanding existing realities (culture, history, formative context) and developing a clear sense of direction for the organisation'.

However, it is necessary to treat the concept of vision or visioning with caution. Seeking to analyse trends and their meaning for the future of the organisation can be seen as a good thing if it engenders debate and if future scenarios become the basis for strategic conversations. Buley (1998: 216) issues a timely warning when discussing the work of Schwenk (1997):

> he argues that a powerful vision can actually do damage to an organization. In his view, by creating and communicating a clear vision, and by creating conditions which require his 'followers' to commit themselves to that vision, a leader is in danger of imposing uniformity of thinking and of stifling healthy debate which can have dire consequences. . . . Imposed values, he argues, destroy dissent and discussion which are essential to creative decision making.

The importance of creating the strategy *with* others, and not just communicating it to others, may be the critical skill that strategic leaders deploy in determining the strategic direction of the organisation, (Boal and Hooijberg 2001; Kakabadse *et al.* 1998). Strategic orientation can be considered to be the establishment of an outward-looking organisation, which builds an understanding of possible future directions, and involves engaging in strategic conversations and debate to focus on the most appropriate direction and approach.

Strategic leaders have the ability to translate strategy into action

In addition to strategic leaders leading the creation of an appropriate strategy for the organisation is the need to translate strategy into action by converting it into operational terms. Kaplan and Norton (2001) argue that this can be done by 'strategy maps' and 'balanced scorecards' and suggest that such approaches 'provide a framework to describe and communicate strategy in a consistent and insightful way' (p. 10). What strategic leaders are able to do is step back and articulate the main features of the current organisation, the strategic architecture of the school, and lead others in defining what the future of the school and the new architecture will be. This is a process that Tichy and Sharman (1993) call the rearchitecturing stage, which involves identifying a series of projects that need to be undertaken to move the organisation from its current to its future state. Tichy and Sharman (1993) put forward a three-stage process that strategic leaders are able to undertake, the components of which are:

- awakening;
- envisioning;
- rearchitecturing.

The awakening stage involves building an agreement within the school that a continuation of the current way of working is inadequate if it wants to be effective in the future. This may involve the process, described in Chapter 5, of enhancing participation and motivation to understand the necessity for change, through strategic conversations. The envisioning stage is building a clear and understandable picture of what this new way of operating looks like. This may initially involve the creation of strategic intent (Hamel and Prahalad 1994) and building the capacity to achieve it. Once this has been completed then the new architecture of the school will emerge and be the organisational basis for action.

Many schools have strategies that are written in different sorts of formal plans. Changing those strategies into action is very difficult. The key assessment of a leader's ability to operate in the strategic domain may be to ask staff in the school how this week's or this term's activities fit into the strategic plan or direction of the school. If the teacher can articulate, in broad terms, where the school is going and what its priorities are, then strategy will have been translated into action. If not, the gap between strategy and action will remain. In our research, with leaders in schools, those who are successful at leading strategy place a large emphasis on strategic awareness and action.

Strategic leaders have the ability to align people and organisations

This ability involves aligning individuals, or the school as a whole, to a future organisational state or position (Davies, B. 2003; Gratton 2000; Gioia and Thomas 1996). A key element of this ability is to encourage commitment through shared values (Boal and Bryson 1988). It would seem that the leader's own personal values and ideas are paramount in this process and the leadership skill involves making it real for others. Leaders therefore need to understand themselves and the values they hold and be able to nurture quality communication. DePree (1993: 99) classifies this 'lavish communication' found in organisations with cultures 'which promote truth and do not suppress or limit the distribution of information'. Stacey (1992) believes that strategy is as much about the creation of meaning for all those in the school as it is about the establishment of direction. Critical in this creation of meaning is the art of strategic conversation and dialogue. Making a vision real for others needs skills of conviction and passion. It involves emotion. Boal and Hooijberg (2001: 516) state that 'strategic leadership focuses on the creation of meaning and purpose for the organisation'. Strategic leadership therefore is concerned with the 'development of the organisation as a whole which includes its changing aims and capabilities' (Selznick 1984: 5).

It is important to find a way to build a connection between thinking and action. The concept of a learning organisation helps here: an organisation of people who are attuned to changes and able to respond to them have valuable insights into how individuals and groups learn and how to convert this knowledge into organisational action. Pietersen (2002: 181) suggests that all learning organisations have developed a 'culture of giving' which 'fosters teamwork, experimentation, learning and knowledge sharing'.

More recent leadership theories focus on transformational and visionary leadership, and they emphasise the interpersonal processes between leaders and followers. Boal and Hooijberg (2001: 526) suggest that research into transformational leaders stresses 'such factors as intellectual stimulation' and 'inspiration'. Cheng (2002: 53) found two recurring elements of leadership in various definitions: 'first leadership is related to the process of influencing others' behaviour; and second, it is related to goal development and achievement.' This view is reflected in the previous discussion on the process of strategy: leaders need the skills to be able to influence people and their actions and they need to direct those actions through setting goals and creating meanings. This has resonance with the perspective of transformational leadership, where a leader is proactive about the vision and mission, shaping members' beliefs, values and attitudes while developing options for the future. Bass (1985) identified that transformational leaders, in educational settings, motivate people to do more than they are originally expected to do in any of the following ways:

> Raising their level of awareness . . . about the importance and value of designated outcomes. . . . Getting them to transcend their own self-interest for the sake of the team, organisation or large polity. . . . Expanding their portfolio of needs and wants from low level (e.g. physiological or safety needs) to high level (e.g. esteem or self-actualization needs).
>
> (Bass 1985: 76)

Alignment is about altering attitudes, values and beliefs, all of which influence the culture of an organisation to unify its sense of purpose and direction.

Strategic leaders have the ability to determine effective intervention points

Strategic leaders are able to define the key moment for strategic change in organisations. This is a concept that Burgleman and Grove (1996) call strategic inflection points. These are critical points in an organisation's development when it is possible to develop new visions, create new strategies and move in new directions. We would call these strategic intervention, or opportunity, points. The key here is knowing not only what to do strategically but also precisely when to intervene and change direction. Boal and Hooijberg (2001: 518) pose the question 'does strategic leadership matter?' Their answer is:

> Strategic leadership does indeed matter . . . it seems to us the real question is not whether it matters but rather under what conditions, when, how and on what criteria.

They believe that *when* a leader makes a decision is just as important as *what* decision or action is taken, a concept considered by B. Davies (2003) through the discussion about the double s-curve. Bartunek and Necochea (2000) define 'Kairos' time as the ability to take the right action at a critical time. Boal and Hooijberg (2001: 528) suggest that strategic inflection points create a 'kairotic moment' and it is during these 'moments that learning and change are possible if only the leader possesses the discernment to take notice and the wisdom to act'. B. Davies' (2003) analysis of the double s-curve and the appropriate point to make the 'strategic leap' to a new way of operating is a useful model here. It may be that both insight and intuition play a significant role in making the appropriate judgement. Strategic leaders, therefore, have the ability to define not only *what* strategically to change but also *when* strategically to change.

Strategic leaders have the ability to develop strategic capabilities

Prahalad and Hamel (1990) use the term 'core competencies' while Stalk *et al*. (1992) use the term 'strategic capabilities'. The focus of much of central government activities in most Western economies is to raise educational standards by measuring student performance in annual tests. The danger of this approach is that it focuses activity on short-term targets. Thus, learning how to teach with the latest 'literacy pack' from the government may improve teachers' specific skills but for sustainability the organisation will need to develop deeper strategic capabilities or core competencies. These can be illustrated with the analogy of a tree, where the branches represent the short-term abilities and the roots are the underpinning fundamental capabilities of the school.

If the school is to develop and be sustainable in the longer term then it needs to develop strategic capabilities. Examples of these would be the fundamental understanding of teaching and learning, rather than the ability to deliver the latest curriculum innovation; a problem-solving culture rather than a blame culture for the staff; assessment *for* learning rather than assessment *of* learning. Creativity in problem-solving and team-working could also be considered resources that give the school deep-seated strategic capabilities or abilities.

These abilities enable the school to meet new challenges successfully by reconfiguring existing abilities and resources rather than having to seek new ones. The questions that strategic leaders ask are: 'What strategic capabilities do I need to sustain and develop for the future?' as well as 'How do I meet current challenges?' By focusing on strategic capabilities, leaders position themselves and their organisations to be sustainable and successful in the longer term.

Strategic leaders have a dissatisfaction or restlessness with the present

This restlessness involves what Senge (1990) describes as 'creative tension' which emerges from seeing clearly where one wishes to be, one's vision, and facing the truth about one's current reality. Strategic leaders are able to envision the 'strategic leap' that an organisation wants to make, while acting as passionate advocates for change. Strategic leaders have the ability to live with the reality that the organisational culture may not be as forward-thinking as they are. They have the ability to live with the ambiguity of not being able to change the organisation fast enough, with the ability to maintain the restlessness for change and improvement. Individuals who are able to do this challenge current ideas and processes to seek better ideas and processes.

Strategic leaders have absorptive capacity

Cohen and Levinthal (1990) define absorptive capacity as the ability to absorb new information and assimilate it, learn from it and, importantly, to apply it to new ends. Hambrick (1989) argues that strategic leadership occurs in an environment embedded in ambiguity, complexity and information overload. It is important therefore for strategic leaders to recognise new information, analyse it and apply it to new outcomes; leaders need the ability to learn. Boal and Hooijberg (2001: 517) also call this 'absorptive capacity' and argue that leaders 'have a unique ability to change or reinforce existing action patterns' within the organisation. Strategic leaders should, therefore, create an organisational context in which learning can take place. This may make use of Argyris and Schön's (1978) double-loop learning. What is important is that strategic leaders filter out the unimportant and make sense of the important for themselves and their organisations. The critical nature of their position often means that their interpretation of reality determines patterns of action within the organisation.

Strategic leaders have adaptive capacity

Black and Boal (1996) and Hambrick (1989) define the ability to change as 'adaptive capacity'. Sanders (1998: 5) supports this view that strategic leaders need the ability to change and learn through asserting that 'mastering chaos, complexity and change' requires new ways of 'seeing and thinking'. Whittington (2001: 43) suggests that 'leaders need an enduring sense of purpose and a continuous sense of motivation'. This can be seen in Hitt, Keats and DeMaries' (1998) term of strategic flexibility. In an era of innovation and continuous learning, where success may depend on a flexible strategic response, this is particularly important and may favour the emergent strategy or the strategic intent approach. Linking to B. Davies' (2003) concept of 'strategic opportunism', leaders position themselves to take significant opportunities as they adapt to new information in a responsive and proactive way. Leaders can adapt and lead new strategic directions for the organisation if they have cognitive flexibility linked to a mindset that welcomes and accepts change.

Strategic leaders have leadership wisdom

Wisdom may simply be defined as the capacity to take the right action at the right time. In a perceptive presentation to the 2002 International Thinking Skills Conference, Robert Sternberg articulated that leaders need wisdom because:

- they need creative abilities to come up with ideas;
- they need analytical abilities to decide whether ideas are good ideas;
- they need practical abilities to make their ideas functional and to convince others of the value of their ideas;
- they need wisdom to balance the effects of ideas on themselves, others and institutions in both the short and long run.

In addressing the nature of wisdom in more depth, he established that wisdom is:

- successful intelligence;
- balancing of interests;
- balancing of time-frames;
- mindful infusion of values;
- balancing of responses to the environment;
- application of knowledge for the common good.

Further, he established that for successful intelligence there is a need to combine practical intelligence, analytical intelligence and emotional intelligence. This provides an insightful and challenging set of criteria for leaders to develop in order to deploy strategic choices with wisdom and effectiveness. Throughout this discussion about wisdom, the personal qualities of leaders have been mentioned. To these we could add, for example, the values they hold, the ability to inspire and stimulate, social intelligence, the ability to be passionate. All of these qualities affect the way a leader learns and is able to change. Boal and Hooijberg (2001: 532) suggest that 'most leadership researchers agree that leaders need to have such important interpersonal skills as empathy, motivation, and communication'. Bennett (2000: 3) expands the importance of personal values:

> If moral leadership is to be exercised and pedagogy re-engineered with any degree of success, then future leaders will need a firm set of personal values. No doubt many will have their own lists, but integrity, social justice, humanity, respect, loyalty and a sharp distinction between right and wrong, will all need to be included. Strategic relationships will soon flounder unless such a value system is held with conviction and exercised on a regular consistent basis.

Although not specifically included in Bennett's comprehensive list, social intelligence is important for strategic leadership because the processes of decision-making, solution implementation and organisational improvement are rarely free of emotion. Social intelligence includes having a thorough understanding of the social context, and is defined by Gardner (1985: 239) as the ability 'to notice and make distinctions among other individuals . . . in particular among their moods, temperaments, motivations and intentions'. Thus, a key component of social intelligence is the ability to discern emotion both in self and in others. Gardner identifies this as both intra- and inter-personal intelligence. The ability to connect the involvement of others and to resolve conflicts will be increasingly vital in a context of developing strategic relationships and finding creative solutions. Bennett (2000: 4) also identifies the importance of strength and courage, stating that 'visionary projects, delivered with passion, will fail unless the leader has the ability to counter adversaries and remain confident until the conclusion has been reached'.

CONCLUSION

Much of the debate about leadership has been focused on transformational leadership with an increasing emphasis on instructional leadership which has been re-branded as 'learning-centred leadership'. Although these are very significant perspectives, there is a danger that learning-centred leadership will be concerned with current approaches and outcomes. While we would support this as it is the core rationale for a school's existence and purpose, we would argue that effective learning-centred leadership needs to be set in a broader organisational and strategic context to be both sustainable and effective in the longer term. To this end, the development of strategic leadership abilities and characteristics plays a significant part. A model of strategic leadership therefore can take the form illustrated in Figure 2.1.

If schools are to sustain student performance and move on to deep learning, rather than just addressing test-based short-term agendas, we need to develop leadership capability that has a strategic dimension. This chapter suggests a framework for identifying the components of that strategic dimension for leadership development.

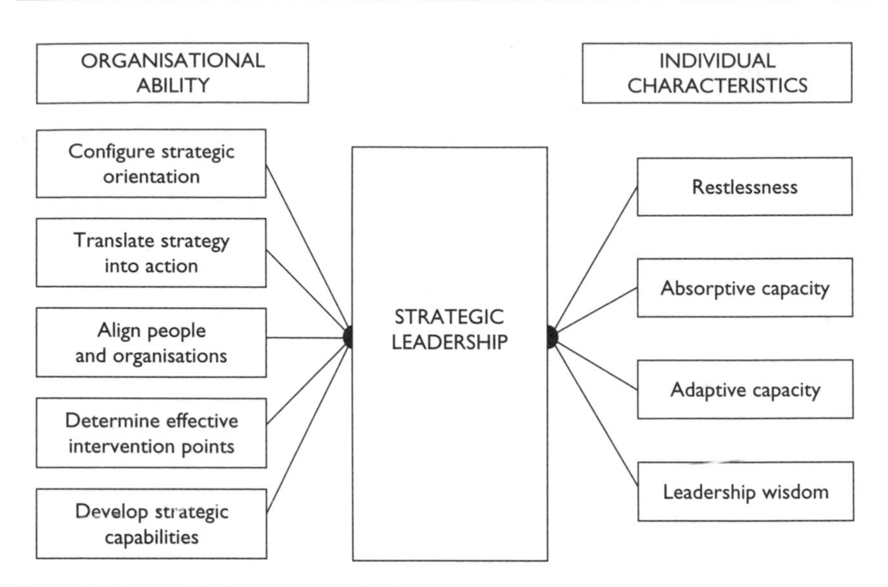

Figure 2.1 A model of strategic leadership

ACKNOWLEDGEMENTS

Thanks are expressed to Carfax Publishing for giving permission for using 'Strategic Leadership' published in *School Leadership and Management*: 2004, 24 (1) as the basis for this chapter.

RESEARCH SPONSOR

The concepts in this chapter were developed as one part of the National College for School Leadership (England) funded research project on developing strategy and strategic leadership in schools. This project aims at exploring in primary (elementary) and secondary (high) schools and special schools the strategic sustainability and leadership aspects of educational organisations.

3 The ethical dimension of leadership

Christopher Bowring-Carr

In this chapter, I look at the ethical dimension of leadership that needs to be at the heart of a school or college, how that dimension might be achieved, and how a school or college might operate if it follows logically and consistently the demands of that ethical imperative. Let us begin by establishing how the term 'ethics' is being used in this book. *The Concise Encyclopedia of Philosophy* (Craig 2000: 256) states:

> What is ethics? First, the systems of value and custom instantiated in the lives of particular groups of human beings are described as the ethics of these groups.

From this quotation we can see that a group of people, everyone in a school or college for example, demonstrates through their values and customs what the ethical code is to which they adhere. Sergiovanni (1992: 102) puts it this way:

> When purpose, social contract, and local school autonomy become the basis of schooling, two important things happen. The school is transformed from an organisation to a covenantal community, and the basis of authority changes from an emphasis on bureaucratic and psychological authority to moral authority. To put it another way, the school changes from a secular organisation to a sacred organisation, from a mere instrument designed to achieve certain ends to a virtuous enterprise.

Let us look at some of the characteristics of the ethical leader, but before doing so it needs to be said that a school will not last very long with unethical leadership, but it can, unfortunately, last quite a long time with an ethically neutral leadership in place. The school, in those circumstances, becomes an efficient processor of people. The message in this chapter is that a very active, up-front stance on a clear ethical code is essential if the school is to be a true community of learners.

What are ethical leaders, or leaders of ethically focused schools? They are people who have, over time, refined and pared from the many experiences encountered in and out of school, a quite small set of values that guide and permeate every action. There is no separation between personal and educational ethics. Above all else, they will be caring people working to establish a caring community. They will be compassionate, looking to protect and honour people. They will understand that there should be no forced choice between the community and the individual because only through the happiness and fulfilment of the individual can there be a contented community, and a contented community will enable the individual to flourish. They will be looking for ways in which to help every individual's growth and development, and enabling every individual to make choices informed by virtue. They will eschew competition, putting interdependence and mutual help in its place. They will not suffer from the current infatuation with efficiency, and will shun the rush to measurement. They will not ask, 'Has Susan learnt X?' but rather, 'What has Susan learnt, what range of learning approaches has she used, and has that learning helped her to grow?' They will know that to be human is to be fallible, and therefore, not being omniscient themselves, will joyfully accept the humanness of others. They know that there will be times when holding on to the basic values will be very tough indeed, but there is no alternative.

What the leader does can be summarised as follows:

- initiating dialogues, discussions, debates on ethical issues, starting with the collegium's establishment of its bed-rock values;
- setting up and maintaining an atmosphere of open challenge and questioning;
- dispersing leadership; there need to be project leaders from among the staff and students carrying out action research into all aspects of the school's life;
- establishing and helping to maintain an active school/community council, made up of staff, students, parents and other members of the community. Such a council has to have real tasks to do, and needs a budget. The council is the voice of the community;
- articulating and manifesting the ethical imperatives of the community in talking to parents, staff, students, all outsiders;
- showing through day-to-day activities what is really important in the place;
- showing that as learning is the core activity, then ethics are intimately bound up with what helps learning;
- standing up for the community against arbitrary diktats from local or central government, protecting it as far as possible against the wilder and frequently contradictory demands of government;
- demonstrating that the community is interdependent;

- showing and asking for total commitment;
- being flexible and living happily with ambiguity within the established ethics;
- being passionate in advocating and celebrating an unpredictable variety of learning outcomes;
- demonstrating at all times that caring for one another is the only way a community can thrive.

The code, the covenant, that informs every activity in the school has to be constructed by the group, with the leader taking the role of gatherer and enabler. An ethical code is not handed down, cannot be taken off the shelf, and cannot be imposed by an outside authority. It is the result of continuous deliberation, but it cannot merely be deliberation. The code of ethics emerges from discussion of what is, for the institution, the bedrock of values and customs, and the values and custom ('how we do things around here') are manifest in and reify the ethics. It is in the organisation and resolution of these discussions that the leader plays a vital part. Let there be no mistaking the difficulty of this process. Leaders rarely get the chance to start with a *tabula rasa*. They are usually faced with a very disparate group of people, including some who love the profession and want to continue to expand and grow and others who merely want a quiet life, to be told what to do, and to get out at 4pm relatively unscathed. Some will be actively against any change and overtly or covertly will do anything in their power to subvert the leader and the ideas. The ethically driven leader will maintain momentum whatever the difficulties. The focus at first will be on those who want to join in. Over time, others will join and slowly all but the few will come to work in the new ways. Eventually, through age or weariness or the desire to find a quieter way of life, the last few will drift away or be so isolated by the remainder of the community that their force will be spent.

The leader creates an atmosphere of trust, in which all in the organisation can feel free to argue, propose, question, and challenge. The confident leader encourages dispersed leadership so that anyone can form a sub-group, investigate a particular aspect of the school's life, research an abstruse point, and then present the findings to the wider group. The leader then has to judge when the discussions have gone on long enough, bring together the disparate ideas, and then articulate the refined essence of what has been said. However, such a dialogue is not, must not be, a one-off event. Life changes too rapidly. Every aspect of the community's life, its values, its culture will be revisited and tested against the changing conditions. Further, that dialogue will not always be calm and reasonable. There will be conflict, but as long as that conflict occurs 'in trust', in an atmosphere which accepts diversity and argument, then the inevitable conflict will be creative. The aim is alignment, not conformity.

One forum for such discussions could be a Community Council. The term 'Community Council' is used rather than 'School Council' deliberately. I believe that in the twenty-first century, a school cannot do all it wants or ought to do for its students on its own. It needs to involve a network of people, some remote and connected to the school by email or video, and some closer, in the community from which the students come. I sketch out what I think education might be for in Chapter 8 and certainly involvement with a wide community is one aspect of a school's activities. In a Community Council there would be representatives from the students, staff, parents, and members of the community. It should have a number of functions in the day-to-day running of the school and in longer-term planning, but the centre of its remit would be to act as the conscience of the school, the place in which decisions are made on whether a course of action, a planned activity, or an individual's behaviour are within the ethical code of the school. In such a forum the leader's ethical stance would be very much to the fore. S/he would be the voice of the school, representing and articulating its best to the Council and hence to the school and community as a whole. It would be in this place that s/he would continually ask before any plan or decision was finalised: 'Is this in the best interests of our students? Does this further our learning?'

Underlying all these discussions is one essential activity; everyone in the school or college is participating in building a community of discourse. Only when the organisation has a community of discourse will there be a shared vocabulary, and only when there is a shared vocabulary will the group be able to articulate its values in the knowledge that all in the group mean the same thing when they talk of, at one level, an 'equitable sharing of resources', or at another level, 'profound learning'. In other words, until there is a community with a mutually agreed language, no one can be sure what one person means by 'happy', or 'learning' or 'work'. When the community of discourse is established, then the code of ethics can be agreed upon. Once it is agreed on, then the leader's role is to articulate and embody that code. The leader's role is to put into clear, unambiguous words the carefully thought-through aspirations of the institution. It is essential that whoever goes into the school, or meets representatives from the school in other places or encounters the school in any of its guises on video or through other media, consistently receives the same message as to what the school stands for, and the person who embodies and reinforces that steadiness is the leader. It is the leader who has the sensitivity to be aware if someone or some action is beginning to sound a note that does not fit with the ethical stance, and it is the leader who then has to intervene.

Achieving an ethical code with the community involved can be difficult. Too often the mores of the community can be in stark contrast to those that the school tries to adhere to. For instance, there are communities in which getting your retaliation in first is the norm – the school's stress on tolerance and gentleness can be seen as weakness. In fact, as experience in Northern Ireland and other troubled places has repeatedly shown, the ethics of the school can be in stark contrast to the ethics of the surrounding people. When such a situation occurs, then the school can do nothing but hold tenaciously to the core principles of care, gentleness and trust that give to the children a chance for emotional security. Too often sections of the wider community appear to lie or equivocate to suit a short-term political end. A school can never do so. Too often sections of the wider community break a promise. A school can never do so. And it is in such circumstances that the leader will be tested. Always acting as representative of the school, the leader will demonstrate over and over again the courage needed to stand for the conscience of the school.

What, for a school, is the starting point in the creation of a code of ethics? The school's central purpose is learning, and everyone in the school or college is a learner. Therefore, the attributes of learning must lie at the heart of the ethical system. In the simplest terms, in a school anything that helps or stimulates someone to learn is ethical. This statement is both very simple and very complex. It is the outworking of the statement that is complex; the concept is comparatively straightforward. It is quite simple to see that an underlying consistent system of justice, an equality of rights and an equitable access to resources are the bedrock of that covenant on which the organisation is built. Overlaying those foundations are such things as cheerfulness, fairness, optimism – approaches to life which invite learners to join together in a mutually supportive community.

One of the attributes of learning is that its outcomes can rarely be mandated. By its nature, learning, by the individual or by the collective, is unpredictable, so if the base for the ethical code of a school is learning, then the leader must be able to live at ease with ambiguity and uncertainty. The school which is formulaic and rigid in its surface demeanour is not a learning school. The leader manifests the flexibility necessary for learners to flourish.

So, at the heart of an ethical school is the school's deliberate construction, over time, of a code of ethics, and this construction is overseen and guided by the leader. The code embodies the ethos of the school. The 'Report of a Survey of Provision for Education for Mutual Understanding in Post-Primary Schools in Northern Ireland' (Education and Training Inspectorate 2000: 7) puts it well:

> A school's ethos does not emerge by chance. It is the result of consultation, careful planning, widespread support, and is lived by all. It takes on its own momentum, but, even in the best practice observed, it needs to be sustained by the school's continuous reaffirmation of its values.

We can, from this statement, derive a definition of 'ethos'. It is that ethical milieu within which young people and adults meet, learn and care for each other.

In a time of very considerable flux, it is essential that the school, and in particular the leader, articulates its code clearly. In previous generations, it was a reasonable assumption that all connected with the school shared a common set of values. These values changed only slowly and did not need careful scrutiny because society was settled and changed only slowly. Indeed, because there were these shared assumptions, the basic values were rarely mentioned. The outward trappings, the sort of behaviour which was expected, the types of clothes that were worn, the forms of greeting and the deference to position were what was emphasised, but the reasons for that way of behaving did not need articulation. Today, however, as is shown in other sections of this book, the rate of change increases exponentially, and that change affects not only the ways in which we live our lives, but fundamentally the ways in which we interact with one another. Therefore, a school needs frequently to re-articulate the code of ethics through which it conducts its business. For example, our understanding of what is entailed in learning is deepening and changing, and therefore we have to change the expectations within which we work in order to accommodate this 'new' learning. It is the role of the leader to sense when some aspect of the changing world makes a re-look at the code necessary, and then to enable a small group to investigate and advise.

There is a spectrum of schools which runs from what can best be termed the 'bureaucratic school' to the 'ethically focused school'. Clearly, there are a number of points along this spectrum; schools which are trying to move from the former to the latter position will take time to shed ways of working and attitudes which have become a part of the fabric over the years. The first type is characterised by being hierarchical, driven by sets of rules to which most in the institution have not contributed, and having an atmosphere in which there is little trust. Inspection and supervision are the main ways in which the day-to-day work of the school is controlled, and the teacher as technician 'delivers' the curriculum. That metaphor, of the teacher as postman, encapsulates all that is wrong with such a system. To 'deliver' is to have no control over the contents of what is delivered, or of its suitability for the individual learner. Such a position is at best ethically neutral.

The 'ethically focused' school is essentially collegial with shared aims, values and vision, and an acceptance that within those values and aims there will be many ways of achieving the school's goals. It is a community which has moved from dependency, which one finds in the autocratic school, through independence to interdependence. It is, as suggested above, a caring place, in which teachers genuinely look after the students and each other, and in which students grow to see that having a care for one's fellows is right. It is also a school which encourages everyone to have a 'voice', an articulated stake in the governance. Flecknoe (2001) uses the terms 'pupil-as-tourist' and 'pupil-as-citizen'. It is, of course, largely the ethos that causes each of those stances but, by establishing an invitational community, young people can be helped to change from one to the other. The former, the tourist, merely passes through the place with little regard for anything except his or her own benefit. The latter is involved, and is encouraged to become more involved. The 'pupil-as-citizen' is a learner and teacher, a mentor for other students, and is involved in the discourse through which the school operates. Hayes (1990: 2) puts it well:

> We draw most of our political concepts from those same Greeks. The dominant theme is that of citizenship. The citizen (polites), a badge of honour denoting entitlement to speak, to be consulted, to be heard before decisions affecting him were taken. And such is the significance of citizenship that only a foolish person could fail to participate. He was called 'idiotes', the loner, the non-political, the etymological forerunner of an 'idiot'.
>
> Greek citizenship, too, involved the concepts of 'aidos' and 'dike' – shame and respect. The force which kept the whole together was the moral pressure of respect for oneself and one's fellow citizens, and shame at falling short of the standards thus set.

Other features of the ethical school are that it is a questioning school, a reflective school. The leader will be the inspiration in that s/he will always be questioning, always seeking out a way of doing things which better enhances learning, and leading the reflective discourse that explores every aspect of the community's life. The school will have developed the habit of examining, regularly, all aspects of its day-to-day running, and the medium- and longer-term plans, seeking to ensure that at every point what is happening and what is being planned fit with the ethical picture that each member of the community has. It is a place in which not only the students are expected to learn, and thereby grow and change, but also all the adults in it as well. And this growth and change will mean that there is an easy acceptance that not always will everything be right first time, but that mistakes will be seen as potential growth points. The leader will demonstrate an ease with uncertainty, and a recognition that making a mistake is acceptable, provided that learning results from this, and provided that the mistake is not repeated.

The school will, however, also be a place which acknowledges that there are two sorts of mistake – 'above-the-waterline mistakes' and 'below-the-waterline mistakes'. The former are those sorts of mistake that affect the superficial workings of the place, but do no harm to anyone – for example, not filling in the register in the usual way, putting the date on the left-hand side of the page rather than the right, wearing coloured socks if the uniform suggests white. 'Below-the-waterline mistakes' are those which contravene the fundamental ethics, which hurt or have the potential to hurt, someone. So, a sarcastic remark, a dismissive comment on a piece of work, a racist or sexist slur or stance, a dismissive attitude towards colleagues – those would cut to the quick of the place and be unacceptable. Again, it is the leader who has, over time, helped the community sift through what is 'above-the-waterline' and what is 'below-the-waterline', and then has the responsibility of articulating that judgement.

That word, 'unacceptable' raises an important point. In an ethics-driven school the business of dealing with a serious error would be undertaken by the collegium, not by a 'line manager'. To suggest that such incidents should be dealt with by the collegium might seem naïve or even asking for the impossible. It is, however, exactly what the quotation from Hayes above is pointing to. It is my absolute conviction that once a mistake or an error of judgement is dealt with in a hierarchical way, then the basic quality of the institution will be impaired and it will revert towards the hierarchical school described above. The problem facing schools today is that so many agencies in the world outside the school believe that control, inspection, 'naming and shaming' are not only acceptable, but are essential ways to control the education system. It must be admitted that it is far more difficult to give trust when one is not trusted. However, the ethical organisation learns to trust itself, because it trusts everyone within it, and relies little on uninvolved outsiders to influence its proper self-regard.

As I have said, the ethically focused school has, at its heart, learning. There has, first, to be an agreement on what is meant by 'learning', and for the purposes of this chapter I will take a constructivist position. Such a position emphasises, *inter alia*, process and that means that the community recognises that good, warm but tough and challenging relationships are the basis for all deep learning. One of the major tasks for the community, therefore, is to ensure that those who in any way disrupt those relationships will feel, through the explicit values explicitly articulated, the disapproval of the community.

However, again because of the tight central control over what goes on in schools, there is another problem that the ethical school has to confront. The problem is that of lists. Barth (1990: 39) sums up the problem:

> This conception of school improvement has led to an extraordinary proliferation of lists. Lists of characteristics of the 'effective principal', the 'effective teacher', the 'effective school'; lists of minimal pupil competencies and of behavioural objectives for teachers; lists of new certification requirements, mandates, and regulations. The list logic has begotten a list sweepstake to see whose is the best list . . . the list logic

> of educational change seems simple, straightforward, and compelling. Its only flaw is that it does not seem to work very well.

He goes on, in developing that chapter, to point to the absolute need for there to be a 'learning community' in which all 'adults and children learn simultaneously and in the same place to think critically and analytically and to solve problems that are important to them' (ibid.: 43).

Part of the list mentality is the notion that there is one clear method to solve whatever problem the politicians are talking about today. Postman (1996), in a discussion of the false gods that bamboozle educators, quotes Mencken. That somewhat irascible commentator, in 1918, wrote:

> There is no sure-cure so idiotic that some superintendent of schools will not swallow it. The aim seems to be to reduce the whole teaching process to a sort of automatic reaction, to discover some master formula that will not only take the place of competence and resourcefulness in the teacher, but that will also create an artificial receptivity in the child.
>
> Postman 1996: 49

The ethical school, therefore, has to look to its own adults and students and work out the best learning and teaching strategies for that community and the best governance for it. The school will certainly come up with a list; we all need lists for shopping, for sending cards at Christmas, for preparing for a holiday, for shoring up the defences against imperfect memory. However, they are our lists, designed by us for our benefit. They are written in our language so that we understand them. They are not mandated by outsiders, to be used as a checklist against which we can be found to be at fault. In this chapter and in others we will suggest lists of possible activities or attributes. They are not mandatory, of course, but rather are there for the reader to choose from, adapt or ignore. The reader can make of them what he or she wills. We are not a hierarchy, but rather, it is to be hoped, we offer prompts and aids to deep learning.

It is ironic that we live in a country that has made the educational system into a rigid hierarchy, with that same hierarchy proclaiming that it is in favour of 'learning', seemingly unaware that shouting at people – telling them to learn and to learn in this particular way, to be tested by that particular test – is a futile exercise, and one that, as I explore in another chapter, leads to memorisation, not learning. As part of this manic central control which education has to suffer, there is an emphasis on specifying 'mandatory learning outcomes'. This is not the chapter for arguing that the phrase is an oxymoron. Rather, the argument here is that the ethical school has to recognise that as it is creating a garden, and is in the business of nurturing, metaphors from business or the factory are inappropriate. Through the deliberations mentioned earlier, the ethical school will establish that its main purpose is the development of learners, interdependent learners. It will, therefore, eschew the idea of specifying in mind-numbing detail the outcomes of learning. Rather it will look to ways of sustaining and encouraging learning by all in the community, removing any barriers that hinder the learning. 'Performance' and certainly not 'performance management' is not what is required; it is a vivid, wide and challenging range of demonstrations of learning that the school is looking to.

This learning does not take place in a vacuum. There must be a purpose for it and the crucial questions that schools will have to answer are: 'Why education?' 'What do we believe we are doing with and for these young people?' (A linear book is not the best way to describe a set of activities that needs to go on simultaneously. What sorts of learning will be enabled and encouraged, what sorts of ethics will inform everyday behaviour, how a definition of the purpose of the institution is arrived at – these and the other core values and aims of the collegium will be debated together, each overlapping and informing the other strands.) Too often, not only in the UK but elsewhere in the world, a good education has come to be equated with a successful economy. We have indeed been told that the purpose of schools is to prepare young people for the economy. This reductionist, and deeply depressing, argument is out-of-date. It belongs to the machine age, and that age is part of history. What we in the developed world need from the education system is the creative, self-starting and self-supporting, autonomous learner, emotionally intelligent, able to work in changing teams, and above all else, someone who enjoys learning for its own sake. Our schools are hampered in achieving those objectives. Indeed, in a recent longitudinal study of post-primary students in Northern Ireland undertaken by the National Foundation for Educational Research (Harland *et al.* 2000: 11), there is the statement:

> According to teachers, while a minority of 'more clued-in' pupils questioned the validity and relevance of their learning, a more mechanical compliance prevailed among the majority.

It might, cynically, be suggested that 'mechanical compliance' is what is wanted by the government. It is not an attitude, however, that is wanted if we are to have a civilised society.

So, what is education for? I would not suggest that I have all the answers, though in many of the chapters in this book we offer an outline of the range of what education should be undertaking. In part answer to the question, I said, earlier, that the ethical school community is characterised by caring. That caring cannot, in the longer term, be confined solely to the school. The sense of guardianship will extend to the community around the school. But a group cannot help to nurture itself and its immediate neighbours without looking further, and perhaps in that looking we can begin to see what education might be for. It might be something to do with helping to establish a world in which the disparities between rich and poor, between the powerful and powerless are fewer, in which the planet itself is better looked after, and in which power is ameliorated by compassion. The leadership in the ethical school has, as part of its role, the need for futures thinking. Bowring-Carr and West-Burnham (1997:136) write of the 'Steward of the Boundaries', and surely any look at what those boundaries of our world at present encompass would give purpose to our education system beyond the mere mechanical acquisition of information. The staff, early on in the establishment of the ethical community, need to look beyond the immediate and take into account the forces that will be affecting our children in the next thirty to forty years. It needs to be able to demonstrate how any activity in school fits in with the larger view. It needs also to be able to demonstrate that it is encouraging those attitudes and expanding those abilities that the students at present in the school will need in order to be able to play an involved part in making their adult society less rapacious than ours.

Trying to prepare our students to attempt to ameliorate the worst aspects of the world might be said to be a totally irrational basis on which a school builds its learning policy. However, step by step we might be able to contribute to the betterment of our community, and we can work to create a series of oases which manifest the best that we are and do within our communities, and those oases might, in time, coalesce. Are we totally naïve if we suggest that the ethics of the school community need to be a microcosm of what will sustain the planet, rather than be a mirror of those forces which at present are destroying it?

The school's leadership also needs, vitally, to keep to the forefront of the collective conscience that one of the over-riding aims of education is to enable people to move from acquiring and memorising information, to using that information to create knowledge, and then, and most importantly, through the application of discernment and experience to move on to wisdom.

We need to look in more detail at what sorts of questions a school community and its critical friends should ask to ensure that it is acting out its professed values. Unlike spring-cleaning, such questioning should not occur out of a sense of ritual at a particular time of year. At any one time, some aspect of the school should be under scrutiny. I am avoiding the word 'audit', as in my mind there is something too numerical in the connotations of the word. There is the feeling behind the word of being called to account by an outside body, so passing the responsibility on to an agency which has power but no personal investment in the school. Also, with the word 'audit', the risk is that we look for items which can be quantified, and as a result those items take on a major importance. The sort of evidence that we are looking for is more qualitative than quantitative.

One way of initiating the enquiry is to undertake pupil shadowing. There is no tool as powerful as this to begin to get a feel for the place as experienced by the student. It takes practice and a deal of sensitivity to begin to feel the school as the student does. It needs openness on the part of the shadower, the student, and those met during the course of the day. It needs what I was saying earlier, the certainty that mistakes will be made which will be starters for development and change, and not matters for blame. It also requires a deal of tentativeness. We cannot be objective in our viewing; it is not possible to say 'I am a camera'. Further, simply by being an observer we change what we observe. In the same way that no two people reading the same text will take the same meaning from it, so no two people observing, say, a lesson will come away with identical comments and views on it. There needs to be the opportunity for the observer to say to the observed (the teacher of the visited class) something along the lines of: 'I think that what you were trying to do was x, and that most of the students were with you.' In the subsequent discussion some approximation of intent and outcome might be agreed on. Similarly, the observer needs to be able to ask the student if the impression that she was interested, involved, bored, bewildered or whatever, was the right one. From such triangulation, practised over time, the organisation can build up a detailed account of the school's activities.

The results of these observations need to be fed back to the collegium, and the leader's task is to help focus and filter the discussions, then articulate the findings, and then help explore what the next steps should be, and then again articulate the conclusions. As the steward of the institution's conscience, it is not for the leader to find fault or award grades or marks out of ten, but rather to come with colleagues to a decision as to what should be done next – to promote what is deemed good practice, or to find how to improve a situation which lets the community down.

I suggest that there are four areas on which the inquiries will be focused. The first, as indicated above, is the area of the *student's everyday experience* of being in the institution. The second is the area of *pedagogy*. The third is how well the *links between the school and the community* are being maintained and expanded. The fourth is an amalgam of the other three but needs to be dealt with in its own right – whether or not the *community as a whole is sustaining its vision, being true to itself.*

What I am trying to demonstrate by outlining the areas for inquiry and suggesting, below, some of the questions to be asked, is how an ethics-driven school moves on from the sorts of questions asked in an ethically neutral school, one in which maintaining the institution and conforming with externally imposed criteria are perceived to be the important considerations. The school determined to act ethically does not look only at the items of functionality – are the rules adhered to, are things done on time, are messages clear and answered? The answers to such questions are needed, but they are only starting points. This school wants to inquire not merely if the rules are being kept, but whether they are the right rules; not if things are done on time, but whether these 'things' are worth doing at all; whether what is being done answers the question: 'Does what we are doing match the ideal that we have set out in our vision statement and in our expressed aims?'

The sorts of questions that will be asked in relation to the first area of inquiry (the students' everyday experience) could include:

- Which students are demonstrating success? In what ways is that success being demonstrated?
- Which students are demonstrating difficulties? What sorts of difficulties are they? Who is labelling them as 'difficulties'? On what grounds? Can these students (who are causing 'difficulties') be grouped, and if so what does such grouping tell us?
- How are students demonstrating their knowledge?
- Are there students about whom we know little, who are quiet and uninvolved? Can we find out why and if so work out what to do? Or is it all right to be quiet?
- Do most of the students for most of the time look cheerful? How often do we hear laughter?
- Are we sure that every student knows at least one adult in the school to whom to turn in times of elation or trouble?
- How often do we enable students to work in teams?
- How often, and in what ways, are students involved in helping to run this place? Could they do more?
- Are the students encouraged to use all their intelligences?
- Do our methods of assessing and valuing students' efforts reflect our aim to be mindful of the whole child?
- Are we encouraging students to refine their emotional intelligence? How?
- What sorts of achievement are we celebrating?
- Do we give time to all our students for quiet reflection every day?
- Are whatever resources we have distributed equitably?
- Are we continuously searching to expand our range of human and material resources?

The sorts of question that might be asked in the second area (pedagogy) could include:

- Are we keeping up-to-date with the material of our subject(s)?
- Do we regularly talk over our approaches to teaching with our colleagues?
- Do we regularly visit each others' classrooms to observe and act as critical friends?

- Do we monitor what sorts of questions we ask?
- Do we regularly challenge and encourage all our students?
- Do we work in teams whenever possible?
- Do we search for and then adopt good practice?
- Do we regularly examine the rationale behind what we do to ensure that we are being honest in our teaching?
- Do we regularly share our widening knowledge about how people learn?
- Do we search out the quieter students and ensure their understanding and participation?
- Do we listen to our students and take seriously what they say?
- Do we listen to the parents and take seriously what they say?
- Do we engage all the intelligences that our students possess?
- Do we reward the outworkings of those intelligences?
- Do we enjoy what we are doing? If not, how are we going to help each other to revitalise our work here?
- What have I learned today?

The sorts of question that might be asked in relation to the third area of inquiry (school–community links) could include:

- Do we encourage the parents to be participants in the children's learning? In what ways?
- Do we regularly discuss with the parents why we do things the way we do?
- Are we committed to going into the community to explain ourselves?
- Do we try to involve the community in validating our students' work?
- Do we actively try to help the community?
- Do we respond fully and in a friendly manner to parents' questions and queries?
- Do we bring in other agencies to help before a problem grows too large?
- Do we act as a focal point for the community?
- Do we use a wide range of approaches to communicate with the community?

The final area (whether the community is being true to its values) might be looked at through these questions:

- Do we care for each other?
- Do we express our affection for each other?
- Before making a decision, do we carefully examine its ethical basis?
- Do we look for opportunities to celebrate and enjoy the work of others?
- Do we regularly revisit our assumptions to ensure they are still valid?
- How do we check that prejudices are not clouding our vision?

- How do we support each other in times of difficulty?
- How do we recharge our batteries?

Of course, the answers to the first three groups of questions will go some way to filling out the whole-school picture.

What I am suggesting here is that the ethical school is a highly self-conscious one, and a verbal one; by that I mean that it is continually examining what it is doing and why, and articulating its questions and answers.

Finally, I know that I am asking a very great deal, and I know that institutions following the suggestions in this chapter will be demonstrating courage. I am very conscious that I am living in an educational world that is obsessed with targets, numbers, checklists, demands, false accountability, tests and control – above all control. The needs of the whole child; the hopes that we, as a society, have to look forward to the next generation being better able to cope with the complexities of the twenty-first century than we were with those of the twentieth; the necessity to have rounded people whose intellectual and artistic capabilities have been challenged and expanded – these hopes are simply not being met in this education system. Creativity, both of adults and of children, has been buried under layers of tests and prescribed syllabuses, and without creativity we are the victims of whatever trite and superficial nostrum the government fastens on next. For a school to stand out against this tide of imposed mediocrity is extremely difficult, but I believe that there is no other choice. Hayes (1984) quoted Koestler, and this quotation sums up our feelings with accuracy:

> What we need is an active fraternity of pessimists. They will not aim at immediate radical solutions, because they know this cannot be achieved in the hollow of the historical wave; they will not brandish the surgeon's knife at the social body, because they know their own instruments are polluted. They will watch with open eyes and without sectarian blinkers for the first sign of the new horizontal movement; when it comes they will assist at its birth, but if it does not come in their lifetime, they will not despair. And meantime their chief aim will be to create oases in the interregnum desert. (24)

There are schools which are breaking out from the rigidities of the past few years. There are schools which are looking to an ethically driven education, an education which focuses on the whole child and not just on those outcomes which can be measured. They might, in some quarters, be termed 'rogue schools'. What needs to occur now is for these rogue schools to band together, in the first instance to support and encourage each other, but in the future to be examples not just of good practice, but of the only practice that is acceptable.

4 The competent leader

Linda Ellison

INTRODUCTION

This book has proposed that leaders need to be both strategic and ethical so that leadership is both forward looking and honest. However, there is a whole range of activities in which a leader has to be competent. Using the perspectives from the competence and competency movement, I will now explore what they bring to considerations of effective leadership. Being effective requires leaders throughout organisations who are aware of their own *knowledge* and *personal qualities* (sometimes referred to as skills, attributes and attitudes) and who are able to carry out their current leadership roles successfully through demonstrating appropriate *actions*. They must also be able to continue to be effective in a changing world and to help other people to develop, for example, pupils, colleagues, parents and governors. Handy (1996: 5) writes of these responsibilities emphasising that 'the task of the leader is to make sure that individuals and groups are competent to exercise the responsibility that is given to them' but he goes on to point out the need for leaders to look to their own development, saying that 'in the new organisations, titles and roles carry little weight until the leaders prove their competence. All authority has to be earned before it can be exercised.'

In response to the drive for effective and efficient organisations, the concepts of competence and competency have been used extensively in the last twenty years to refer to the skills and characteristics which enable people to carry out successfully the tasks required of a role, yet there is still confusion about the terms. This confusion is complicated by the fact that, in several countries, 'standards' have been developed for various leadership, management and teaching roles in schools. Within this standards-based system, the terms competence and competency are not always used, yet one or other of these concepts underpins many of the expectations.

EXPLORING THE TERMS COMPETENCE, COMPETENCY AND STANDARDS

While definitions and examples of these concepts are provided here, the reader needs to remember that the terms are often used interchangeably by some writers and in some contexts, so it is probably more important to consider what is actually being discussed, rather than forming a view based merely on which term is being used. With that caveat out of the way, I will provide below the most common explanations of the terms, pointing out, where possible, any alternative usage which might be of significance.

A useful way of distinguishing is to think of competences as describing the ability to carry out a particular task to an identified *minimum* standard. In other words, they relate to *outputs*. Competencies, on the other hand, relate to *inputs*, the things that a person brings to the job or activity in order to be successful, i.e. a set of underlying characteristics which can be drawn on in a range of situations in order to achieve *superior* performance. However, we may also refer to a person who has 'what is required for the job' as being competent in an overall sense so that those who wish to create benchmarks for success in a job would often write these as standards which are a combination of competence and competency, i.e. those things which the person brings to the job and those outputs which they demonstrate as they carry out the job. Some sets of standards are threshold, i.e. indicate a minimum acceptable level, whereas other sets may be designed to describe excellence in the role. In addition, we talk about organisations as having core competences, i.e. core capability or expertise in a particular aspect of work which can be applied and developed in a variety of ways. The way in which these four terms might be seen to combine in an organisation is shown in Figure 4.1.

This section is structured in order to explain individual competence, individual competency, standards and organisational core competence.

Competence

The term competence has been used in Britain for many years and recognises a person's demonstrated ability, in terms of skills and knowledge, to meet the minimum standards to fulfil a role in a particular occupation. It therefore relates to the achievement of 'outputs', i.e. a person's ability to produce satisfactory 'results' through carrying out the role.

In the UK, the term competence is particularly familiar through its use in the National Vocational Qualification (NVQ) and Scottish National Vocational Qualification (SNVQ) frameworks, work-related qualifications which are based on National Occupational Standards, i.e. statements of performance standards describing what effective people do as they carry out particular occupations from hairdressing to accounting. The standards

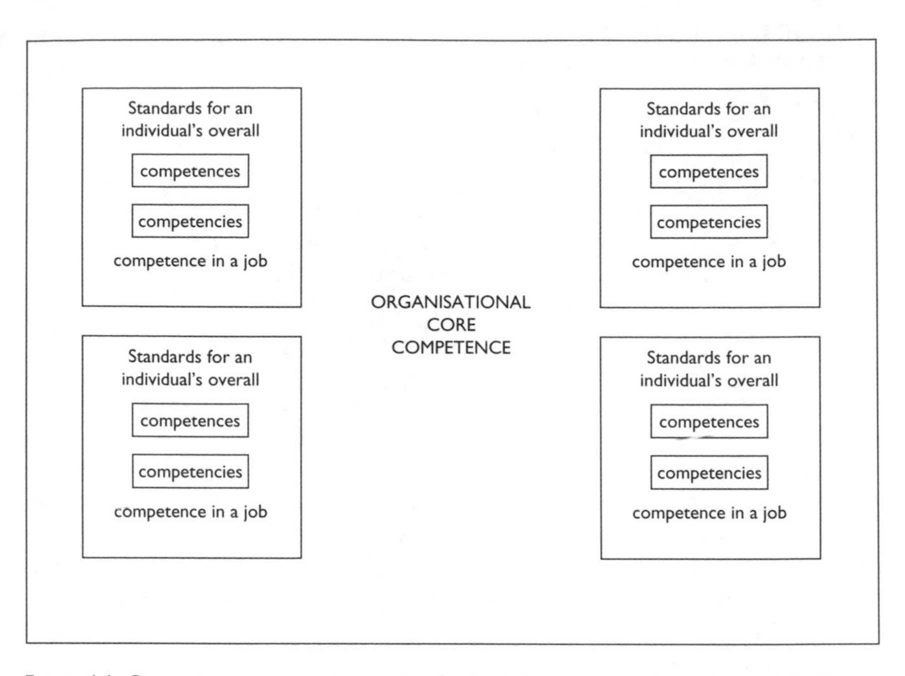

Figure 4.1 Competence, competency, standards and core competence in combination

relate to practice, rather than theory; they cover all the main parts of the job including best practice, knowledge and understanding, and the ability to adapt in a future context. They are broken down into elements and, in terms of level, they go from routine and predictable activities ('Foundation' – at Level 1) to complex, unpredictable activities with high levels of responsibility and autonomy ('Chartered, professional and senior management roles' – at Level 5). The acquisition of NVQs is intended to ensure that employees have the skills and knowledge to meet the organisation's needs.

The standards of the Management Standards Centre (MSC) provide a similar, standards-based approach for the various levels of management. MSC standards are at Levels 3, 4 and 5 (where Level 5 is equivalent to a degree in management). The MSC concept of competence relates to the ability to carry out specific job requirements to a particular standard but also considers the issue of transferability of the skills and knowledge to a new situation.

In a similar way, a competence approach is used in order to specify the standards which should be achieved by beginning teachers, i.e. those whose initial training is complete (whether in a higher education institution or through a school-based scheme). The standards were devised by the Teacher Training Agency (TTA) in the 1990s to provide a common framework of expectations with the most recent version being 'Qualifying to Teach' (TTA 2003b). This document states that the standards are 'outcome statements that set out what a trainee teacher must know, understand and be able to do to be awarded QTS' (TTA 2003a: 3). For the later career stages in England, in 1997 and 1998 the TTA developed frameworks which are more of a hybrid and which are discussed in the section on standards below.

Competence frameworks such as NVQ and MSC are created by a specific procedure so that once the performance criteria and situations have been specified for a role, workers can be trained and assessed against them. The whole process is a logical, systematic approach providing a comprehensive guide for assessment and development. It involves the following stages:

- identify the key purpose of a job, of key roles within it and of key units within each role;
- specify the performance criteria which are appropriate and the situations in which these must be demonstrated;
- train staff, usually on the job;
- assess to see if the competence standard has been met.

In order to gain accreditation through NVQ or MSC, the person develops a portfolio (or equivalent) which demonstrates the successful achievement of the standards for a particular level.

The concept of competence in relation to school leadership and management has not been widely adopted although there were, in the early 1990s, several projects which built on the work of the School Management Task Force (DES 1990). The most notable of these projects, as clearly described by Esp (1993), would be those of Peter Earley for School Management South and Tony Beck and Geoff Bowles for Manchester Polytechnic. Their work provided a valuable stimulus to discussion about the skills, knowledge and understanding needed for effective leadership and management but it was often felt that something was missing from the model in that it disaggregated what seemed to many to be an holistic process.

The competence approach has been widely criticised because it sets out minimum standards which give the expectations of a threshold level of performance and are therefore not necessarily going to guide the development of excellent performance. The approach also seems to suggest that jobs are static by focusing on the characteristics of a job rather than on the characteristics of people who can be successful in the job, both now and as it changes in the dynamic context. Another criticism of the competence approach is that the same job can be very different in different circumstances, e.g. small school or large school, successful school or one which is struggling.

The standards are felt by many to be too detailed and fragmentary with roles being over-analysed into many small parts with no discrimination between the routine and the significant. Such an inflexible and prescriptive approach may not be appropriate for complex roles such as the various leadership positions in education where successful people need to be able to combine knowledge and skills with an understanding of their own and others' behaviours and attitudes in a wide range of emerging circumstances. Although requirements have changed, the time-consuming collection of evidence for accreditation has been found by some in education to be a 'paper exercise in proof' rather than being developmental.

Although many organisations use the actual MSC models of managerial competences, others feel them to be too inflexible for the higher levels of management and leadership work and have adapted them to fit their needs or just used the lower level standards such as those for team leading. The emphasis in educational leadership on flexibility and on people skills has led to the rejection by many of the competence approach and the seeking of solutions via the competency model.

Competency

This term originated in the US, particularly through the work of the psychologist David McClelland and the McBer organisation (later Hay McBer and now the HayGroup) who carried out the first study of competencies in 1973 and on whose work much of the current NCSL thinking in school leadership is based. In a similar way, many large companies have employed psychologists to develop competency models to meet their needs.

In this approach, 'a competency is a measurable characteristic of a person that is related to effective performance in a specific job, organisation or culture.' (HayGroup 2001: 1) The term thus refers to the underlying characteristics (i.e., the inputs) that an individual brings to the job and which result in successful or superior performance. A competency is not, therefore, a task, but a characteristic that enables a person to carry out the tasks of the job. This is a valuable approach because contexts change and it would seem that those who have the right characteristics for the role would be best able to adapt to new situations. It needs to be reiterated, however, that competencies can be developed as opposed to being fixed from birth.

Competencies are determined by observing and interviewing those who have been acknowledged by peers and experts to be outstanding performers in their jobs. (It may be difficult to obtain consensus on this in schools!) The process has been carried out for hundreds of different jobs, such as nurses, sales personnel, headteachers, company directors, and it allows for the identification of the characteristics which distinguish those outstanding people from the rest. Each competency is expressed in terms of behaviours, 'those thoughts and actions of outstanding performers'

(HayGroup 2001: 1). The competencies for a particular role can be identified by the following process:

1 clarify the major requirements and performance criteria for a particular job
2 identify successful job performers i.e. the best 10 per cent
3 observe them in the role and identify key characteristics, areas of concern and actions
4 compare their characteristics and behaviour with that of other job holders
5 formulate the key competencies
6 cluster the competencies into groups for ease of reference.

An example of a competency which was developed through this process, originally for the Leadership Programme for Serving Headteachers (LPSH) programme, is shown in Table 4.1 (HayGroup 2000). Although this relates to headship, a similar process would be used in relation to other school leadership roles and could result in some similar behaviours, although the scale of influence may be different.

As suggested in Table 4.1, the competency approach can appear to produce a list of characteristics which are found in excellent performers and this can seem daunting to those who have not been recognised at such a level of excellence or those who aspire to these positions. It is important, therefore, to use the approach sensitively when developing leaders and potential leaders. As the example shows, it is necessary to understand why a competency is significant, rather than just to copy the behaviours so that a leader is then able to use discretion in the working context, rather than imitate the competency mechanistically. This understanding of the purposes and principles can help to overcome the criticism of the competency approach that simply replicating the characteristics of these excellent performers will produce clone-like behaviour with standardised and insincere responses in other individuals in particular situations.

It is most important that any study of the competencies needed for a particular role has been carried out well, since otherwise the appointment and development processes in the organisation will not produce effectiveness in the role. For example, can a study of 'leaders' be useful across different organisations or does it need to be context-specific? Are the characteristics of effective ward or regimental leadership different from subject or whole-school leadership, in terms of the generic characteristics of leadership? One research project compared the leadership required of effective headteachers with that of senior executives in private enterprise and found that the two working environments are coming closer together but that there are lessons to be learned on both sides. For example,

> While business leaders are more adept at strategy and vision, headteachers' strengths lie in raising capability. Technology can render a strategy irrelevant in a matter of months – capable, motivated employees will never go out of fashion.
>
> (Forde, Hobby and Lees, 2000: 4)

Table 4.1 The expression of a competency (based on HayGroup 2000)

Cluster	Creating the vision
Title of competency	Initiative
Definition	The drive to act now to anticipate and pre-empt events
Core question	Does the individual have a bias for action and does he or she think ahead to anticipate and act on future needs and opportunities?
Why it matters	Heads need to be able to take decisive and immediate action when there are difficulties, or to prevent a situation escalating. Prompt action enhances the credibility of the headteacher. Headteachers also need to be proactive in the medium and long term so that opportunities are not lost and problems not left to drift. Critically, they need to be proactive in shaping and reshaping provision to take account of fast-moving societal changes and educational initiatives.
Levels of action (these are sometimes known as Behavioural Statements)	*1 Acts decisively* Is decisive in a crisis situation. Defuses potential problems before they escalate. Questions to probe significant detail.
	2 Thinks and acts ahead Thinks and acts ahead of time, to seize an opportunity or to sort out a problem.
	3 Prepares for future opportunities Anticipates and prepares for possible problems or opportunities that are not obvious to others. Takes action to create an opportunity or to avoid a future problem.
	4 Acts now to achieve long-term payoffs Anticipates situations a long way off and acts to create opportunities or avoid problems that are not obvious to others.

Some critics feel that leadership and management takes place in such a dynamic context involving varied and changing relationships that it is impossible to suggest 'ideal' characteristics. It is likely that certain competencies will be particularly significant for effective leadership in the future but, as the approach is based on observing effective performers of today, it cannot be used accurately to predict the competencies of the future. Researchers, therefore, can only speculate but it is a flexible approach so models can be updated by further research. We already know that modern workplaces require more collaboration, autonomy and creativity than control and conformity and that there are, increasingly, variations in the background and previous experience of the workforce so that different combinations of competencies may be significant according to the situation. We can also look at those competencies (shown in Table 4.2) which seem to be linked with success in times of rapid change and in an increasingly competitive global context, so that leadership development work can provide opportunities to develop these.

Table 4.2 Competencies for the future

Self-confidence	Information seeking
Achievement orientation	Collaborativeness
Conceptual ability	Impact and influence
Initiative	Strategic orientation

There are similarities between the competency approach and emotional intelligences. Goleman's research (1998) found that emotional intelligence was twice as important as a discriminator of success in leadership than technical skills and general intelligence and he is now working closely with those in the competency arena such as Richard Boyatzis and the HayGroup.

Standards for an individual's overall competence for the job

In general conversation, we often refer to a person as being competent or incompetent in a particular role. In relation to leadership, this implies that a leader needs to have 'what it takes' to carry out the whole job. Standards are often, therefore, developed for a particular role in order to determine whether an individual has the overall capability to fulfil the role (i.e., 'is competent') and to guide professional development. While some sets of standards are a series of output statements (i.e., competences), others are expressed as a mixture of competences and competencies and comprise the *knowledge* (sometimes with 'understanding' listed separately), *skills* and *attitudes* that are required to carry out a particular role.

Following the development of the standards for Qualified Teacher Status in the late 1990s, the Teacher Training Agency (TTA) in England consulted widely and developed sets of standards for various roles in the teaching profession, for example National Standards for Subject Leaders (TTA 1998a), for Special Educational Needs Co-ordinators (TTA 1998b) and for headteachers (TTA 1997). They recognised that success in each of these roles involved more than just a tick list of actions and that there was a need to set out the professional knowledge, understanding, skills and attributes necessary to carry out effectively the key tasks of that role. Other than the compulsory ones (for QTS), the sets of standards have been used with varying degrees of acceptance or enthusiasm. The headteacher standards were not used very much at first, except in the National Professional Qualification for Headship (NPQH) programme. Work by NCSL has reshaped the standards for headteachers in England so that they are expressed as the required knowledge, professional qualities and actions (see page 50), placing greater emphasis than before on competencies. The standards for subject leaders have had a mixed response, especially when applied to subject leadership in primary schools, where the expected requirements were not felt to be feasible. More recently, the various standards have been used to inform performance management discussions and as part of professional development programmes.

Some standards are written to reflect threshold or entry level performance in the role while others are designed to reflect excellent performance. In this way, for example, success in the NPQH suggests that a person is ready to begin headship, although it does not guarantee later success. However, the revised standards for headteachers (DfES 2004) have been designed to indicate what is expected of an effective headteacher, not one who is entering at threshold level nor one who is excellent. They differ from the previous ones in that they reflect an increased focus on professional qualities which are framed as competencies, while still including knowledge and actions which are framed as outcome measures or competences.

Examples drawn from various standards for overall competence are given in Table 4.3.

Organisational core competence

The core competences of an organisation represent an intermediate level of capability between the capabilities of the individuals within the organisation (discussed above) and the overarching metacompetence, such as 'education' or 'public relations'. Thus, a core competence could be defined as 'the bundle of skills and technologies' (Hamel and Prahalad 1994: 199) or capabilities that allows an organisation to be a leader in the provision of a particular range of products or services that are of benefit to its customers such as the core competence of Canon in optics, Honda in engines and Sony in miniaturisation.

Hamel and Prahalad (1994) maintain that there are likely to be between five and fifteen core competences in an organisation and that, in order to be considered 'core', the competences must have:

- customer value, i.e. people will choose the organisation over others, even if it is sometimes difficult to explain why – the concept of a 'happy school' comes to mind here;

Table 4.3 Examples from standards for overall competence (extracts only)

Standard	*Aspect*	*Description*
Revised National Standards for Headteachers in England (DfES 2004)	Developing self and working with others	Knows about strategies to promote individual and team development. Is able to develop, empower and sustain individuals and teams. Acknowledges the responsibilities and celebrates the achievements of individuals and teams.
The Standard for Headship in Scotland (Scottish Executive 2003)	Interpersonal abilities	Demonstrates confidence and courage. Creates and maintains a positive atmosphere. Inspires and motivates others. Communicates effectively. Empathises with others. Values and works through teams.
Original version of National Standards for Subject Leaders in England (TTA 1998b)	Decision-making skills	Able to: Judge when to make decisions, when to consult with others and when to defer to the headteacher or senior managers Analyse, understand and interpret relevant information and data Think creatively and imaginatively to anticipate and solve problems and identify opportunities

- competitor differentiation, i.e. competences not held by all in the sector such as capability in global partnerships, vocational provision, university partnerships for students and so on;
- extendability, i.e. the ability to be applied to new products or services, for example, current capability in differentiated approaches to learning and in community and family links could lead to a future application through provision for learners of all ages 'from cradle to grave' and through leadership of multi-agency provision of services.

The core competences are not always very obvious. They are below the surface, rather like the roots of a tree or the submerged part of an iceberg, and they are unlikely to be exclusive to a particular person or small team. The way in which the capabilities of the individuals are integrated to form a core competence is seen as the 'distinguishing hallmark' (Hamel and Heene 1994: 11) of an organisation. For these reasons, effective leaders need to understand how the various stakeholders such as students, staff, governors and parents make their contributions to overall success.

The next section of this chapter examines some of the different systems which are available to identify and develop individuals with particular capabilities and which may be of relevance in education.

COMPETENCE AND COMPETENCY SYSTEMS OF RELEVANCE TO SCHOOLS

The section which follows examines the features of some of the many specific systems which are available in the UK and internationally for the development of competent professionals in schools. In addition, some systems are included which relate to other roles because the leadership dimension in schools extends beyond the teaching profession. The first two examples relate to systems which are largely based on competence while the remainder are closer to competency in their philosophy.

The Management Standards Centre

The Management Standards Centre (MSC) is an independent unit of the Chartered Management Institute and, since 2001, has been responsible for revising and implementing competence standards in leadership and management which can be used across all organisations in England. The Centre has taken over the standards that were put in place by its predecessor, the Management Charter Initiative (MCI) which was established in 1988 following reports (Constable and McCormick 1987; Handy 1987) highlighting the need for a higher level management development in the UK.

In early 2004, the MSC was in the final stages of consultation about revised 'new world-class occupational standards for management and leadership' to improve capability in the UK, stating that

> The new standards will identify what individuals with management and leadership responsibilities are expected to know and understand and be able to do in relation to management and leadership functions/activities.
>
> (MSC 2004: 1)

In the proposed new system, 'Version 2' of the consultation process puts forward six functional groupings:

- managing self and personal skills
- providing direction
- facilitating change
- working with people
- using resources
- achieving results.

Each grouping contains a cluster of units, forming 51 units in all. Table 4.4 shows the nine units for one grouping ('Providing direction') and the headings which are used to define each of the units. Further details can be obtained from www.managers.org.uk.

Table 4.4 Draft units for an MSC function

Functional grouping: Providing direction	
Made up of nine units	Each unit is expressed as
Map the environment	Title
Develop vision and strategy	Overview
Develop plans for your area of responsibility	Outcomes of effective performance
Guide the implementation of strategy	Behaviours which underpin effective performance
Lead people	Knowledge and understanding
Ensure compliance with legal, regulatory, ethical and social requirements	Skills
Develop organisational culture	
Manage risk	
Promote diversity	

Source: MSC 2004

The model provides very detailed specifications of what a manager should be able to do and should know. It is interesting to note the inclusion of 'behaviours' in the new standards and also that some of the skills are more related to what people bring to the job than previously, thus reflecting a move towards the competency approach.

The standards provide a framework of benchmarks for development and recognise existing achievements in experienced staff. They are assessed by a file or portfolio but now more innovative approaches to assessment are available such as video, audio, or 'walk and talk assessment', as long as the evidence can be noted by the assessor. Those who demonstrate that they have achieved particular levels in the standards can become eligible for Associate or Membership of the Institute of Management Development.

Although the standards are generic across types and sizes of organisations, as explained earlier in this chapter, they are little used in schools. They could, however, form the basis of discussion and could be used for those in a variety of school support positions whose leadership and management roles are not covered by the TTA or NCSL standards and could facilitate the ability of such staff to take their qualifications into other employment sectors.

TTA standards

A number of standards have been introduced from the early 1990s onwards in order to provide benchmarks so that all concerned are clear about what is required of teachers at particular career stages or in particular roles.

The standards for beginning teachers with Qualified Teacher Status (QTS) are output statements or *competences*, originally developed in the early 1990s, which have been regularly refined and are used to judge whether a trainee can be designated as a newly qualified teacher (NQT). The most recent standards are published as 'Qualifying to Teach' (TTA 2003a) which states that:

> The Standards for the award of Qualified Teacher Status are outcome statements that set out what a trained teacher must know, understand and be able to do to be awarded QTS.
>
> (TTA 2003a: 3)

They comprise three interrelated sections: professional values and practice; knowledge and understanding; teaching. As well as forming a baseline for entry to the profession and guiding those involved in initial teacher training, the standards can also prove useful in other circumstances, particularly to act as guidance for those who are struggling to be effective for whatever reason. (For a full copy of the standards, see www.tta.gov.uk.)

In addition, the TTA has developed a set of induction standards (TTA 2003b) which were published for use from September 2003. These set out the standards (classified under the same three sections as for QTS) which relate to working with students, colleagues and parents. These must be met by the end of the Induction period and, in addition, the NQT must continue to meet the standards for QTS as above. Most teachers in England will, at a later career stage, wish to be assessed for additional salary increments through the threshold system. As this system is still under development, with 'Upper Pay Spine 3' on the horizon at the time of writing, it is likely that national standards will be developed here as well.

As discussed in the earlier section on standards, the TTA standards for Subject Leaders were disseminated in 1998 and have not had a very high profile. They relate to:

- core purpose of the subject leader
- key outcomes of subject leadership
- professional knowledge and understanding
- skills and attributes
- key areas of subject leadership.

(TTA 1998b)

It is to be hoped that, in the near future, these standards will be reviewed in the same way as those for heads so that they are seen as more relevant by the profession.

Although many teachers wish to move to team and whole-school leadership roles, there are other ways in which leadership can be displayed, including through the role as an Advanced Skills Teacher (AST) or master teacher. The DfES has listed six broad sets of criteria, known as national standards of excellence, for eligibility as an AST. They relate to outcomes, knowledge, planning, teaching, evaluating and, crucially, supporting other teachers. Assessment involves observation, interviews with pupils, parents and staff and the production of a portfolio of evidence.

It is therefore important that those in leadership roles in schools, whether at senior or middle levels, are aware of these sets of standards and the guidance which is provided for leaders about their implementation, especially in relation to motivation, monitoring progress and informing professional development.

The HayGroup

The HayGroup, formerly known as Hay McBer and the McBer organisation, has been researching characteristics or *competencies* across a wide range of jobs since it was formed as a consultancy company by David McClelland. The concepts are based on McClelland's (1988) view that three tendencies or *motivations* (for achievement, affiliation and power) are the main determinants of the way in which a person demonstrates and uses his or her skills and knowledge. The characteristics of these three motivations are set out in Table 4.5 on p. 46.

This work resulted in the identification by McBer of a number of behaviour indicators which were clustered under headings as follows:

ACHIEVEMENT AND ACTION
Achievement orientation
Concern for order
Information seeking
Initiative

HELPING AND HUMAN SERVICE
Interpersonal understanding
Customer service orientation

MANAGERIAL
Developing others
Directiveness
Teamwork and co-operation
Team leadership

COGNITIVE
Analytical thinking
Conceptual thinking
Technical/professional expertise

IMPACT AND INFLUENCE
Influence
Organisational awareness
Relationship building

PERSONAL EFFECTIVENESS
Self-control
Self-confidence
Flexibility
Organisational commitment

Many of the indicators and clusters have been found to be fairly common across various occupations but there are some job-specific ones such as low fear of rejection in salespeople or a sense of humour in nurses. The HayGroup is constantly examining the characteristics demonstrated by effective managers and leaders (at various levels in the organisation) and refining the model for a changing world. For outstanding mid- and first-level managers working laterally and upwards in the organisation as well as downwards, the current model clusters the competencies as shown in Table 4.6. This approach is relevant across many organisations, rather than being context specific and could be applied at middle leadership level for teachers as well as for leaders of support staff as an alternative to the MSC approach.

Table 4.5 McClelland's (1988) motivations

Motivation	*Characteristics*
Achievement	• sets challenging targets • finds ways of improving things • values personal responsibility • seeks objective feedback in order to improve • prefers working with experts to friends
Affiliation	• likes to spend time with friends • keeps in contact with people • puts people before tasks and friends before experts • would rather work in a group than alone • likes co-operating
Power	• looks for chances to lead • influences others to obtain leader roles • willing to help others towards own or their goals • gets involved in organisational politics • seeks and uses information to influence events

Table 4.6 The manager model for first- and second-level managers

Cluster	*Competency*
Managing yourself	Empathy Self control Self confidence
Managing your team	Developing others Holding people accountable Team leadership
Managing the work	Results orientation Initiative Problem solving
Managing collaboratively	Influencing others Fostering teamwork

Source: HayGroup (2001)

Recent work by the HayGroup has focused on four competencies which they believe are essential to effective leadership and seven which are essential to effective management. This is an interesting development in that it appears to recognise that, except in very large organisations, leaders also need to be managers to some degree. The list of leadership competencies focuses very much on the strategic, placing many of the competencies which we might consider to be 'leadership' in schools into the 'management' category. What is important is that these competencies are developed in a school, even if there is dispute among authors about terminology.

Table 4.7 Leadership and management competencies

Leadership	*Management*
Information seeking	Achievement orientation
Conceptual thinking	Developing others
Strategic orientation	Directiveness
Customer service orientation	Impact and influence
	Interpersonal understanding
	Organizational awareness
	Team leadership

Source: HayGroup (2003a, 2003b)

Instruments are available to assess an individual's performance in relation to these competencies, the Leadership Competency Instrument and the Management Competency Questionnaire respectively (HayGroup 2003a, 2003b).

National College for School Leadership Models of Excellence

These models were originally developed by Hay McBer in 1998 when the company worked in partnership with the TTA to develop the Leadership Programme for Serving Headteachers (LPSH). The programme subsequently passed to the DfES and then to the NCSL where responsibility for delivery currently lies and under whose auspices further revisions have been carried out. The Models of Excellence were developed as a result of research into effective headteachers, using the standard Hay McBer procedure of observing the work of effective people in the role. Models for deputy headteachers were added later. The Models comprise fifteen characteristics presented under five headings known as clusters and are linked to the National Standards for Headteachers, although the latter do not relate to excellent performance.

In addition, the HayGroup did further work on effective heads and identified their leadership styles. This work has been criticised as not necessarily being transferable across the range of heads although the writers do acknowledge that it was based mainly on the work of five 'maverick' heads who are very experienced and well known in England. Contingency theory (Fiedler 1967) reminds us to take account of the situation, the task, the leader and the followers so, although the report gives food for thought, it would be wrong to assume that these characteristics are going to be applicable in all situations.

Table 4.8 The models of excellence

Cluster	*Characteristics*
Personal values and passionate conviction	Respect for others Challenge and support Personal conviction
Creating the vision	Strategic thinking Drive for improvement Initiative
Planning for delivery: monitoring, evaluation and improving performance	Analytical thinking Initiative Transformational leadership Teamworking Understanding others Developing potential
Getting people on board	Impact and influence Being and holding people accountable
Gathering information and gaining understanding	Understanding the environment Information seeking

Source: HayGroup (2000)

Emotional intelligence

Goleman's (2000) studies in the workplace reflect the competencies approach, seeing emotional intelligence as 'the ability to manage ourselves and our relationships effectively' (Goleman 2000: 80), an essential aspect of effective leadership. Indeed, he is now working with Boyatzis and the HayGroup on new ways of linking aspects of their work. Goleman sets out four fundamental capabilities and then lists the specific sets of competencies which make up each as shown in Table 4.9. It is clear that these competencies can be applicable in a range of contexts, both within and beyond education.

Table 4.9 Capabilities and competencies

Fundamental capabilities	*Sets of competencies*
Self-awareness	Emotional self-awareness Accurate self-assessment Self-confidence
Self-management	Self-control Trustworthiness Conscientiousness Adaptability Achievement orientation Initiative
Social awareness	Empathy Organizational awareness Service orientation
Social skill	Visionary leadership Influence Developing others Communication Change catalyst Conflict management Building bonds Teamwork and collaboration

Source: Goleman 2000

The Gallup Organisation

Gallup has developed a process which examines outstanding individuals in a particular job in order to identify 'talents' and 'strengths' which are then used to produce a template that can be applied to selection or development. This approach has some similarities to the competency approach but Gallup believes that everyone's habits and behaviours are different and that natural talents should be built upon, i.e. areas of talent are developed into strengths, rather than trying to remedy 'weaknesses'. The work is more commonly used in the US and can be seen in the book, *Now Discover Your Strengths* (Buckingham and Clifton 2001).

Standards for headteachers

In England, a set of standards was originally developed by the Teacher Training Agency and introduced in 1997. The standards were revised in 2004 (DfES 2004) because it was perceived that the role of heads had changed significantly. The revised standards relate to the following areas of the head's role:

- shaping the future
- leading learning and teaching
- developing self and working with others
- managing the organisation
- securing accountability
- strengthening community

Each is subdivided into:

- importance to headship (the significance and distinctiveness of each area)
- knowledge (what the person knows and understands)
- professional qualities (skills, dispositions and personal capabilities brough to the role)
- actions (what the person does to achieve the core purpose).

Although the lists appear to be separate, it is the NCSL's view that there are connections and interdependencies across the six areas. As explained in the first part of this chapter, there is now a greater focus on the competencies required for success, rather than on an output or competence model.

The standards are intended to 'capture the challenge of headship' (NCSL 2003: 3), 'articulating the role of effective headship in the 21st century' (NCSL 2003: 6). They provide a framework for the development of aspiring heads (for self-development and for NPQH) as well as for heads in post and can aid the performance management process. They are stated to apply to effective headship and do not, therefore, discriminate between threshold or entry levels and excellence, nor is there currently any attempt to differentiate between the headship of different types of schools.

CONCLUSION

This chapter has outlined some of the different approaches which are available to provide a framework for the development of effective leadership in schools. Senior staff and governors need to take a view as to which are the most appropriate frameworks for the school, bearing in mind context, transferability, legislation and economics. Leadership development should be considered as a journey and not an event. The purpose of this chapter has been to provide a map of that journey. We wish our readers well as they undertake their own personal journeys.

Part II

Leading strategic change

5 Leading the strategically focused school

Brent Davies

WHAT IS STRATEGY?

Strategy as a concept can be, and often is, misunderstood in the way it is commonly used. Strategy is seen as a 'good' concept, being so often erroneously attached to many leadership and management activities. For example, in searching the Office for Standards in Education (OfSTED) database of 100 reports on primary schools for mentions of strategy and planning, this statement was found in an OfSTED report of a school:

> From this informed base, good strategic planning is undertaken. The school improvement plan is comprehensive and has a clear focus on raising standards for Years 1 and 2 and sustaining standards for Year 6. Currently, the plan does not run for more than a year.
>
> (OfSTED 2002: 12)

The problem with the OfSTED quotation is that it is about the short-term agenda of target-setting and the statement 'Currently, the plan does not run for more than a year' betrays the lack of understanding of the longer-term direction-setting nature of strategy.

How does this idea check against concepts of strategy? Traditionally, strategy has always been associated with the idea of direction setting for the organisation. It is necessary to understand the history of the organisation and its current situation to be able to attempt to set the direction of the organisation. This is articulated by Mintzberg (2003) in defining strategic thinking as 'seeing ahead', 'seeing behind', 'seeing above', 'seeing below', 'seeing beside', 'seeing beyond', and significantly 'seeing it through'. Another concept is that strategy is about the broad major dimensions of the organisation and another would be that it deals with the medium to longer term. It is possible to consider that strategic activity deals with broad aggregated data, and operational activity with the disaggregated detail of the shorter term. Davies and Ellison (2003) use 1–2 years for the shorter-term action planning, 3–5 years for the strategic medium-term and 5–10 years for the futures-thinking longer term. Clearly, the interpretation used in the above OfSTED report is at variance with these concepts as it focuses on shorter-term standards-raising agendas. What else apart from scope, in terms of broad aggregated data and time scale, are the concepts we associate with strategy? Instead of being associated with a linear plan, strategy might usefully be thought of as a perspective, as a way of looking at things. Such a view would bring together the idea of broader direction setting over the medium term to create a strategic orientation. In other words, strategy provides the template against which to set shorter-term planning and activities. Having established some of the elements in a conceptualisation of strategy, the chapter will now establish a three-part model for developing a strategically focused school.

A MODEL FOR CREATING A STRATEGICALLY FOCUSED SCHOOL

One of the challenges facing schools in the UK and other countries is that they are confronted by a central government agenda that focuses on short-term targets and achievements. While in themselves these shorter-term improvement agendas may be beneficial, they may totally dominate a school's activities. The danger is that schools will orient their teaching and organisational processes to achieve these targets but will neglect the activities and processes they need to build sustainability; to make them successful in the longer term.

As a result of researching schools that are strategically oriented and sustainable in the longer term, three dimensions have become apparent. First, there are strategic processes evident within the school; second, these processes work through strategic approaches; third, these processes and approaches help to establish characteristics of a strategically focused school. This chapter will examine these three dimensions in detail but a brief description will initially be given.

Initially, the strategic processes evident in strategically focused schools manifest themselves in four domains: conceptualisation processes; people and development processes; implementation processes; strategic articulation processes. These four factors work together and while they will be described separately, they should be considered as part of an integrated process.

Next, these strategic processes work through different strategic approaches to build a strategically focused school. The four strategic approaches that will be discussed are: the rational or traditional approach of strategic planning; the flexible and reflective approach of emergent strategy; the devolved or decentralised approach of strategic intrapreneurship; and the building of strategic intent. Finally, there is the establishment of a strategic focus for the school and this, in part, involves the development of the strategic architecture of the school, which enables the school to focus on the longer-term key elements of the school's development. This is one of the characteristics of a strategically focused school that will be discussed later in this chapter.

The model in this chapter focuses on the importance not only of creating strategy but also of addressing the two crucial factors that, if neglected, can lead to the failure of strategy. These factors are the ability to translate strategy into action and second to align the organisation and the individuals within it to achieving that strategy. While the chapter argues that strategic processes work through different strategic approaches to build a strategically focused school, it would be simplistic to think of this as a straightforward linear process. Rather, it is an iterative process with a feed-back loop operating continuously. Strategic leadership is at the centre of this activity in developing the successful school in the long term, as can be seen in Figure 5.1.

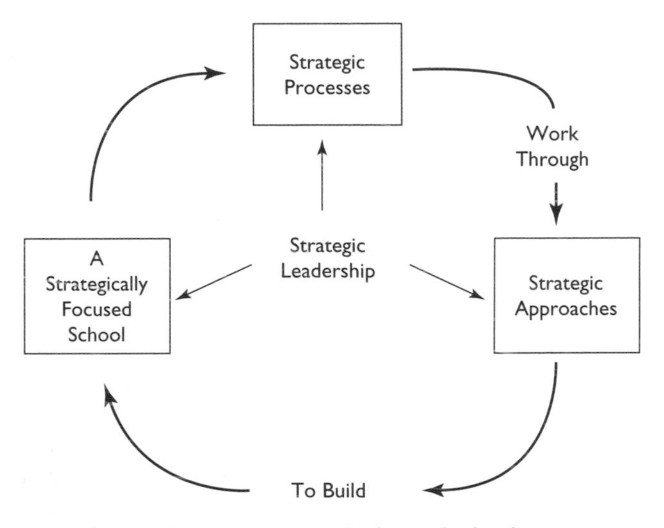

Figure 5.1 A model for developing a strategically focused school

Source: Davies 2004: 13

STRATEGIC LEADERSHIP

In Figure 5.1, strategic leadership is the central activity that facilitates and drives the strategic cycle. The nature of strategic leadership will be briefly considered, but the reader should refer back to Chapter 2 for an in-depth review of the nature and dimensions of strategic leadership, before the chapter moves on to discuss strategic processes and approaches. In any consideration of strategic leadership, it is important to consider whether we are talking about an individual strategic leader or a wider group of people who contribute strategic leadership insights and perceptions to organisational decision-making. This chapter considers strategic leadership to involve a number of individuals, throughout the school, who have strategic leadership abilities and who contribute to the process.

Strategic leaders have a coherent and perceptive map of the existing state or position of the organisation and are able to envisage how that map needs to change and develop into the future. They use this knowledge to build a vision of where the organisation needs to be. However, to turn that vision into reality, they need to be able to communicate the map and vision to others so as to engage them in the process of shaping the future direction of the organisation. They achieve this collaboration by working to build engagement, capability and alignment. Engagement is about the process of motivating all staff in the school to believe in the purpose and need for change and development so that it is meaningful to them. Capability is about building the skills and understanding to both comprehend the necessary developments and have the ability to put new approaches and systems into practice. Alignment is the difficult challenge of bringing together both individuals and organisational perspectives to work in a focused directional way to achieve agreed objectives.

An interesting consideration is whether the ability to utilise strategic leadership capabilities in an organisation is dependent on the stage of leadership development in the individual or on the stage of the life cycle of the organisation. Do leaders develop administrative and managerial skills first and when they are comfortable with their skill level take on the challenge of deploying more direction-changing strategic skills? Similarly, do leaders have to ensure that the organisation is working effectively and maximising its outputs in the current paradigm before they can think of operating in a different way? Such a mode of operating might be thought of as sequential strategic development. Does strategic activity only follow operational activity or, as Davies, B. (2003) suggests, can it be part of a 'twin-track' parallel approach that uses the double s-curve as a means of concurrently managing the known and developing the new? This double s-curve is illustrated in Figure 5.2.

Figure 5.2 suggests that strategic leaders operate a twin-track approach. Concurrently they attempt to extend the effectiveness of the current way of working by extending the existing s-curve through improvements in practice while at the same time building the capability and capacity to move to a significantly new way of working by making a strategic leap. These two activities combine the management task of 'doing things better' and the leadership task of 'doing things differently'. (See Barker, 2003; Davies, B. 2003; Davies and Davies 2003; Wise 2003). A consideration of when to start 'doing things differently' leads to the critical factor of strategic timing. The research would suggest that outstanding strategic leaders operate a concurrent approach.

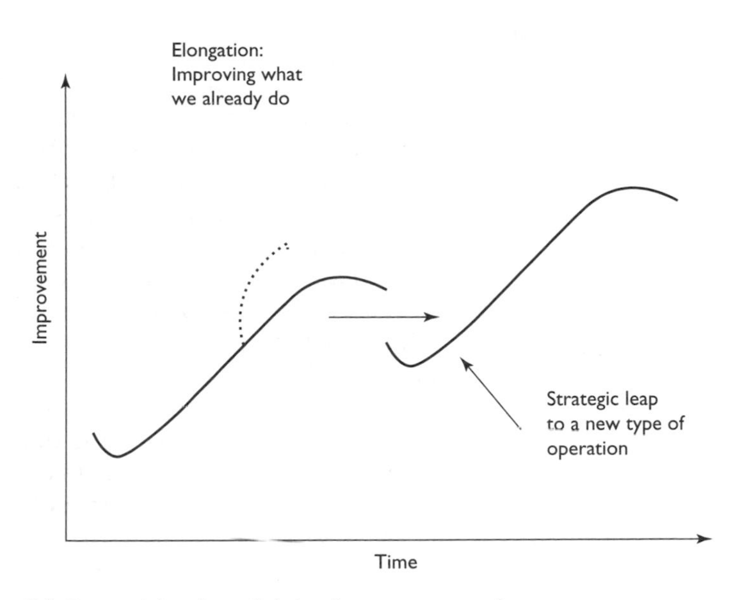

Figure 5.2 Sequential and parallel development approaches
Source: Davies, B. 2003: 306

Another characteristic of strategic leaders is that they are strategically opportunistic. It is important to distinguish between opportunistic leaders who may or may not take the opportunities that arise, such as bidding for a particular government initiative, and those who are strategically opportunistic. Being strategically opportunistic involves developing the major directional thrusts for the school and configuring them to be in a position to take on specific opportunities that fit that configuration as they arise. It also involves the concept of abandonment, giving up some activities to accommodate the new ones. A key characteristic of strategic leaders could be the intuition and judgement which enable them to choose the optimum time to make changes. Such ability is what can be described as strategic timing. A final characteristic may well be that leaders are optimists as well as opportunists in that they are positive about the future.

STRATEGIC PROCESSES

Strategic processes can be defined in four categories, each of which is examined in more detail below:

- conceptualisation processes;
- people interaction and development processes;
- articulation processes;
- implementation processes.

Conceptualisation processes

In researching the development of strategy in schools, a key factor that has emerged is that individuals within the school have to engage in a fundamental rethinking of the way the school operates and the way it needs to operate in the future. The next significant step is deciding how to move from the present state to the desired future state. The research suggests that the leaders in strategically focused schools engage in a three-staged personal and organisation conceptualisation. This process starts with reflection, and being reflective enables the leader(s) to analyse the situation and develop strategic thinking within themselves and the school, and in doing so, to build new mental models of how to operate. The reflection processes are built on the leader's ability to make sense of the internal and external environment. Headteachers in the research made the point of making time to 'see' in these different ways in order to understand what to do. This process obviously creates the ability to think differently and strategically as Garratt (2003: 2–3) describes:

> 'Strategic thinking' is the process by which an organization's direction-givers can rise above the daily managerial processes and crises to gain different perspectives of the internal and external dynamics causing change in their environment and thereby give more effective direction to their organization. Such perspectives should be both future-oriented *and* historically understood.

The advantage of creating a new mental model is that mental models make sense of complex reality and provide a framework to explain key concepts to others in the organisation. An example of this conceptualisation process would be building a new understanding within the whole community of what learning is and how to develop optimal approaches and conditions that will maximise children's learning.

People interaction and development processes

In building strategic capability, the most significant resource, that of human capital, is of fundamental importance (Gratton 2000; Grundy 1998). The research interviewees articulated a process that was based on strategic conversations which built participation and motivation within their school to improve strategic capability.

These four stages of development can be conveniently displayed sequentially in Figure 5.3 but it is more probable that they work in an iterative way.

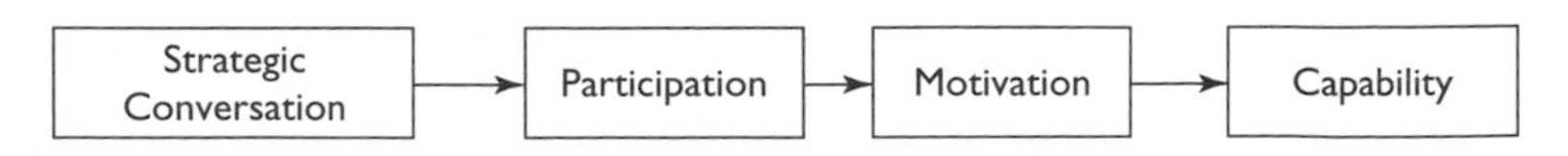

Figure 5.3 People interaction and development processes
Source: Davies 2004: 16

These four stages can be more fully described as:

(a) Strategic conversation. As described by Hirschhorn, (1997), van der Heijden (1996) and Davies (2002), developing strategic conversations and dialogue involves discussions about holistic whole-school issues and the trends that face the school over the next few years as well as the shorter-term operational issues. These strategic conversations enable people to develop a strategic perspective of what the school might become. Without such conversations, however tentative they might at first be, the future will, literally, not be articulated. Such conversations are difficult because short-term accountability demands mean that there is a danger that meetings and discussions focus just on immediate issues. Leaders have to split business and future developments into separate meetings and ensure that attention is focused on the larger and longer-term agendas as well as the immediate ones. Also, the importance of the day-to-day interactions cannot be neglected as they can contribute to stimulating discussions and ideas. It is this process that develops scenarios and strategic thinking to lead the school forward.

(b) Strategic participation. By definition, the conversations lead to greater knowledge and participation in discussions. It can be a difficult and slow process from the previous state of being concerned only with the short term to the new state of being involved in the broader and longer-term strategic issues. It can be a process of reculturing (Fullan 1993; Hargreaves 1994; Stoll, Fink and Earl 2002) the organisation. The process of greater awareness and participation in discussion is a key means of developing the ability of the organisation to build leadership in depth. The key ability here is to build involvement in the longer-term development of the school. Strategic organisations use the abilities and talents of wider staff groupings to involve all in building and committing to the strategic direction of the school. One of the research schools uses staff groups that cut across roles in the school (teachers, learning support staff, administrative and premises staff) to take on a major future-oriented change issue. The aim is to build capacity and participation in reaching strategies and solutions for the school's development.

(c) Strategic motivation. Developing a strategic cause in which individuals are motivated to contribute leads to an improved commitment and effort. Gratton (2000: 19–20) advocates developing 'emotional capabilities', 'trust-building capabilities' and capabilities to build a 'psychological

contract' as means of engaging and motivating staff. Building a commitment to values and long-term ambitions provides individuals with a vision and sense of direction that allows them to put short-term problems and challenges into context. This can be the key to seeing long-term activities sustained. Covey's (1989) 'keeping the end in mind' is as important in the long term as it is in the short term because it is a vital strategic activity in driving through the immediate situation in order to achieve long-term goals.

(d) Building capability. The strategic conversation and enhanced participation build greater personal and organisational capability and capacity. Given that the major resource of any organisation is the quality of its human capital, then enhancing that quality is a major organisational focus. It is useful to differentiate between capability and capacity. Capacity can be considered the resource level that is available at any given moment to achieve an objective. Capability is that mix of skills and competencies possessed by the people in the organisation which is needed to achieve the task. The right number of people may not, at a particular juncture, have the right skills. However, when they do, then it can be said that both capacity and capability are present. Boisot (1998: 5) states that 'we shall use the term capability to depict a strategic skill in the application and integration of competencies'. A useful discussion of capability is provided by Stalk, Evans and Schulman (1992). These definitions come out of the business literature, while much of the educational literature uses the word 'capacity' as an overall term to mean capability and capacity (see Harris 2002; Stoll and Myers 1998). The challenge for strategic organisations is not merely getting more people but getting the right people or developing the existing staff to develop new skills and competencies. Establishing in a greater number of staff the broader skills set necessary to build sustainability and renewal and not just the ability to cope with current operational needs is a major task of strategically successful schools.

Articulation processes

Articulation of strategy can take place in three main ways:

(a) Oral. How do those in leadership positions articulate the key messages to staff about values, vision and the direction of the school? One of our case study heads reported, 'Once a half-term I do a brief focused presentation to all staff (teaching and support) about the direction and challenges facing the school to build a strategic view and language to extend their operational knowledge.' He went on to say, 'this provides the cornerstone for all the informal strategic conversations to take place between colleagues and myself and between colleagues themselves'. The way that meetings of staff are conducted is significant in building a strategic perspective. Do they start with a celebration of learning or a discussion of future policy or are

those items tacked on to the end of the administrative items? 'Walking the talk' is vitally important with strategy if the culture is to change.

(b) Written. The written documentation needs to be of two types. First, there needs to be a separate dimension or section to the planning documentation in the school that addresses not only the school improvement/ school development issues but the broader strategic development issues and challenges over the medium to long term. Davies and Ellison (2003) specify that there should be a strategic intent statement as well as a strategic plan in a section of the overall school plan which is separate from the operational or action-planning element. Second, individuals in the school should be conversant with the strategic as well as the operational plan and it should not just be a document on the shelf in the headteacher's office. If an external visitor talks to a member of staff about how his or her work is guided by the plan, and there is not a coherent answer, then the plan may be useful as an external audit document but not as a piece of writing that affects practice in the school. Written documentation should be a guide for action, not just a formal record, if it is to affect the strategic direction of the school.

(c) Structural. How do the organisational structures in the school reflect its strategic objectives as well as current managerial needs? Wise (2003) reports:

> The separation of the 'Operational Management Team' from the 'Strategic Policy Team' has proved to be a great success. Too often Senior Management Teams become bogged down in operational matters with little or no time to discuss important strategic issues. The separation of strategic and operational functions has resulted in a separation of the urgent from the important. No longer does the urgent drive out the important; both are now catered for. In addition, the various groups provide a unique 'time horizon' management structure with: i) Operational Management Team, focusing on the next 0–12 months, ii) School Development Plan Team, focusing on the next 6–24 months and iii) Research and Development Team, focusing on the next 2–5 years.
>
> (Wise 2003: 117)

Similar structural arrangements that articulate the strategic focus of the school are reported by headteachers in our research project:

> we have six cross-school change teams. They consist of teaching and non-teaching staff and there are about 20 members in each team. They are each tasked with one significant area of strategic development each year. It is part of the organisational structure and aims to get all

staff to be involved in creative thinking directed at the medium-term future of the school.

Another headteacher reported, 'We have restructured the governing body committee framework to have a strategic committee looking at where KS1 and 2 should be in five years' time.' These examples of strategic structures highlight the significant factor that articulation must be an integrated approach. The documentation must not be seen in isolation from how leaders talk and discuss strategic issues or from the organisational structures they set up to facilitate the development of a strategically focused school.

Implementation processes

The challenge of implementing strategy involves four key tasks: translating strategy into action; aligning the individual and the organisation to the new strategy; deciding between sequential and parallel implementation approaches; finally the issue of strategic timing.

(a) Translating strategy into action. Although this sounds an obvious activity, it is sometimes one of the most difficult to do. Whereas discussing and writing plans cause some organisational tensions, the implementation can produce significant tensions and resistance to change. The deployment of the conceptual processes on p. 60 above may assist the process. However, successful strategic organisations pay similar amounts of attention to how strategies are to be implemented as well as to what those strategies are. Three key points (adapted from Gratton 2000) are critical here:

- keep the process simple;
- measure success through the richness of the strategic conversations;
- focus on the few themes that will make a real difference.

(b) Alignment. One of the key challenges in this implementation process is aligning both individual and organisational values, culture and ways of working to the new strategy. This alignment requires both initial and ongoing attention from the strategic leaders in the organisation to 'cement' the new way of working into the organisational practice and culture. Pietersen (2002: 54) forcefully argues:

> You'll need the ability to align every element of your entire organization – measurement and reward systems, organizational structures and processes, your corporate culture, and the skills and motivation of your people – behind your strategic focus. This is a monumental leadership challenge; without success here, no strategy can succeed.

Thus realigning both the corporate and individual 'mind set' to the new direction of the organisation and being committed to it needs extensive staff development and training.

(c) Sequential and parallel implementation approaches. One way of considering organisational development is that schools, for example, move from one phase of their development to another in a sequential way. A common argument (Marsh 2000) is that once the improvements in the current operation have been achieved, the leadership in the school has both the courage and the experience to take more fundamental strategic moves. Another and alternative perspective is to consider a twin-track approach which was illustrated earlier in Figure 5.2.

(d) Strategic timing. The leadership challenge of when to make a significant strategic change is as critical to success as choosing the right strategic change to make. The issue of timing can rest on leadership intuition as much as on rational analysis. When individuals in the organisation are ready for change, when the organisation needs the change and when the external constraints and conditions force the change all have to be balanced one against the other. As Figure 5.2 shows, the leader's skill, his or her critical strategic judgement, lies in knowing when to make the leap to a new way of operating. Such judgement is manifested in not only knowing what and knowing how but also knowing when (Boal and Hooijberg 2001) and, equally importantly, knowing what not to do (Kaplan and Norton 2001).

STRATEGIC APPROACHES

There are numerous categorisations of strategy (see Volberda and Elfring 2001). The one that has been used in this research project is a conceptual framework by Boisot (2003) who identifies four types of strategic approach. These are:

Strategic planning. The traditional 'planning school' approach (see Mintzberg, Ahlstrand and Lampel 1998) assumes that the future can be predicted and that linear, rational, pro-active plans can be drawn up. This is a situation in which although there is significant change, it is not overwhelming and there is a clear understanding of what to do. In a school setting, it assumes you know where you want to go, how to manage the journey and what the desired outcomes are. This certainty would apply to part of a typical school's activities. For example, at any given time, one can know student numbers, and plot the students as they grow older and move through the school; or one can estimate teachers' salary costs as they move up the incremental scale. While strategy is, in the terms of this chapter, associated with the medium term (3–5 years), the basic principles of strategic planning have been used for shorter-term school development planning (SDP) or school improvement planning (SIP). However, while SDP and SIP use the predictable nature of targets and managing the journey to achieve them, they deal with detail and not the broad aggregated data of a true strategic approach and they also operate in a much shorter time-frame.

Emergent strategy. As the name suggests, this strategic approach is one that emerges through practice. Organisations faced with significant but not overwhelming change and with little initial understanding of how to react, work through a policy of trial and error. As successes become apparent they are replicated, whereas failures are not. Over a period of time a portfolio of successful approaches is built up that becomes a coherent pattern for future behaviour and hence a strategic approach emerges. In a school setting, this strategy resonates with many initiatives that are forced on schools by central government. With little time fully to implement the changes, many schools work through an emergent strategy of learning by doing. Whittington (2001: 4) summarises this as 'seeing strategy best as an emergent process of learning and adaptation'.

Decentralised or distributed strategy. This is what Boisot (2003) calls intrapreneurship, a situation where the central leadership and management of an organisation set down a very limited number of planning frameworks and leave the detailed planning to the sub-units within the organisation. Typically such planning would occur in an environment of rapid or turbulent change. In this environment, the central leadership of the organisation cannot understand in detail the rapidly changing context in which it operates. To lead and manage in such a framework requires the ability to lay down the key values and operating targets and then decentralise the organisation and implementation to the sub-units. In schools, this delegation would represent a situation in which school leaders leave a great deal of the planning to the curricular or Key Stage sub-groups.

Strategic intent. This form of strategy is very useful in a period of considerable change or turbulence. The planning framework is one in which, although the senior leadership is able to articulate what major strategic shifts or changes it wishes to make, it is unsure of how to operationalise these ideas. In brief it knows where it wants to go but not how to get there. Determining the intent may be dependent on leadership intuition (Klein 2003; Parikh 1994) as well as leadership analysis. The key to deploying this form of strategic approach is to set targets in the form of strategic intents that stretch the organisation to perform at significantly different or increased levels. It then engages in a series of capability- and capacity-building measures to 'leverage up' the organisation to produce at the higher level. The intent is the glue that binds the organisation together as it focuses on how to achieve this new strategic outcome. Work by Hamel and Prahalad (1994) and Davies, B. (2003) illustrates the significance of this approach.

The mistake from reviewing these four types of strategic approach is to think that schools use one strategic approach to the exclusion of all others.

In practice a school may use a portfolio of strategic approaches in differing circumstances. Strategic planning may be the preferred approach when there is full knowledge and a time frame that facilitates it. However, given a need to implement a significant change at short notice with little prior knowledge of the area, then the strategic approach needs to be built up drawing on the experience of implementing the change; thus an emergent strategy would be evident. When the school is attempting to build a major cultural and organisational change by developing the capacity to achieve a significant shift in performance it would build a series of strategic intents. All these approaches could be used concurrently in response to the challenges and possibilities which face schools, so deploying a portfolio of strategic approaches would be the appropriate response.

CHARACTERISTICS OF A STRATEGICALLY FOCUSED SCHOOL

The initial research discussions and findings from the case study schools have started to isolate features that strategically focused schools display. These are considered below.

They build in sustainability

The first and most important characteristic of a strategically focused school is that it builds sustainability into its processes. While many schools have effective school development or improvement plans, these are by their very nature short-term. While they may contribute to short-term effectiveness, they do not necessarily ensure the longer-term success or viability of the school. Similarly, having longer-term plans would be pointless if the immediate viability of the school was threatened. What is needed is a balance which is represented in Figure 5.4.

In Figure 5.4 the desirable position is in the upper right-hand quartile where both short-term target setting and operational plans are complemented by the medium- to longer-term strategic plans. While many initiatives from government such as literacy and numeracy strategies have short-term targets, there is concern as to whether these are sustainable by simply working harder to achieve increased results in one-dimensional tests. What is needed is a focus on deeper educational learning and organisational capabilities that are sustainable over the longer term, often described as strategic capabilities (Stalk, Evans and Schulman1992) or core competencies (Hamel and Prahalad 1994). There needs to be a set of strategic sustainable objectives in the planning process.

Operational Processes and Planning (SDP and Target Setting)			
	Effective	Functionally successful in the short term but not sustainable long term	Successful and sustainable in both the short term and long term
	Ineffective	Failure inevitable both in the short term and long term	Short-term crises will prevent longer-term sustainability
		Ineffective	Effective
		Strategic Processes and Planning	

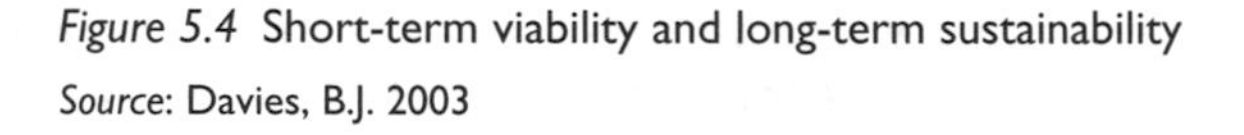

Figure 5.4 Short-term viability and long-term sustainability
Source: Davies, B.J. 2003

They develop set strategic measures to assess their success

For an individual on a diet the maxim may be 'you are what you eat'. The organisational equivalent of this may be 'you are what you measure'. While all schools have ways of measuring whether short-term goals such as Key Stage and examination targets are realised, how many have strategic medium-term goals and the measurement techniques to judge whether they are reached? Initial research evidence suggests that strategically focused schools have medium-term broader education measures of success, as well as short-term goals that are measured by the raw numbers demanded by many agencies.

They are restless, not complacent

There is a strong correlation between individual characteristics of the leader and the collective nature of the school team. While not dismissing current approaches and strengths, strategically focused schools are constantly looking for the next development idea or phase and they realise that what is good enough for now will not remain so. They are forward looking and futures oriented. They see the future as affording better opportunities; they see change as desirable, not undesirable; they see challenges rather than problems. In brief, they are improvers, not maintainers. They see a constant need to keep up to date and draw in ideas on how they may challenge current patterns and do things differently in the future.

They are networked: locally, regionally, nationally and internationally

Our research shows that strategically focused schools invest considerable time and energy in building and sustaining networks. These are not confined just to benchmarking current practice but are forums for ideas where visioning and future-oriented dialogues are facilitated. They are constantly seeking new ways of thinking and working and they seek to build their own solutions from a wide range of sources. In summary, they are outward looking and believe that, however good they are, they can never be good enough and need to make strategic alliances and networks with other people and organisations to develop broad sets of ideas and knowledge capital.

They use sophisticated multi-approach planning processes

The planning approaches in this chapter have been analysed and a perspective established that schools do not use one approach or another but use a portfolio that combines some or all four main approaches so that depending on circumstance and context the school will utilise a sophisticated multi-planning approach. This is a key attribute as planning should serve the organisation and not the reverse. It also allows the school to cope with complexity and rapid change.

They build the strategic architecture of the school

The need for 'strategic architecture' requires a school to identify the main pillars of its existence and build a strategic map of the current situation and how those key pillars will develop into the future. Davies, B. (2003) outlines the strategic architecture of the school shown in Figure 5.5.

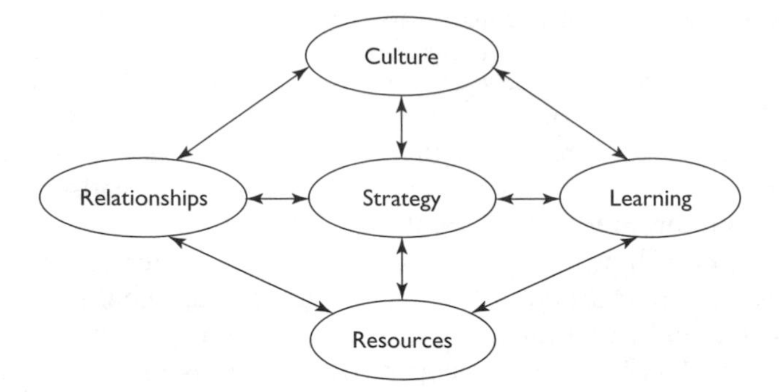

Figure 5.5 The strategic architecture of the school
Source: Davies, B. 2003: 308

The significance of the strategic architecture is that it outlines the main features of the school and focuses attention on them and projects them five years into the future. The challenge then is to adopt strategic approaches that will assist the school to move from the current to the future strategic position. For a more detailed analysis of the architecture of the school, Davies, B. (2003) provides an analysis of the strategic activities and processes, using a balanced scorecard approach (Kaplan and Norton, 1996, 2001; Niven 2002) that is necessary to turn strategy into action.

They are strategically opportunistic

Strategically focused schools position themselves to be able to build the right capability to take advantage of future opportunities. It is possible to consider positioning as a key to enabling the school to be strategically opportunistic. There is a significant difference between schools which simply respond to happenstance (i.e. they bid for initiatives as they come along) and being strategically opportunistic. Strategically opportunistic schools position themselves to make a choice between alternative opportunities and choose the one(s) that fits their strategic direction and development framework.

They deploy strategic timing and abandonment

When to make a strategic shift and what to give up are difficult and challenging decisions. Strategically focused organisations give equal attention to 'when to change' as to 'what to change'. This dual focus is linked to the double s-curve (see Figure 5.2) and when to make the strategic leap to a new way of operating. The danger of taking on too many new initiatives is that the organisation loses focus and overburdens the leadership capacity of the school. Key to maintaining focus and operating within capacity is the concept of abandonment. The schools make clear decisions to undertake the difficult challenge of abandoning some areas of development and activity to create organisational capacity to undertake the new challenge, which involves a constant process of focusing on priorities and making strategic choices.

They develop and sustain strategic leadership

The linking theme in this chapter is that of strategic leadership. Initially it flagged the idea that we need to focus not just on the leader but also on leadership in the school. Strategically focused schools develop leadership in depth which is sometimes called 'distributed leadership'. A focus on how this type of leadership is maintained and enhanced is a feature of strategically focused schools. This concept was articulated more fully in Chapter 2.

CONCLUSION

This chapter has addressed the key concern of how leaders are able to sustain and develop schools through the deployment of effective planning strategies. The central need in the education service is to recognise that many of the gains in student achievement as measured in test scores may not be sustainable if we continue to be fixated on short-term outcomes and plans. There is a need to switch the focus on to two critical areas. First, in order to achieve sustainable development it is necessary to have more effective strategic medium-term planning. Second, if school development and improvement are to be sustainable, it is vital to focus equal attention on the planning processes through concepts such as strategic conversations, participation and motivation as well as to the formal documentation of planning. Leadership that is strategically focused is a key facilitator of this process.

ACKNOWLEDGEMENTS

Thanks are expressed to Carfax Publishing for giving permission for using 'Developing the Strategically Focused School' published in *School Leadership and Management*: 2004, 24 (1) as the basis for this chapter.

RESEARCH SPONSOR

The concepts in this chapter were developed as part of the National College for School Leadership (England) funded research project on developing strategy and strategic leadership in schools. This project aims at exploring in primary (elementary) and secondary (high) schools and special schools the strategic sustainability and leadership aspects of educational organisations.

6 Leading and managing change

Viv Garrett

INTRODUCTION

The leadership and management of change is fraught with tensions: tensions between desired change and imposed, often unwanted, change; between planned and unplanned change; between systematic planning and evolutionary change. And change can usually be guaranteed to cause a great deal of disturbance in a school system. Now this is not always a bad thing if it is well led and managed. But what is the best way to lead and manage change? Is there in fact one best way, or should it depend on our circumstances? Where do we start? One way may be to understand as much as possible about the process of change in order to have a fair chance of leading and managing it effectively.

The purpose of this chapter is to help give you that fair chance. First I will discuss two key aspects of understanding change, then examine the dilemma of planning for change in a dynamic environment, and finally explore some important considerations for leading and managing successful change. In order to do this, I will draw on my own experience and on interviews and discussions I have had with a range of headteachers and teachers. All agree that change is normal, is persistent, and is becoming ever more complex. When one considers the number of changes affecting schools over the past twenty years or so, one can see that change is now so frequent as to be almost continuous. In addition, it is multi-dimensional in that it has an effect on several, if not all, parts of the school system. If one adds to that the normal unplanned disruptions to school life, such as the turnover of staff, illness, disagreements and the like, it becomes impossible to predict accurately the complexities of any particular change. That is not, however, an excuse for a laissez-faire attitude; it is a reason for *managing* the change instead of merely allowing it to happen. Fullan (1993: viii) acknowledges that those people with 'a knowledge of how to view, cope with and initiate change' will manage it better than others. He argues that change mirrors life in that one can never be perfectly happy or in harmony. He further (2003: 24) warns us to 'give up the idea that the pace of change will slow down' and to 'develop a more relaxed attitude toward uncertainty'. The ability to lead and manage change, therefore, is an essential skill for all those in schools, whether they are working at classroom level, middle leadership or senior leadership. This chapter, then, is for anyone involved in the leadership and management of change. I acknowledge that not all those charged with managing change will be change leaders, although most change leaders will also be involved with its management. For the purposes of this chapter, I will address all concerned as *change managers*.

KEY ASPECTS OF UNDERSTANDING CHANGE

Understanding the individual

One of the first considerations is to understand how change can affect the individual. Let us look first at the tensions between planned and unplanned change, and whether changes are wanted or unwanted. All changes involve some form of transition from an old state to a new (Adams, Hayes and Hopson 1976). These transitional events may be both *desired* and *expected*: examples of this could be starting at university, getting married, having children, or starting a new job. They may be *desired* yet *unexpected* like winning the lottery, or meeting up with old friends. These two kinds of change are generally pleasing to the individual. On the other hand are changes which are *not desired*, yet are *expected*. Examples of these are the death of parents, saying goodbye to close friends, or the end of a project. The most stressful of all are those changes which are *neither expected nor desired*, like a sudden crisis such as unexpected illness or redundancy. All of these changes will cause a certain amount of stress to the individual but it will not necessarily always be negative stress. As change managers we need to be aware of these dimensions of desirability and predictability in individual responses and approaches to the change process.

Change events happen to individuals whether they like it or not; whether they learn and grow from the experience is up to them. What does change mean to the individual? How does it make them feel? In order to answer these questions, it may be worthwhile reflecting on your own experience. What sort of feelings did you experience during a period of change? Did those feelings alter during the process? Change can mean stepping out of a position where you feel confident, where you know the rules and the script, and where you are able to function comfortably, into an altogether more uncomfortable position where there is uncertainty about role, relationships and responsibilities, and where you have less confidence in having the skills and knowledge necessary to function effectively. Plant (1987) refers to these positions as *firm ground* and *swampy ground*. It is the area of swampy ground that offers the greatest opportunities and challenges; later on, individuals will note that the greater choice is offered here too, although that might not be apparent at first. It is a big step for people to move into the unknown and can be likened to visiting a new part of the world. Will I like it? How will I cope? It is risky – and exciting. Different responses are normal and to be expected. They can range from the 'I'll try anything for a bit of excitement', through the more normal initial reticence until persuaded, to the 'I'm not going anywhere, and you're not making me'. These attitudes may well be affected by what else is going on in a person's life. Everyone has a need for a certain amount of stability – whether it is personal or professional. The stress factors of moving house, getting married (or divorced), or starting a new job are well documented. How reasonable is it to expect a teacher who is experiencing a combination of these stresses to view yet more change with enthusiasm? By recognising that need for some stability, change managers can show understanding and provide support.

Support can also be provided by taking note of individuals' responses to the transition into a changed state. It has long been accepted that a person's self-esteem can be affected by change, particularly undesirable change (Adams, Hayes and Hopson 1976; Hopson, Scally and Stafford 1992) and seven stages of changes have been identified (see Figure 6.1). Internalisation of the change is the aim, when 'people's hearts and minds need to change, and not just their preferences or routine behaviours' (Heifetz and Linsky 2002: 60).

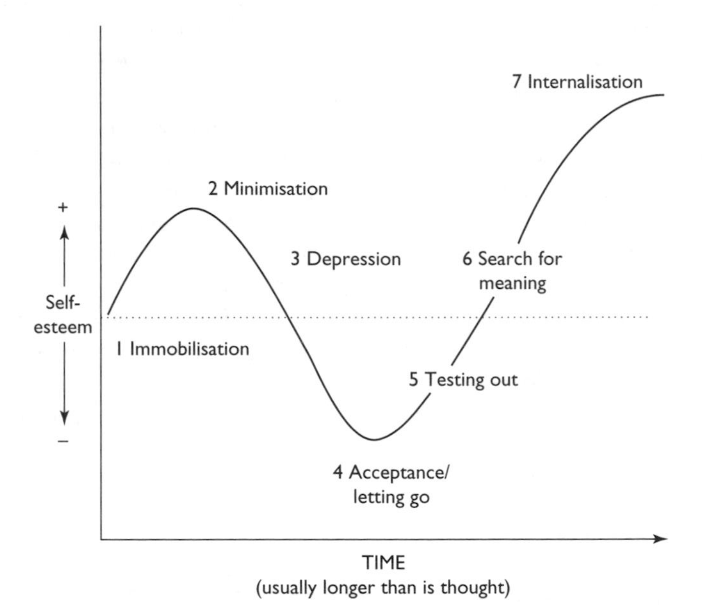

Figure 6.1 Self-esteem changes during transition

Source: Adams *et al.* 1976

These stages can be explored in the following way:

Immobilisation. As individuals start to piece together the information they have been given along with the rumours they are collecting, they begin to form a picture of what the change might be. First reactions are ones of shock and may well include disbelief and the feeling that things could not possibly be that bad, so they do nothing.

Minimisation. As the picture is confirmed, and people try to fit it within their own frames of reference, they may well attempt to minimise the effect it will have on them as individuals or as a group. They may even deny to themselves that change will take place.

Depression. As reality sinks in, the individual may feel particularly unhappy, confused and unappreciated. They may be trying very hard to make sense of the change, trying to reconcile it with their own values and beliefs, and trying to find where they actually fit into the new reality. They may feel powerless and not in control.

Acceptance/letting go. This happens at the lowest point when individuals do at last accept reality. While they do not know what the future holds, they accept that there will be a future and that they cannot go back.

Testing out. Individuals start to examine ways in which they can work with the change. This may involve discussions with peers or with senior managers, or trying out new materials or techniques. 'Where do I stand now?' is the prime question.

Search for meaning. This is the stage when self-esteem starts to rise again as individuals begin to understand the new ways and to see how they can use them and adapt them. They may continue to test out ways of working until they feel comfortable and ready to move to the next stage.

Internalisation. The change has now been understood and adopted. Individuals have the confidence to further adapt and develop what is now an accepted way of working. They can now start to build on their newly developed strengths.

The crucial thing for the change manager to understand is that everyone will go through this process at their own pace, and that they should be allowed time for this process. Change managers have to allow others to make sense of the change in exactly the same way as they had to; it could take others longer if they are at different starting points. People come from different backgrounds with different experiences and this needs to be acknowledged. Change managers cannot force people to act and think differently but they can show understanding and support at the key points in transition. Fullan (1993) quotes Marris (1975: 166) to demonstrate this:

> When those who have the power to manipulate changes act as if they have only to explain, and when their explanations are not at once accepted, shrug off opposition as ignorance or prejudice, they express a profound contempt for the meaning of lives other than their own.

> For the reformers have already assimilated these changes to their purposes, and worked out a reformulation which makes sense to them, perhaps through months or years of analysis and debate. If they deny others the chance to do the same, they treat them as puppets dangling by the threads of their own conceptions.

In providing support it should be noted that the stage from *depression* to *acceptance* is an important one and needs to be monitored. Patient reassurance and help should be given so that individuals do not feel they are suffering alone. While some will come through this stage relatively unscathed, others will undoubtedly suffer. This is the stage of change when some professional development is usual; however, this can cause even more anxiety in cases where the individual feels they cannot cope. Once the individual indicates that they will let go of the past, then further professional development will be beneficial and will hasten the last stages.

This understanding of individuals' response to change is crucial and needs to be considered along with the second key aspect of leading and managing change: that of understanding the organisation.

Understanding the organisation

An understanding of the organisation in which the change manager works is essential to the successful leadership and management of change. That is, not only the pattern of formal meetings and lines of reporting and accountability, but also the more informal ways of getting things done. Schools may all have a similar purpose in that they provide an education for the students in their care, but the ways they go about this are very different. It may help to refer to the iceberg diagram adapted from Plant (1987) and shown in Figure 6. 2.

The visible part of the iceberg indicates the formal organisation of the school: the ways in which the school is structured, its pattern of lessons and meetings, the explicit parts of its philosophy and purpose, i.e. *what is immediately apparent*. The underwater portion depicts the informal or hidden organisation: the ethos or culture, the ways things really happen, i.e. *what becomes apparent after a period in the school.*

The *formal organisation* is the normal vehicle for the working of the school. Schools have always been complex organisations, and become more so as they become more outward-looking and work with a wide range of stakeholders. A deceptively simple way of describing a typical school is to think of it as made up of a number of transparent layers. The first layer is the physical environment: the buildings and grounds. The second is the organisation of the students and the teaching: the students are divided into classes, the curriculum is divided into subjects, the timetable is divided into lessons, and the teachers are divided into subject or year

Figure 6.2 Organisation iceberg
Source: Adapted from Plant 1987

groups. They are surrounded by a framework of supporting personnel, including administrative and clerical/technical staff, welfare and classroom support staff and volunteer helpers, and those taking care of the physical fabric and environment of the school. On top of this is a layer of responsibilities and reporting structures; a further layer of strategies contains communication procedures and meetings, and this is then covered by a blanket of stated policies and procedures on the running of the school. This multi-layered kaleidoscope is then managed by the governors, headteacher and team, and influenced by parents, community, education officials and government, as well as staff and students.

The *informal organisation* is the cultural dimension of the school. This hidden part of the organisation includes the way individuals and groups relate to each other in an informal sense, and establish power groups which are apart from the formal structure of curricular areas and working parties.

The most powerful staff members may not hold formal positions of responsibility in the school, but nevertheless teachers look to them for leadership in times of decision-making. They may be particularly charismatic individuals, they may be acknowledged experts who attract a certain level of respect, or they may hold influential positions outside the formal school structure. Examples of these might be a teacher union representative, a teacher with several years of experience who does not hold a post of responsibility, or a teacher well-known for expertise in areas outside the school. Interest groups may have developed within the staffroom: the staff football team, a group with similar values or political beliefs; and outside the staffroom: those who prefer to take their breaks elsewhere in bases around the school, and the outcast smokers. Each of these groups will have its own unstated, yet understood, code of practice which may well include how its members react to new initiatives. While change managers may be using the formal structure and procedures of their schools to introduce and implement a change, they need to be very aware of the informal rules and relationships current in the school and take account of this dimension both in their planning and in their day-to-day management. Hargreaves and Fullan (1998: 27) have an insight on this:

> Your own organisation has its own special combination of personalities and prehistories. There is no one answer to the question of how one brings about change in specific situations. You can get ideas, directions, insights, and lines of thought, but you can never know exactly how to proceed. You have to beat the path by walking it.

Walking that path and the place of planning is something to be addressed in the next section.

PLANNING FOR CHANGE

The process of the planning of change should always be the topic of discussion and debate. Should the implementation of changes be incremental and controlled? Or should changes be allowed to evolve in an unplanned way? Where is the powerbase for change? Wilson (1992: 12) explores these issues in his discussion of approaches to organisational change, and comments that planned change relies upon a model of organisation in which there is uncritical acceptance of the managerial role, which has been particularly true of North America and the UK. He compares this situation with other countries and cites Sweden and Japan where ideas can emanate from all parts of the organisation and planned change requires careful consultation with the workforce. This is an interesting issue with regard to education in the UK. There is no doubt that government policies favour the acceptance of the hierarchical model of management with planned incremental change.

However, the majority of school leaders would not accept that the onus of change lies solely with senior school teams; I know of several schools which have systems in place to actively encourage staff involvement in the initiation and implementation of change. I would argue that effective implementation of change relies on the active involvement of staff at each stage of the process; otherwise the change will never become fully operational and incorporated into everyday practice. Morgan (1993) addresses the empowerment of staff in his innovative book *Imaginization*:

> We are leaving the age of organised organisations and moving into an era where the ability to understand, facilitate, and encourage processes of self-organisation will become a key competence.
>
> (Morgan 1993: frontispiece)

Of course, school staff are not the only people to be involved in the change process. There may well be other individuals and groups outside the organisation who have an interest or stake in the changing situation. Fullan stresses the need to take into account all participant and stakeholder views as the change progresses. He warns us of the dangers of planning down to the last detail and reminds us that 'change is a journey not a blueprint'(1993: 24): one can never accurately predict what is going to happen. The active involvement of key stakeholders in the change process is crucial for effective implementation. The more say individuals have had at each stage of the process, the more likely they are to support developments. It is worthwhile referring to Berman's (1980) work at this point and noting his concept of *adaptive implementation* which is reliant on stakeholder input and participation. By allowing participants to adapt, form and reform their approaches to initiatives, internalisation of the change is more likely. This loosely coupled attitude is in contrast to his alternative concept of *programmed implementation* which has, as its core, tightly controlled incremental steps towards agreed goals. These are but two ends of a continuum; actual practice takes place at various stages in between and has to be dependent on the nature of the change, the internal situation and the external environment.

Fullan takes these perspectives into account and suggests that we do not spend too much time on strategic planning at the outset of complex change processes. He supports Louis and Miles' (1990) *evolutionary perspective*:

> The evolutionary perspective rests on the assumption that the environment both inside and outside organisations is often chaotic. No specific plan can last for very long, because it will either become outmoded due to changing external pressures, or because disagreement over priorities arises within the organisation.
>
> (Louis and Miles 1990: 193)

As a result of the turbulent environment in which we now find ourselves, Fullan has proposed a particular order of events in preparing for educational change: *Ready! Fire! Aim!* (Fullan 1993: 31). He argues that the *Ready!* state encompasses the idea of preparedness and direction, *Fire!* is the stage of enquiry and action where knowledge is formed, and *Aim!* is the stage when vision, mission and strategic planning are addressed. This is a direct challenge to the systematic approaches to change which first encourage us to shape the vision, then define the mission, then formulate the strategic plan, and only then follow it by action, i.e. Ready, Aim, Fire.

Fullan maintains that the *Ready!* state encompasses a notion of direction but that one should not become bogged down by vision, mission and strategic planning before learning about the dynamic reality (Fullan 1993: 31). An example which immediately comes to mind as an illustration of these three stages is the OfSTED inspection. Any school which has not been inspected for a while is in a state of readiness; the staff have an idea of the direction in which they should be going. Once the school has been informed of a date for inspection, the lead time enables the staff to complete informal audits of their information systems and their teaching and learning processes in preparation for the formal procedure. *Fire!* is the process of the inspection itself where all concerned share in a great deal of learning; and *Aim!* is the agenda discussed and formulated as a result.

I will use this framework of *Ready! Fire!* and *Aim!* to examine how these states can be translated into concepts and strategies for the school workplace. I will then explore some key considerations for the successful management of change.

A state of readiness

We have seen above that Fullan (1993) believes that vision-driven change is an old paradigm, that vision should emerge from, rather than precede, action. He stresses the importance of the shared vision, and believes that the process of merging the personal and the shared visions takes time, and can be achieved only after much discussion and interaction. In my experience, schools are addressing this state of readiness and vision creation in different ways. All have become very conscious of the power of the marketplace and this becomes one of the key drivers of the ready state. What does a state of readiness actually mean for schools? I give three examples below of schools in various stages of creating readiness for change. The first school has raised awareness by initially focusing on classroom practice; the second by voluntary involvement of staff in regular think-tanks; the third by a new headteacher appointed to turn a school around.

The first headteacher stresses that the intellectual stimulation of change is quite critical for the success of a school, but emphasises that the need for change has to be based on a knowledge of what is happening – that change *evolves* from a felt need. But where does this knowledge come from? He acknowledges that anticipation about particular situations comes from two sources in the school: from middle and senior leadership and from the classroom. He has a very strong philosophy that the key function of a school is what happens in the classroom, and that the quality of interaction between the teacher and the pupil is one of his most important responsibilities. In order to learn about this, he and his assistant heads target faculties in the school, observe lessons and hold discussions with staff. In checking out the different subject areas, they ask questions and pose challenges and make this part of accepted practice. In this way they have become sensitive to the need for change. As teaching has improved and examination pass rates have increased, the staff in turn have learnt about their situations and have become far more sensitive and welcoming to the idea of change. The concept of professional development plays an important part in the life of this school.

Another headteacher stresses the importance of continuous thinking about the future and harnessing the best ideas from any member of the school, students included. She holds regular think-tank meetings with open agendas at which anyone can present a paper and share their ideas. The only proviso is that each area of the school must be represented at the meetings. These ideas are then discussed at various levels within the school. During this process, the ideas are shaped and reshaped before being given to a small working group to investigate. This headteacher feels it extremely important to indulge in the process of innovative lateral thinking: to focus on what is best for students and not to get demoralised by working to others' agendas all the time. An emphasis on the development of individuals through the performance management process and training programmes, together with a climate of support, ensures that there is a buzz of involvement and achievement in the school.

Both of the headteachers cited above are very experienced and run very successful schools. But what of a headteacher taking over a school categorised by OfSTED as having serious weaknesses? This third school is at a very different stage of development. The new head has a different starting point in attempting to achieve a ready state in her school. She not only has to bring in new ideas to make a difference to the school in a short length of time but she also has to work on the culture of the school and improve staff morale. She concedes that she has had to adopt a fairly autocratic style in order to introduce the necessary challenges for thinking about the future. The question of leadership style is an interesting issue in this context: this head differs very much from the first two examples of heads in established schools. In preparing this school for a state of readiness, this head has had to take into account various situational factors: those of *relationships* within the school (trust, respect and support for her and for one another), of the *nature of the tasks* to be undertaken, and of the *maturity* of the staff in terms of ability, experience and motivation. It is largely the factors of relationships and levels of maturity which may differ in the three schools described. Long-established theories from researchers such as Fiedler (1967) and Hersey and Blanchard (1982) bear out these influences on leadership style. As this school is working through its agenda and individuals are developing in maturity, so the head is able to soft-pedal on the telling dimension and encourage a more participative climate. In practice, the perceived and real culture change, as a result of the appointment of a new headteacher, often results in a turnover of staff which can contribute to the development of maturity in the organisation. In this school, over 60 per cent of the staff now have less than five years' experience; although they may be lacking in maturity in terms of experience, change is normal to them. Professional development plays a significant role in this school with the benefits of increased staff confidence in the development and implementation of new ideas.

Each of these schools is working towards a culture of readiness for change in which individuals feel they have responsibility for their part in the overall agenda for school improvement.

Let us now consider the next part of the framework.

Prepared to fire! Investigating wicked problems

This is the stage of enquiry and learning; the action preceding the stage of strategic planning. Before making detailed plans for the future, we must ensure we learn as much as possible about our particular problems. The term 'wicked problems' was coined by Rittel and Webber (1973) and could have been devised especially for the problem situations faced in schools. A wicked problem is one that does not have an easy solution; in fact it is probably not solvable. There is no right answer to the problem, and any possible action will be dependent on the nature of the problem, the situation and the individuals involved. The danger is that we get so close to our problem that we lose sight of the whole picture and make assumptions as to its real nature. When a problem occurs, we automatically search our frames of reference and slot in our previously tried solutions – we use our programmed knowledge. This ready application of programmed knowledge is not always appropriate in complex situations and denies learning taking place until after a solution has been tried out, sometimes unsuccessfully. Fullan (1993: 26) has a comment to make on this:

> we cannot develop effective responses to complex situations unless we actively seek and confront the real problems which are in fact difficult to solve. Problems are our friends because it is only through immersing ourselves in problems that we can come up with creative solutions.

We need to focus actively on the problem itself and try and build up the richest possible picture of the situation rather than begin by focusing on the possible solutions. In order to do this, we need to learn to ask questions of ourselves and others and explore the situation afresh. As Pascale (1990: 14) states 'Inquiry is the engine of vitality and self-renewal'.

This questioning is an integral part of Action Learning, an approach to management education identified by Revans (1983) and further developed by Pedler (1996). Questioning and careful reflection should precede the use of programmed knowledge; learning is achieved when both are added together. This technique is used in Action Learning groups which bring together small groups of committed people on a voluntary basis in order to help and support one another through the wicked problems of the workplace. By the use of careful questioning, an individual is helped to explore the fullest possible picture of a problem, then to focus in on possible ways forward. Strict rules regarding technique and confidentiality apply. A commitment to action completes the first stage of the process with follow-up meetings to check progress and provide continuing support. Action Learning groups are used in and across a wide range of organisations and are particularly valuable in providing support to individual leaders who would otherwise feel very isolated in their organisations.

Action Learning can be used in schools in a number of ways. A group of classroom teachers or members of a department can explore ways to improve teaching using their real experiences of problem situations; a group of heads of department can explore the problems besetting the introduction of new assessment methods; young teachers can develop their confidence in dealing with difficult situations; a senior management team can actively support one another in their responsibilities. In addition to extending their knowledge about the particular situations being addressed, individuals will learn more about themselves and their styles of leading and managing, and experience the challenges of commitment and accountability to the group.

Other groups and working parties can be set up in schools in order to investigate problem areas more deeply, to consider proposals and suggestions, to consult, and to conduct feasibility studies. All these functions are examples of further enquiry and learning and fulfil the necessary components of the *Fire!* stage.

Aim! Now can we plan?

The investigative processes outlined above begin the process of shaping and reshaping ideas to form a vision of the future. By further developing the circles of involvement and participation, knowledge and understanding is increased, not only about the vision but also about the changes that may be necessary. Each stakeholder has had the opportunity to provide some input into the shared vision of the future. The personal vision presented to the school think-tank, described earlier, has now been investigated, and has been shaped and reshaped as it has been discussed formally and informally in various corners and at various levels in the organisation. Although this process can be lengthy and difficult as individuals form and reform their positions, implementation now has more chance of success because of the early involvement of those affected. The planning in turn can be less affected by the negative actions of individuals who feel their opinions have been ignored, or, worse, were never sought. There is also more chance of the implementation involving more creative changes and challenges to the normal accepted pattern of the school. These more far-reaching changes have been described as *revolutionary transformation* (Wilson 1992) or *second-order* changes (Cuban 1988).

Wilson (1992: 20) has identified four levels of organisational change:

Level 1	Status quo	staying the same (or even running to stand still?)
Level 2	Expanded reproduction	doing more of the same
Level 3	Evolutionary transition	making changes within the existing structures
Level 4	Revolutionary transformation	making fundamental changes to the structures of the organisation

Each level of achievement may be the result of a conscious decision. It may be that a school decides, after much consultation and reflection, to maintain the status quo in a particular area for the time being (Level 1). Discussions of a successful pilot scheme may well result in replicating it elsewhere in the organisation: doing more of the same (Level 2). Similarly, fine tuning of extensive developments may be necessary, i.e. making changes within the existing structures (Level 3). However, it is the level of making fundamental changes to the structures of an organisation which is the most difficult to achieve (Level 4). Cuban (1988) has a simpler model of *first-order* changes similar to Wilson's Levels 2 and 3, and *second-order*, similar to Level 4. He comments on the difficulties of second-order changes in relation to his analysis of school reform in North America:

> Most reforms foundered on the rocks of flawed implementation. Many were diverted by the quiet but persistent resistance of teachers and administrators who, unconvinced by the unvarnished cheer of reformers, saw minimal gain and much loss in embracing second-order changes boosted by those who were unfamiliar with the classroom as

> a workplace. Thus first-order changes succeeded while second-order changes were either adapted to fit what existed or sloughed off, allowing the system to remain essentially untouched. The ingredients change, the Chinese saying goes, but the soup remains the same.
>
> (Cuban 1988: 341)

We can learn from his experience and should never lose sight of the fact that educational change involves people. Systems seldom fight back, but human beings can and will! Heifetz and Linsky (2002: 30) have a comment on this:

> Adaptive change stimulates resistance because it challenges people's habits, beliefs and values. It asks them to take a loss, experience uncertainty, and even express disloyalty to people and cultures. Because adaptive change forces people to question and perhaps redefine aspects of their identity, it also challenges their sense of competence. Loss, disloyalty, and feeling incompetent: That's a lot to ask. No wonder people resist.

MANAGING SUCCESSFUL CHANGE

It is tempting to say that once the three stages of *Ready!, Fire!, Aim!* have been addressed, there is every chance that the change will be successful. However, as Heifetz and Linsky point out above, we need to recognise that resistance to change can be normal and natural. It is important for the change manager to be sensitive to this and to be aware of the barriers which can exist (Dalin 1978; Pugh 1993; Aspinwall 1998). There may be *personal* barriers built up as a defence where an individual feels that their values and beliefs are being threatened or undermined or *psychological* barriers in response to an inherent unwillingness to change. There may also be *organisational* barriers where the structure of the organisation is not flexible enough to permit particular changes, or *power* barriers where individuals or interest groups are unhappy about possible redistribution of power.

There are two diagnostic tools which may be of use in raising the awareness of the change manager and others to the barriers which exist in a particular situation. These are: force field analysis, and micro-political mapping (see Aspinwall *et al.* 1992). Force field analysis (see Figure 6.3) is commonly used to identify whether there is a critical mass of support for a proposed change, and to analyse the reasons for any blockages later on. An open discussion of the driving forces and hindering forces of a change can be of considerable advantage and can aid identification of ways forward. By ensuring overt analysis, change managers open up the problem to encourage participation and ownership of possible solutions.

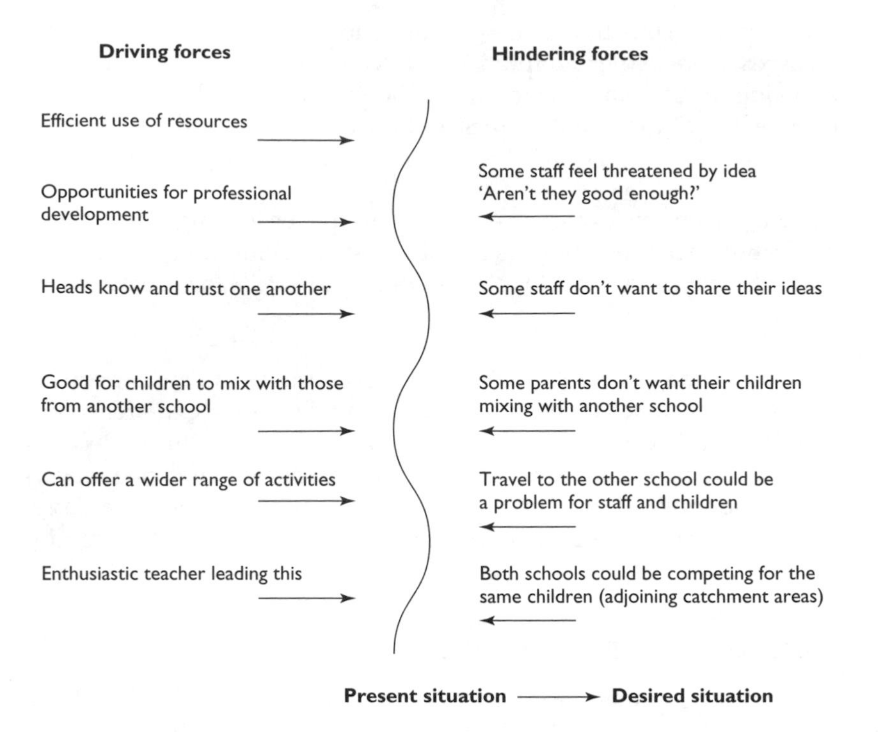

Figure 6.3 Force field analysis: two schools wishing to combine resources in the form of some teacher expertise and accommodation

The second tool, micro-political mapping (see Figure 6.4) focuses more on people and their behaviour. This exercise aids the identification of individuals in terms of their power or influence, and their concern or support for the change in question. This mapping of the distribution of power and the identification of winners and losers is a useful exercise to undertake as an individual change manager, or as a small group managing a change. However, it should be noted that the analysis can be quite subjective, and any results should be sensitively handled.

Both of these exercises can help to identify areas, and agents, of resistance. The next stage for the change manager is to try to understand the reasons for resistance and to introduce strategies to remedy the situation. One particularly common reason is the *perceived* lack of communication. 'Nobody's told me what's happening' is commonly heard and is a good excuse for non-involvement. Ensuring that all have the necessary knowledge and understanding of the proposed changes is the first step. Yet communication does not finish there. There are further questions which are often overlooked. What are the procedures for communicating progress and achievements to others? Are there mechanisms for feedback? A busy change manager can become so caught up in the intricacies of imple-

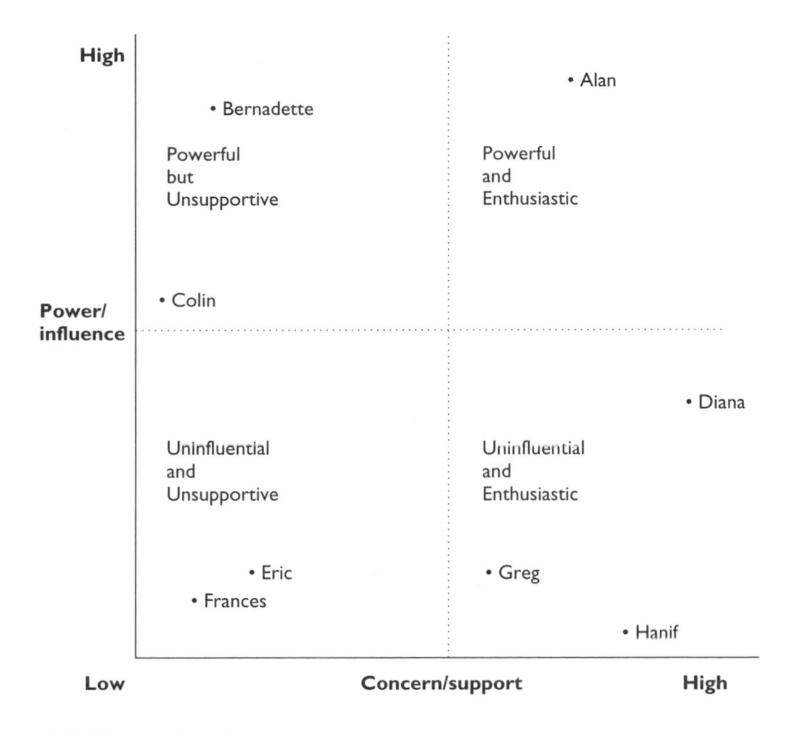

Figure 6.4 Micro-political mapping

mentation that the business of reporting and receiving feedback can seem relatively unimportant. Yet it is the sharing of the successes and difficulties that ensures the continued involvement of people. 'Communicate like never before' (Plant 1987) and 'Communicate like crazy' (Clarke 1994) are the constant cries of advice. This applies not only to the supply of information *down* through, and *across*, the organisation, but also to allowing information, comment and feedback *upwards*. Only then can all feel properly informed. There is always the danger of not providing enough information: in those cases, the resultant vacuum provides opportunities for rumour and assumptions. Then additional work is required of the change manager to discover the truths and deal with the false situations which have arisen.

Even if communication is satisfactory, there will still be some individuals or groups who can be identified as resistors. This is when the change manager needs to consider specific strategies to overcome the negative attitudes displayed. A short-term strategy of immediately counteracting any negativity can prove its worth and nullify mischief making, but requires considerable vigilance by the change manager and can absorb much time and energy. An understanding of 'what makes people tick' can help to identify additional strategies for providing support where needed, helping to build confidence, working together and sharing hopes and concerns: remedies for the difficulties of the transition curve described earlier in this chapter.

Although the above may be effective strategies for managing resistance to change, they do not address the cultural issues of helping a school to achieve Fullan's (1993) *Ready!* state. It is in the quality of people and their interactions that ultimate success lies. We have agreed that change depends on people, on their feeling confident enough to take on change: confident both in the role they are playing and in their relationships with other people. We have discovered that we need to be sensitive to the need for support, particularly when individuals are anxious or afraid. We have established that we need to nurture the skills of individuals and help them to develop to achieve their potential both as individuals and as members of the larger organisation. We need to empower them to do this.

Professional development plays an important part in any organisation, and leaders have to try to achieve a balance between the needs of the individual and the needs of the organisation. In a period of scarce resources, it has become increasingly the case that the needs of the organisation come first; although any wise leader will take account of the individual's interests and needs in developing their role in the organisation. The performance management or appraisal system should provide a vehicle for the effective integration of personal and organisational needs. The resultant consolidation of personal and school development plans provides the basis for a programme of professional development. A key group of staff who are benefiting from targeted professional development are the middle leaders (e.g. the 'Leading from the Middle' programme from the National College for School Leadership). It is acknowledged that these leaders can be a significant influence in schools: both on classroom practice and on whole-school leadership and management. Professional development can play a large part not only in providing them with appropriate teaching and leadership skills, but also in helping them with the wider issues of developing confidence, clarifying their role, and being prepared to take on their responsibilities. As one head said to me, 'You can never have enough help for all the changes a school needs to take on board.' A leadership development programme for middle leaders run by a university with local schools provides an example of learning that can be achieved by the sharing of experiences across and within schools. As well as gaining a qualification, the middle leaders are providing a support group for each other in which they can safely work through their ideas and frustrations, as well as contributing to the development of a critical mass driving and supporting the improvement agenda in their schools.

It is now generally acknowledged that the quality of ideas and creative thinking is greater in a collaborative situation where individuals can bring and share their specific knowledge and expertise. 'People need one another to learn and to accomplish things' (Fullan 1993: 17), which is demonstrated by the forming of relationships, teams, partnerships and alliances. But these are not static: relationships by their very nature will change and develop. Collaboration is a dynamic process requiring awareness of the potential of forming and reforming relationships all the time. Collaboration means accepting that everyone's contribution will be encouraged and valued. It does not, and should not, mean that everyone will always agree, because the quality of interaction will depend on the contributions of the individual. These in turn depend on the individual's experience, their values and beliefs, their intuition, their capacity for independent thinking and their confidence in themselves and in the collaborative situation. Sometimes the contribution may be an initiating one; at other times, it may move matters on by involving others inside and outside the group. It may also be a dissenting one, advising caution or proposing a different mode of action. This position of dissension is not a comfortable one, but the resulting conflict is essential for healthy group working and learning. 'You can't have organizational learning without individual learning, and you can't have learning in groups without processing conflict' (Fullan 1993: 36). Tuckman's (1965) writings show agreement with the importance of conflict and he argues that the process of *storming* is an essential one for effective group performance. It is only after a group of people have been through the uncomfortable experiences of initiating and responding to personal challenge that they can call themselves a *team*.

Belbin (1981, 1993) is one writer who, over the years, has taken this idea of teams further. His research is based on the belief that individuals fulfil a team role as well as a function within the organisation. He identifies nine such team roles. Plant; Resource-investigator; Co-ordinator; Shaper; Monitor–evaluator; Teamworker; Implementer; Completer–finisher, and Specialist. Some of these roles are inward-looking towards the maintenance and development of the team; others look outwards towards the organisation and the wider environment. It is not expected that any one person would be able to fulfil all of these roles; the team role will depend on the pattern of behaviour in the team situation. This behaviour pattern is established by a combination of the factors of personality, mental abilities, values and motivations, field constraints, experience and role learning (Belbin 1993). There is an art to building a team and, for a team to be effective, each of these team roles should be covered. That is not to say that each team should have a membership of nine people, but that each role should be represented within the membership. For example, one team member may fulfil a dual role of monitor-evaluator and completer-finisher, another of resource-investigator and plant, and another may fulfil the specialist role alone.

It is recognised that one cannot always set up teams from scratch, and that it is often politically desirable to include certain members in a team, but it is worthwhile using Belbin's framework to analyse problems of non-performance and then taking remedial action. One headteacher who uses short-term working parties to initiate and implement change selects a small nucleus of workers: 'doers', 'facilitators' and 'thinkers'. The working party is then opened up for free membership to enable everyone to have the opportunity of serving. The importance of a clear brief is established with agreed dates for reporting back. In this respect, the role of the completer-finisher is important; different skills and roles are useful at different stages of a change process.

Provided that teamwork is not forced upon people, or worse, that people pay lip service to teamwork by merely appearing at meetings, there are very real benefits. Most individuals have an affiliation need – they like to feel part of something. Success or adversity can help the bonding of individuals into a team; OfSTED inspections can play their part in this. Several schools organise informal social activities to encourage bonding and the breaking down of barriers. They can aid the development of an understanding that everyone in the organisation is a human being with different needs and different vulnerabilities even though they may hold different positions of responsibility. Improving relationships within the staff group as a whole can facilitate team working throughout the school. In turn, as individuals begin to realise both their and others' potential in small working groups, so a better level of understanding and appreciation of others' strengths can influence relationships within the larger organisation.

But what happens when a short-term working group disbands? The members have succeeded in working well together to achieve their targets and have begun to realise their potential. They do not want to break up as a group; they are back on Plant's (1987) *firm ground*. However, there is a good opportunity here to use the expertise developed. Individuals can be encouraged to use their teamwork skills to develop other working groups. And the group as a whole can be used, in one headteacher's words, as a 'building block' for the future, for example a successful group working with other groups on relevant change issues.

However, it is not only inside the organisation that collaboration takes place. Working with the wider environment can provide new perspectives and the stimulus necessary to view the future creatively. Although this means moving into Plant's (1987) *swampy ground*, this can be particularly beneficial for the smaller school where the staff may feel under more pressure to be creative and might welcome an influx of new ideas. Fullan (1993: 87) is continually advising teachers to 'connect with the wider environment':

> There is a ceiling effect to conceptualising inspiring visions, to investigating and solving problems, to achieving greater and greater competencies, and to engaging in productive relationships, if one does

> not connect to varied and large networks of others involved in similar and different pursuits.

Schools cannot develop in isolation from their environments. The best schools will always take account of the local and wider context in recognising opportunities for development, but without losing sight of their fundamental beliefs and values. This may range from school staff being active members of local community groups, through joint management of a sports centre, to the setting up of a Community School. The development of an interactive relationship with external bodies can be very challenging as well as potentially extremely rewarding. It is essential to respect each other's cultures and ways of working; it is by recognising and incorporating the strengths of those cultures that learning and development occurs. But ease of working together does not happen overnight. It can take some time, and much hard work, to build up, particularly if the cultures are very different. However, once a working relationship is established, the results are worthwhile and can provide the impetus for further developments and future alliances. It is by learning to work with others that we start to learn more about ourselves. As schools work with new partners both inside and outside the education system, they can also begin to discover how others perceive them. Some perceptions and assumptions may be wrong and can then be challenged and corrected; others may well be uncomfortable but correct. Some schools have joined together for mutual support in all sorts of areas, for example, a more efficient means of offering training courses, or a sharing of specialist facilities.

A paradox here is the idea of collaborative working, and the establishment of alliances and networks, set against the reality of competition in the marketplace. This is another interesting tension leading to the careful choice of partners. But it is worthwhile seeking out more challenging partners and establishing an atmosphere of trust: the ultimate sharing may be beneficial to all. Some schools are taking advantage of the wider national and international context to further enhance their development opportunities.

This widening of individuals' experience is borne out by Fullan (2003: 27) who writes of the 'big picture dot-connection' . . . to integrate 'new horizons and moral purpose':

> The goal is to create new policies, strategies and mechanisms that enable people to enlarge their own worlds in order to provide greater ideas and place the meaning of their work in a much larger perspective. When people do this they have a chance of changing the very context that historically constrains them.

CONCLUSION

All of the above strategies refer to empowerment of individuals: ensuring they have involvement in the processes of change, ensuring they are able to work together in collaboration with others, and ensuring they have the necessary skills to implement any change. This form of power-sharing is crucial to successful implementation and eventual internalisation of the change, but it does require a school leader who is secure enough to continue to see the whole picture and to live with the feeling of possible loss of control. Headteachers can empower others by giving individuals the opportunity to share the power and control of a change. Individuals can empower themselves by learning about the change process and taking responsibility for their part in it. This acceptance of the potential of individuals is summed up in DePree's (1990: 142) description of *elegance*:

> Most of the time, when we consider ourselves and others, we are looking at only parts of people. The measure of individuals – and so of corporations – is the extent to which we struggle to complete ourselves, the energy we devote to living up to our potential. An elegant company frees its members to be their best. Elegant leaders free the people they lead to do the same.

7 Leading and managing staff in high performance schools

Max Sawatzki

THE NEED FOR BOTH LEADERSHIP AND MANAGEMENT

It needs to be acknowledged from the outset that, in this era which is high on both complexity and rate of change, there is a need for high levels of both leadership and management in striving to develop and maintain world-class organisations. Hence, there is little point in debating the virtue of one versus the other, or even bothering to dwell greatly on defining the difference between them, even though Kotter (1990) does this very neatly through the analysis illustrated in Table 7.1.

Suffice it to say that in this high performance era it is pointless talking about managing staff, without at the same time talking of leading staff.

EMERGING TRENDS IN LEADERSHIP

While it is not possible to examine fully here the nature of effective leadership, it is worth reflecting briefly on the changes to the concept of leadership that have occurred over a number of years. The American Telephone and Telegraph definition, for example, as presented by Moses (1990) has changed significantly in this time, as illustrated below:

1956 *A man can lead a group to accomplish a task without arousing hostility.*
1970–80 *An individual can lead a group to accomplish a task.*
1990– *An individual elicits high performance outcomes from others.*

Apart from the significance of the changed wording to include female leaders, which in itself is a major leap forward, the trend in this development is clearly towards the leader as facilitator of team performance, rather than as knight on white charger, or director and supervisor; and towards a situation wherein leadership is about the creation and maintenance of a climate and conditions for the achievement of goals and the attainment of high performance – a situation in which leadership involves working with and through others.

Table 7.1 Distinguishing leadership and management

	Management	*Leadership*
Creating an agenda	Planning and budgeting – establishing detailed steps and timetables for achieving needed results, and then allocating the resources necessary to make that happen	Establishing direction – developing a vision of the future, often the distant future, and strategies for producing the changes needed to achieve that vision
Developing a human network for achieving the agenda	Organising and staffing – establishing some structure for accomplishing plan requirements, staffing that structure with individuals, delegating responsibility and authority for carrying out the plan, providing policies and procedures to help guide people, and creating methods or systems to monitor implementation	Aligning people – communicating the direction by words and deeds to all those whose co-operation may be needed so as to influence the creation of teams and coalitions that understand the vision and strategies, and accept their validity
Execution	Controlling and problem solving – monitoring results vs. plan in some detail, identifying deviations, and then planning and organising to solve these problems	Motivating and inspiring – energising people to overcome major political, bureaucratic, and resource barriers to change by satisfying very basic, but often unfulfilled, human needs
Outcomes	Produces a degree of predictability and order, and has the potential of consistently producing key results expected by various stakeholders (e.g. for customers, always being on time; for stockholders, being on budget)	Produces change, often to a dramatic degree, and has the potential of producing extremely useful change (e.g., new products that customers want, new approaches to labour relations that help make a firm more competitive)

Source: Kotter 1990

This does not suggest for a minute that the leader is simply a co-ordinator, for this is certainly not the case. Leadership is a far more active and deliberate process than this. Indeed, leadership will always be about helping the group move forward by utilising the efforts of individuals who complement and enhance each other's skills, 'linking the group to the strengthening unit of a common purpose . . . making the parts whole' (Adair 1986: 116).

Looking at these changes in another way, it is worthwhile reflecting, as Sharpe (1995: 17) does, that 'education for the 21st Century is coinciding with a renewed interest in the concept of leadership'. Tracing the emergence of the concept through two-dimensional leadership (1960s), situational leadership (1970s) and transformational leadership (late 1970s), Sharpe concludes that in the late 1990s leadership regained its rightful place in the scheme of things, having been relegated to second place by the 'more mundane and at times sterile diet of management efficiency' in the 1980s.

This analysis supports a currently dominant view of the need for what DePree (1990: 1) describes as *Strategic Leadership*. In his terms, 'the first requirement of a leader is to define reality. The last is to say "Thank you". In between the leader must become a servant and a debtor.' Within the schooling context, Caldwell and Spinks (1992: 92) define strategic leadership as:

- keeping abreast of trends and issues, threats and opportunities in the school environment and in society at large, nationally and internationally; discerning the 'megatrends' and anticipating their impact on education generally and on the school in particular;
- sharing their knowledge with others in the school's community and encouraging other school leaders to do the same in their areas of interest;
- establishing structures and processes which enable the school to set priorities and formulate strategies which take account of likely and/or preferred futures; being a key source of expertise as these occur;
- ensuring that the attention of the school community is focused on matters of strategic importance;
- monitoring the implementation of strategies as well as emerging strategic issues in the wider environment; facilitating an ongoing process of review.

Consistent with, but somewhat an extension of these views, is the conception of leadership provided by Manz and Sims (1994). In their publication, *Superleadership* they conclude that the leadership which is required today is best described as 'leading others to lead themselves' through, among other things, modelling effective leadership behaviours, and through establishing self-leadership systems – culture, socio-technical designs, and teams. In their terms, 'superleaders have super followers', a view which is endorsed by Chaleff (1995: 46) who argues that 'We need a dynamic model of followership that balances and supports dynamic leadership . . . a proactive view of the follower's role, which brings it into parity with the (formal) leader's role.' In essence, we are therefore drawn to a model which suggests that leadership lies in all of us, and the high performing organisation will be one in which each member of the team is a self-led, growing and dynamic individual, prepared to contribute to the greater good of the team and the organisation.

But what of the *formal* or designated leader's position within this scheme of things? The final piece in the mosaic is provided by Wilson *et al.* (1994)

who show visually the changes that have occurred over the years, arriving at the *highly empowering* leader who acts as mentor to a number of self-managing work teams. This formulation is shown in Figure 7.1

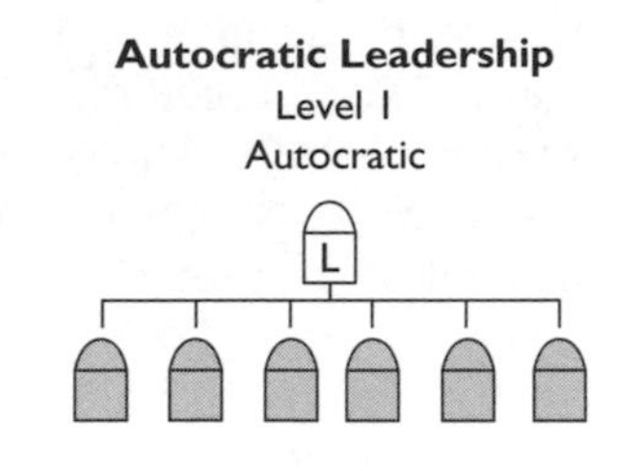

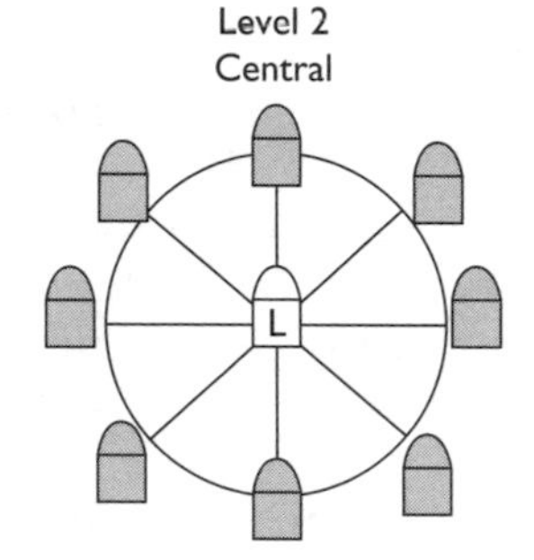

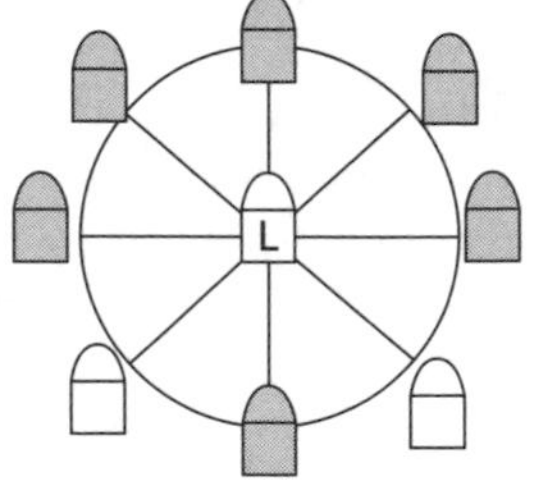

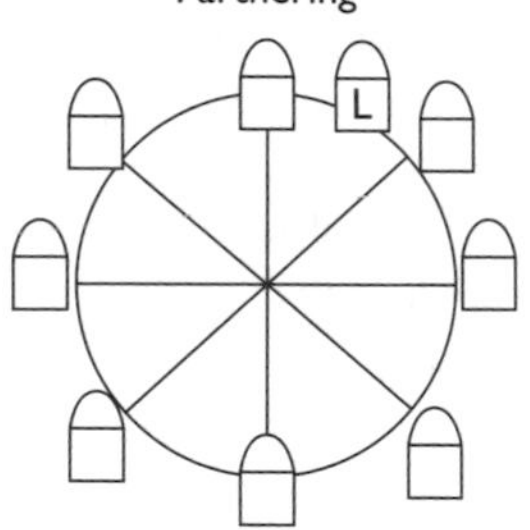

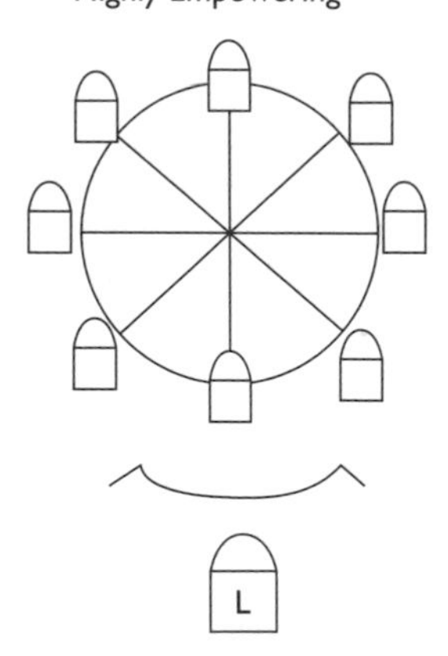

Figure 7.1 Five levels of leadership

Source: Wilson *et al.* 1994

As portrayed in Figure 7.1, the transition in conceptions of leadership commenced with earlier bureaucratic and often autocratic forms; moved through more participative leadership forms in which the designated leader allowed others to exercise a leadership responsibility; through to more recent high involvement models under which the leader is either a partner in leadership or in its most highly developed form, a mentor to the self-led team.

Again, I emphasise that under these arrangements the role of the formal leader is no less important. Indeed, the opposite is true, as he or she must carry out his or her role by establishing and communicating the vision, by modelling, and by mentoring and coaching. This approach is consistent with Bennis and Nanus' (1985: 46) view that 'Leaders acquire and wear their visions like clothes. Accordingly, they seem to enrol themselves (and then others) in the belief of their ideals as attainable, and *their behaviour exemplifies the ideals in action*' (italics added).

Such views of leadership also rely heavily on the concept of *empowerment* whereby the designated leader 'empowers others to translate intention into reality and sustain it' (Bennis and Nanus 1985: 80). Such empowerment, urge Bennis and Nanus, involves four major elements:

- significance – a feeling of those involved that they are doing something important and significant – 'of being at the active centre of the social order' (*ibid*.: 82);
- competence – development and learning on the job;
- a sense of community – a sense of 'family', of being 'joined in some common purpose' (*ibid*.: 83);
- fun and enjoyment – derived from the work and interactions with others involved in it.

In summary therefore, rethinking leadership in high performing schools of the future involves developing a form of leadership which is highly involving and highly empowering, which relies on leading others to lead themselves, and which consequently has significant implications for the second major part of our picture, namely Management.

EMERGING TRENDS IN THE MANAGEMENT OF STAFF

Of the many issues that could be addressed under this heading, I propose to concentrate here on three: creating and developing high performance teams; utilising on-the-job development systems including mentoring and coaching; and developing performance feedback mechanisms.

Creating and developing high performance teams

As we saw earlier, new conceptions of leadership involve the formal leader acting as a mentor to largely self-led, self-managed work teams. The outstanding emphasis being placed on these increasingly popular organisational forms mirrors Moses' (1990) view that in the high performance era *the team, and not the individual, becomes the major unit of analysis.*

It should come as little surprise that such an arrangement is currently enjoying increasingly high levels of support from organisations of all kinds. This is because it is a manifestation of the belief that in high performing, responsive, customer-focused organisations striving for success in this era, power, information and resources need to be allocated as close as possible to the point of delivery of services; and the team represents a strong organisational form which can provide the basis for such an arrangement.

The emerging model suggests that for high performance teamwork to occur, this alignment of power, information, resources and indeed rewards with the team structure is a fundamental prerequisite. This is in contrast with earlier approaches in which teams were sometimes used to deal with specific issues and/or solve particular problems, without, necessarily, having large amounts of power and resources at their disposal. Under the new scenario, effective teamwork becomes far more than a nicety aimed at improving working conditions of staff, or even achieving improved outcomes, and moves to the central position of major driver in pursuit of high performance.

Putting it another way, we can talk all we like about teams and teamwork (when we may well often mean groups and group work), but unless we are prepared to put our money where our mouth is, we are not likely to achieve high performance teamwork, i.e. teamwork that produces, in the main, consistently high levels of performance, or higher levels of performance than would normally be expected given all the circumstances.

If this is true of organisations generally, it is even more pertinent for schools and school systems within which the dominant paradigm is rapidly becoming one in which the school itself is the major self-managing team. Under this arrangement it is important that the paradigm shift that has seen the transformation of large, bureaucratic education systems to new arrangements involving a strategic core steering a system of self-managing schools, is in fact institutionalised at the school level, so that the school itself consists of a strategic core steering a system of self-managing teams.

Carmichael (1993) portrays the change at institutional level as shown in Figure 7.2. Under the arrangement outlined, the hitherto bureaucratic scientific management model applying world-wide in years gone by, is rapidly being replaced by a new arrangement featuring a very lean strategic core 'steering' a system of self-managing work units, with responsibilities as shown.

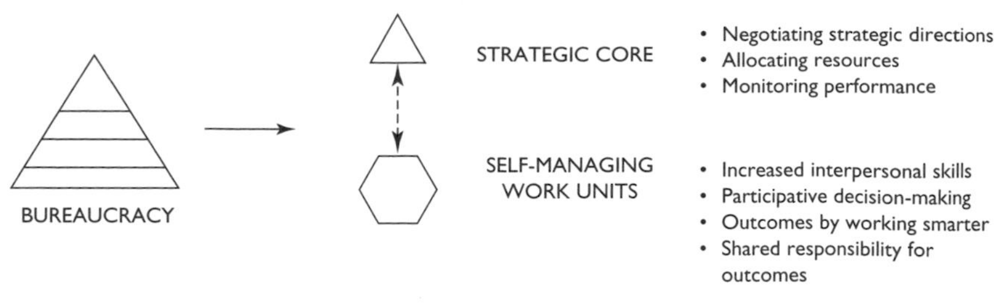

Figure 7.2 The paradigm shift

Source: Carmichael 1993

Hence this is where the real challenge lies for schools; because while many school heads or principals endorse the move from the centralised organisational arrangements which were typical at the system level in a previous era, many have, as yet, to come to terms with the new paradigm as it applies at the school level.

What to do?

In implementing this central idea there are four key steps which need to be taken:

- reorganising the school
- forming the teams
- building high performance teamwork
- aligning rewards and incentives with team performance.

Reorganising the school

The first of these steps, as suggested above, is to organise the school so that teams become an integral part of it. In other words, the school, as a self-managing work unit, needs to comprise a strategic core, steering a system of smaller self-managing work units or teams. Visually, the overall changes may be portrayed as in Figure 7.3. Depending on the nature of the school, the arrangements will vary.

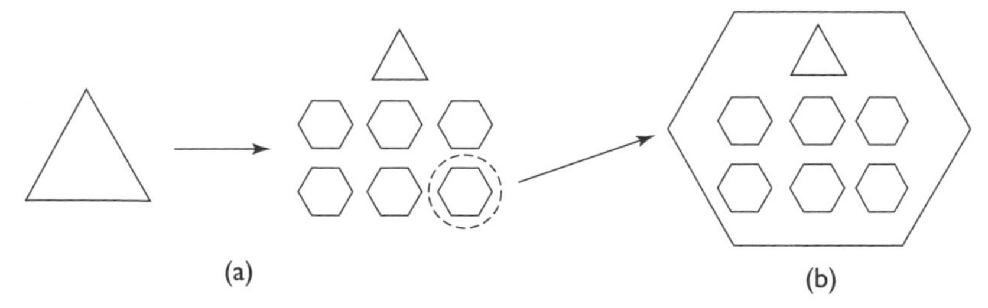

Figure 7.3 Restructuring (a) the system and (b) the school

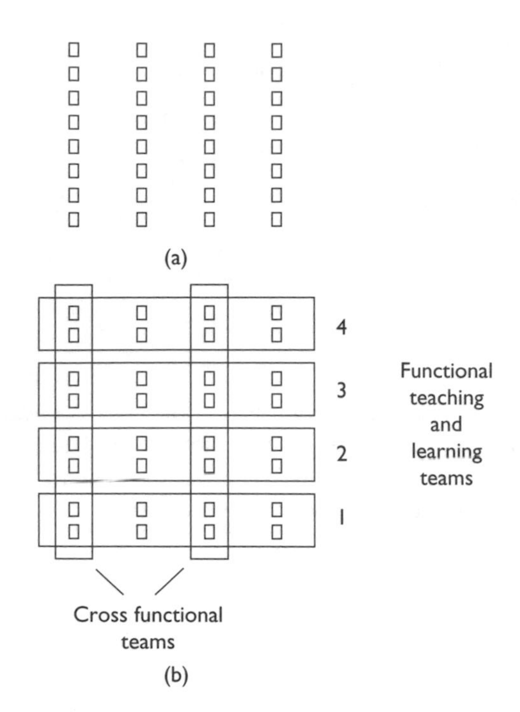

Figure 7.4 School reorganisation: (a) the previous arrangement and (b) the new arrangements at Huntingdale Primary School, Western Australia

One example of such an approach is that of Huntingdale Primary School, Western Australia, where principal Murray Randall organised the school into functional and cross functional teams responsible for the teaching and non-teaching aspects of school life respectively. Visually, the organisation changed from a set of more or less free-standing individual units as shown in Figure 7.4 (a), to one based on horizontal and vertical teams shown in Figure 7.4(b). Under this new arrangement, there are four teaching and learning teams of six to eight people, and cross functional teams to cover areas such as school management, curriculum and so on.

In explaining the very thorough culture building process the school went through, principal Murray Randall said they began by talking and moving towards a shared understanding and a common language. They then held a strategic planning workshop for the three members of the School Administration (Senior Management) Team, including sorting out their roles. Next they raised the level of debate through presentations at staff meetings, through holding targeted workshops, and providing release time, for staff to plan and think. They gradually moved to implementation of Total Quality Management principles, and made a number of important modifications to teaching and learning.

Peer coaching is a significant feature of the new arrangements, and new leaders have emerged very clearly. What began as a good idea has become a vibrant new organisational structure which has overcome initial barriers, and as Murray tells it, the 'fierce individualism' that existed previously. The next move is to provide each team with its own budget which will operate within the framework of the overall school budget. This will provide the cement that binds the mosaic together.

Forming the teams

The second step that needs to be taken is to form the teams that will provide the basis for the organisation. Like the definition of team and leader, there are many theories on forming teams based on complementary roles, behaviour styles, personality styles and the like. Analytical instruments and psychometric tests range in sophistication and technicality from the more extreme such as the Myers–Briggs Type Indicator and the Margerison–McCann Team Index, to far simpler versions such as the Briggs–Stratton behaviour styles inventory, the Belbin self-perception inventory, and the Gregorc style delineator. Each of these latter three has a different role to play in helping with teamwork. The first deals with dominant behavioural styles, the second preferred team roles, and the third dominant thinking styles.

Of course care needs to be exercised in the use of such instruments as they are merely *indicators* of dominant styles at a particular point in time. These can change over time, and any one individual can display the characteristics of more than one style at any particular point in time. Hence caution must be exercised in granting to the instruments a level of accuracy and immutability that cannot be justified. Similarly, in arranging the mix of styles it is important to recognise the limitations of the instruments and our own ability to combine complementary styles in order to make the 'perfect' team. In short, this is not an exact science, and it should not be treated like one.

Having said all this, the fact is that instruments such as those mentioned above can play an important role in team building, and whether we use the simple versions or the complex ones, whether we read widely and deeply to increase our own knowledge and understanding, or indeed use other methods, the major messages remain the same, namely that in building effective teams, we need to:

- be aware of our own dominant behaviour styles, thinking styles, and preferred team roles;
- be aware of the range of styles and roles that exist in others;
- appreciate and respect other styles and roles as valid, indeed important to the success of the team;

- compose teams using complementary behaviour styles, thinking styles, and preferred team roles;
- assign individuals to appropriate roles, based on their individual styles, characteristics, and preferences;
- vary team composition according to the nature of the task;
- share functional team leadership according to the nature of the task.

And if high performance teams need very good leadership, leaders of high performing schools need to be thoroughly sensitised to this issue of diversity and complementarity, in order to ensure that the teams which are formed, the people who are recruited, and the systems which are developed, take account of these significant issues. This may require some form of technical analysis from the many that are available, but the least it will require will be conscious observation of the behaviour of team members or potential team members, and heightened sensitivity to their particular styles, characteristics, and individual needs.

Building high performance teamwork

Having formed the teams, the third step is to create the conditions for the achievement of high performance. What are some of the issues that need to be considered here?

First, one major discriminating characteristic of teams that ultimately reach high levels of performance is their preoccupation with outcomes, as well as their focus on measurements of performance. In essence, for such teams feedback is the fuel that powers performance and they are very active in gathering and analysing data in order to take their performance to even higher levels. Hence whether it is data relating to the extent of achievement of goals, whether it is data relating to the performance of individuals within the team, or whether it is data relating to performance of the team as perceived by the individuals within it, one critical element of high performance is that of data gathering, analysis and feedback.

A second major element relates to the unification of the team around a common cause or, more often, a difficult or highly challenging task. Those of us who have experienced teamwork in a personally challenging outdoor or wilderness environment appreciate fully the team cohesiveness and synergy that results from an extremely difficult and/or dangerous situation, whether it be in white water or on a sheer rockface. There are few other experiences which reduce individuals to a sense of common cause and genuine feeling and concern for other members of the team than this one. And of course there are many parallels in organisational life, with particularly challenging missions and their associated levels of risk having similar effects upon team members.

The point is, however, that without this single unifying challenge or threat teams can rarely rise to levels which might genuinely be called 'high performance'. Hence, it is in my view unrealistic to expect all teams within an organisation to be *high performing*. And yet, if there are insufficient such teams, the overall organisation is likely to lack the get-up-and-go to reach the very high standards necessary for the high performance era.

Critical questions that must be addressed, therefore, are what are the *real* challenges in this organisation? What are the issues which desperately need to be addressed? Who are the best people to address them? And how should we configure them as a team in order to achieve the outcomes required in as effective and efficient a manner as possible? Having said this, there is no good reason why all teams should not aspire to the features of high performing teams and it is therefore important to emphasise that while not all will be high performing, there is no reason why they cannot still be highly effective 'real teams'.

Thus, in building high performance, as well as forming teams effectively, it is also critical to do the following:

- identify clearly the specific challenge that needs to be addressed;
- develop a clear focus on outcomes and performance;
- collect and use high quality data to underpin judgement and action;
- foster a culture of continuous improvement;
- create a climate of development and learning on the job;
- adopt common and agreed processes of decision-making, problem-solving, and innovative thinking;
- develop a sense of caring for the team and individuals within it, that transcends personal success or well being;
- create a working climate which offers fun and enjoyment;
- celebrate success.

Aligning rewards and incentives with team performance

The fourth and final step relates to *alignment* – alignment of resources to programme outcomes and alignment of incentives and/or rewards to team outcomes. This is indeed a real challenge, indeed one which is occupying a lot of thought in organisations that have, since time immemorial, remunerated individual performance. Even now, with an increasingly high degree of emphasis on teamwork and team performance, the dominant reward paradigm continues to be based on the individual.

So how might it be done differently? In short, only with difficulty unless the school has the power to allocate a certain amount of its salary and/or other budget to a reward pool that may then be applied on the basis of performance. Like most things, the best approach would be one based on common sense – one that has as its basis individual salaries and perhaps even an element of individual performance reward, while at the same time building in a capacity for incentives and/or rewards for teams, not necessarily in cold hard cash, but in whatever form is negotiated between the team and the principal or his/her strategic core team. This could include, for example, professional development opportunities, fact-finding or benchmarking investigations, special technology for use by the team, or even celebratory events to mark the accomplishment of noteworthy high levels of performance.

From manager to mentor; from commander to coach

Under the arrangements outlined above, it becomes clear that approaches to leadership and management will be quite different, with a major emphasis being placed on mentoring and coaching both of teams and of individuals within teams. Consistent with Figure 7.1 earlier, it seems reasonable that the principal and his/her strategic team might be responsible for mentoring and coaching one or more teams within the school and might, in addition, be responsible for setting up a school-wide mentoring and coaching system which involves everyone in the school.

Within the overall context of performance development, the concept of mentoring and coaching has always offered great promise for supporting individual growth and development but in the high performance era, the concept which might hitherto have been seen as an organisational frill, becomes integral to performance. Little wonder that in *The Return of the Mentor*, Caldwell and Carter (1993) note that mentoring as an issue has recently taken on far greater prominence as workplaces seek to respond to the needs of the emerging era, and the demands for service-driven, highly efficient organisations. They also note that this prominence spans a wide range of both private and public sector organisations, including many in Health and Education that seek to create what Senge (1990) refers to as *the learning organisation*.

Some commentators are inclined to use the terms 'Mentor and 'Coach' interchangeably, but I prefer to differentiate between the two. In a sense, mentoring is a more inclusive, more embracing term which often includes the activity of coaching, but can be much more than that. Hence for me a Mentor is a trusted experienced professional, who is willing to assist a less experienced person by listening, sharing experiences, advising, guiding, and coaching; a coach is more of a trusted colleague who is willing to assist by observing performance, gathering and analysing data, and providing meaningful positive feedback. As suggested above, coaching may be thought of as a subset of mentoring, and while a mentor may well coach from time to time, he or she will do far more than this. Other activities may include helping the person to identify and refine developmental needs, assisting with the creation of a personalised individual development plan, reflecting with the person on his/her handling of specific activities or initiatives which the mentor may not have seen personally, but which can provide the opportunity for what Hersey (1990) calls *reflective review and coaching*.

Whatever the tasks agreed upon, it is critical that the protégé takes responsibility for managing an individual developmental plan, while the mentor acts as supporter, helper and encourager. Consequently the role involves far more listening than it does talking, and is much more subtle than giving lots of good advice and suggestions based on experience. Indeed, the skilled mentor is able to assist the individual to draw his/her own conclusions about performance by having him/her articulate the issues, incidents, solutions and so on, and by working in a way that allows distillation of appropriate action plans.

It is important to note here that this concept of 'mentor' is a far cry from the earlier colloquial versions of the term which implied opening doors for fortunate individuals or giving them a leg up the organisational ladder, often at the expense of others who were not lucky enough to have key decision-makers as their 'mentors'. On the contrary, the model envisaged here is a very professional one, aimed totally at assisting the individual to grow and develop.

Developing performance feedback mechanisms

As has already been established, the quest for high performance needs to be built upon a platform of goals, outcomes, and feedback about performance, both at the organisational level and at the level of individuals within the organisation. Since this chapter deals predominantly with leading and managing staff, it is to this latter point that we now turn.

It has long been recognised that feedback about performance is essential to organisational improvement, and organisations all over the world are increasingly seeking such feedback from their clients/customers and from other key stakeholders. This is in fact one major characteristic that distinguishes high performance organisations and/or teams from others – the extent to which they gather effective data, feed it back, and use it to drive the organisation to increasingly higher levels of performance.

Such approaches involve collection of performance data about a whole range of variables in the course of normal operations. Most also involve gathering customer response data through survey questionnaires and, increasingly, through face-to-face focus group meetings. Many organisations have found this approach to be highly effective, not the least of which are Qantas, Australia's largest airline, and BA. Both represent excellent examples of organisations that use feedback to drive their performance.

It is not just external customers that can provide this crucial feedback. Many high-powered organisations are seeking feedback from employees, sometimes using very informal and/or unstructured approaches while others are using more structured approaches based around specially developed questionnaires such as the Service Organisation Profile (Georgiades 1990). The basis of such feedback models is the belief that employee satisfaction provides the basis for customer satisfaction. Hence when an organisation obtains a clear view of its performance in terms of key variables such as Leadership, Service Mission, Management Practices, Group Climate, Job Satisfaction, Role Overload, Career Development and the like, and when this is shown relative to a world-wide database, the feedback can be extremely powerful in stimulating change and, ultimately, heightened performance.

Within education, increasing emphasis is being placed on annual survey data, with many school systems and individual schools gathering important data which they can use to improve their performance. As in other organisations, the trend is towards gathering these data from a wide range of stakeholders about a broad set of variables relating to school performance.

Feedback – an essential ingredient for the people of the organisation

If feedback is essential for driving organisational performance, it is just as critical for the individuals within the organisation. Outside education, increasing importance is being placed upon what is now being termed '360 degree feedback'. Under this approach, each individual systematically gathers data about his or her performance from a range of people, either once or twice a year, using specially prepared and agreed instruments. The range of people from whom comments are sought typically includes the person's manager, his/her 'peers', and his/her 'subordinates', whom we now prefer to refer to as 'team members', a term better suited to the flatter, team-based structures of today. By gathering data from these various sectors, the individual gets a multifaceted, rounded, or '360 degree' view of performance, as seen from a range of perspectives.

Surprisingly, analysis of a range of models and instruments reveals that many omit reference to the client or customer served by the individual, either internal to the organisation, or external. No doubt this is somewhat related to the difficulty of gathering meaningful data from the client sector, but for organisations that champion service excellence this appears to be a serious omission, and one which schools can hardly afford.

Hence within schools it is suggested that data should be sought from the person's manager, and an appropriate sample of peers, team members, parents and, where appropriate, students. The person also needs to analyse his/her own performance in order to compare perceptions with the feedback received from others. Thus the 360 degree feedback model might be pictured as in Figure 7.5, with the individual at the centre of the process,

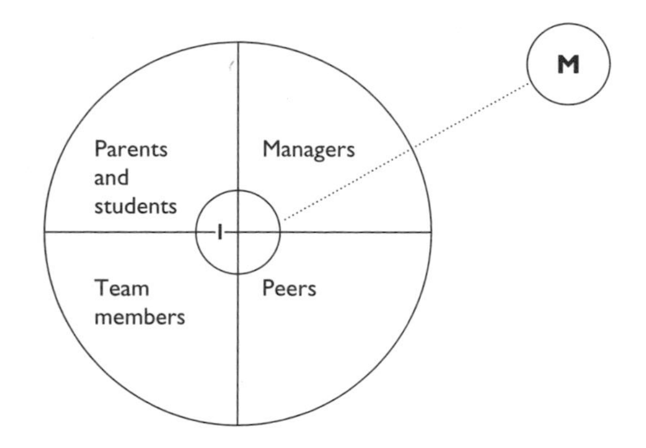

Figure 7.5 The 360 degree feedback model

and the person's mentor on the side, with the task of helping the person make sense of the feedback and determine appropriate growth plans.

It is important that the process be kept simple, through the use of an instrument which asks simple questions, and which is easy to complete and return. It is also important that respondents be free to rate the person in accordance with their true opinion in answer to the questions asked, by providing the feedback anonymously.

Thoughtful construction of the data gathering instrument and accompanying analytical approaches can result in the individual receiving very specific feedback which can be presented in a simple and easily understood graphical format. One example of such an approach was provided by the Principal Development Inventory (PDI), developed by Performance Development International with input and assistance from a large number of experienced principals (PDI 1995). The PDI was created especially for members of the principal class, i.e. principals and deputy/assistant principals. It focused on a range of critical variables identified by practitioners as essential to successful functioning as a school leader, thereby providing the basis for high performance feedback and individual development planning.

In addition to inviting the individual to complete his/her own assessment using the forty-item questionnaire, the PDI was used to gather 360 degree feedback from a full spectrum of stakeholders. Following analysis by Performance Development International, the individual was provided with feedback in graphical format, with results shown against those of an international database including principals and assistant principals from a number of countries. The forty items clustered around key variables including Leadership, Management, Teamwork, Communication/ Interpersonal Skills, Personal Attributes, and Overall Job Competence. Performance on each variable as perceived by each of the respondent groupings (parents, teachers, manager and so on), was shown, relative to the perception of the individual, thereby providing a solid basis for analysis and for development planning.

Of course, the place to start with all this is with the designated formal leader and his or her leadership team. Apart from the fact that the performance of school leaders is such an important variable in school performance, there is another major reason for doing so. In Australia we call it *leadership by example*. As noted earlier, others such as Manz and Sims (1994) call it *Superleadership*, or *leading others to lead themselves, by modelling effective leadership behaviours* while Bennis and Nanus (1985) simply call it *exemplifying ideals through behaviour*.

Whatever we call it, it means being prepared to put ourselves on the line by demonstrating our own personal commitment to high performance and growth – and, having done this, by then holding the quite reasonable expectation that all other staff will follow the lead. The overall outcome of this will hopefully be a learning, growing, dynamic, high performing school of the twenty-first century – a school which is nourished by feedback, the fuel that powers performance.

DRAWING THE THREADS TOGETHER

This chapter has presented a range of issues relating to leading and managing staff in high performing schools. It began by emphasising the importance of both leadership and management, and the leadership theme has permeated the whole chapter. It has also acknowledged that the changes required are more than fiddling at the edges or simply tweaking the systems. For many schools the changes envisaged represent a bold, adventurous step, and one that can only be met by comprehensive overhaul.

Hence, major emphasis has been placed on creating and building high performance teams, on aligning rewards and incentives with team performance and on adopting approaches to leadership and management which place responsibility for performance with the team and the individual; which encourage performance feedback and developmental planning; and which begin with the leadership team leading by example in search of a new, great tomorrow in the truly high performing school of the twenty-first century.

NOTE

Minor alterations have been made to this chapter written by the late Max Sawatzki in the mid-1990s.

Part III

Leading learning

8 Leading learning

Christopher Bowring-Carr

The central message that runs throughout this book is that the core activity of a school is learning. Of course, it is not just the students who learn; to suggest that is to imply that learning is imposed on one group by another, and that the other group has completed all the learning that it needs. In a world changing as fast as this, such a suggestion is profoundly silly. Everyone in a school is a learner. The objective that every school should strive for is to become a learning community, and the word 'community' is chosen deliberately rather than 'organisation'.

> Since community means different things in different disciplines, I proposed that for schools we define the term as follows: Communities are collections of individuals who are bonded together by natural will and who are together bound to a set of shared ideas and ideals. This bonding and binding is tight enough to transform them from a collection of 'I's' into a collective 'we'. As a 'we', members are part of a tightly knit web of meaningful relationships. This 'we' usually shares a common place and over time comes to share common sentiments and traditions that are sustaining.
>
> (Sergiovanni, 1996: 48)

Not merely does this community have individual learning at its heart, but it embraces the idea that learning is a social activity, and, as the learner grows in experience, becomes an interdependent activity. The community and the individual learn with and from each other. Therefore, one of the themes running through such a community is that it is helping to produce learners who are autonomous, learners who can and want to learn, and know how to do so.

Before looking at the implications of the notion of an autonomous learner, we need to try to explain our belief as to what learning is, and what it is for. Taking in information, remembering more and more facts are only distantly related to real learning. Real learning, or deep learning, alters the way in which we see the world, alters us as people. When we look back at the mass of material that we processed while at school and university, what percentage can we honestly say fundamentally, or even slightly changed us? How much of it was anodyne? How much of it, in retrospect, was plain wrong? That great Irish essayist, Butler (1990: 125) described learning vividly:

> Real learning is dynamic, dangerous, exhilarating. It is built on curiosity not knowledge.

One of the important activities for any leader is constantly to be inviting discussions about what learning is and how it can be demonstrated. It must be remembered in the learning community that although learning occurs almost all the time, it is channelled and limited by the culture and the mythology of the community. Also, it is distorted by the micro-political interests of the individual. And finally, it is frequently prevented by the personal defence mechanisms that we all erect to protect us from the discomfort of the new, and from the fear of failure. What is needed, therefore, is for the leader to encourage in the community an attitude of self-awareness and openness, an acceptance of the unpredictability of learning, of self-consciousness about how we learn, and how we do not, what fosters and what blocks learning – in other words, the topic of learning needs to be the centre of staff meetings on a regular basis, not relegated to the occasional in-service development day.

Clearly, the ultimate purpose of learning is going to dictate the type of learning that will be fostered, and the type of leadership that will be required. Are our schools maintained in order to transmit society's values to the next generation? Are they in place in order to produce willing workers and consumers to maintain our economy? If they are, then schools are there merely to transmit information, not to enable the next generation to grow into being reflective, questioning people. I believe that schools exist in order to help children become better at thinking, imagining, understanding, questioning, challenging the status quo, and adapting to change. I believe that what we need is for the community to be able to interrogate that mass of information which is now available – it needs the right questions, so that it can turn information into knowledge, and then knowledge into wisdom. There are a great many people in the world who want to ensnare citizens with their particular brand of information – ensnare them politically, commercially or emotionally. The learning community needs to be able to question these people rigorously and persistently. For the students to be able to make the most of their lives, they need to be able to probe, both for work and for pleasure, that mass of information that is so easily available, and to shape it, order it, and make good sense of it. And for schools to be able to do those things, everyone in them must be eager to question and think, reflect, care and imagine. After all, as Kohn (1999:

121) puts it, not many parents, if asked what they want for their children to gain from school, say

> 'What's most important to me is that my kid will be able to convert a fraction into a decimal' or 'will know the difference between a simile and a metaphor'.

The problem is that the dominant language of those who control our schools focuses on tests, test scores, league tables, standards (not clearly defined) – the paraphernalia of measurement. Moreover, the problem has an impact out of all proportion to its intellectual worth because that official language is unavoidable. Or at least at first sight it is unavoidable. However, there are a number of schools which, while successfully fulfilling the demands of the testing regime, are putting (have put) in place organisations which enable deep learning to occur.

Let me make clear what is needed for deep learning to occur, and then look at the implications for leadership. First, a list of nine aspirations, some of which are realistically achievable in the short term, while others might take a little longer.

1 Schools are physical and virtual learning resources at the heart of their communities. The days when the school was defined, limited, by the fence around its grounds, and when the community sent its children there to be taught and disciplined, should be ended. Schools are expensive resources open at the moment for about 16 per cent of the year. They need to be the monasteries of the twenty-first century – centres of learning, of caring, of sustenance.
2 Access to the building blocks of learning is now available 24 hours a day, 365 days a year. Schools need to adjust to this fact.
3 Learning programmes need to be individual. We all learn differently, at different speeds, in different rhythms and for different reasons. The idea that thirty students can be mandated to learn a sequence of facts at the same time, grouped together for no good reason other than their date of birth, is outdated.
4 Learners should be able, from time to time, to choose areas which they want to investigate for their own purposes.
5 Teachers are coaches, mentors, guides and resources who co-ordinate the work of learners and those who support them. The teacher should be seen more as a team leader, the team being a group of people with many different strengths and specialisms enabling students to learn. Teachers are no longer the main transmitters of information.
6 Learning is a community-wide responsibility.
7 Modes of assessment are negotiated.
8 Funding is public, private and individual.
9 Accountability is based in local democracy.

There are certain basic requirements without which we cannot begin to have deep learning, but instead would be forced to continue with the regime of short-term, superficial memorisation which is so rewarded and exhorted at present. These requirements are:

- No hierarchies – when there are hierarchies there is a focus on position and the status quo, both inimical to learning. Instead, there will be informality – all the people in the learning organisation are relaxed in each others' company, open to new ideas, supportive of each other and accepting of an equality of regard. There has to be accountability, of course, and legally there has to be one person who bears that responsibility. However, being accountable and instituting a hierarchy do not need to go together.
- No fear – in an institution in which there is fear, the individuals in it will minimise taking risks and doing something new; learning implies taking risks and moving into unknown ground.
- Emphasis will be primarily on the process, rather than on the end result. In other words, grades, marks, the results of tests will take on decreasing importance. As Bruner wrote (in Kohn 1999: 191) students should 'experience success and failure not as reward and punishment, but as information'.
- The learning community knows that intelligence is not individual but social, and that learning is not best achieved through solitude but through social interaction. The implication is that the organisation of the daily routines emphasises and encourages people to meet, to work in small or large groups, and for varying times.
- The learning community also knows that intelligence depends on the richness of the resources available. The library, the software, the networks – the antennae of learning will be given the highest priority.
- The learning community knows that learning comes from asking questions, not having the 'right' answers. The best questions will be those that no-one has an answer to right away, and in any one day the students will be asking far more questions than the teachers. Also, learning comes from self – from questioning one's mistakes, learning from them, and taking the pains to work through that difficult self-discipline.
- The learning community knows that learning cannot be hemmed in by artificial subject barriers. Although for the sake of the imposed tests, some attention will be paid to the old-fashioned subject labels, the deepest learning will come from students working together across a number of disciplines.
- The learning community knows that people see the world through different lenses, and they use different intellectual, physical and emotional strengths to make sense of the world and build their reality. Learners will have each strength fostered and rewarded.

- The learning community, most importantly and urgently, needs to return to a living language about education. In its discussions about learning and pedagogy, it has to ditch the dead language of the government and look afresh at what it – this living community – wants to describe and analyse. It will have to subvert the unthinking acceptance of the sterile metaphors such as 'targets', 'Key Stages', 'levels', 'standards'. The language in the public arena used to describe and proscribe education is the language of managerialism; it is a language bereft of passion, power and precision. In the extract that follows, Martin and D'Agostino (2003: 5) look at the language of the National Curriculum's prescription for the teaching of reading.

  > In reading, pupils should be taught strategies to help them read with understanding, to locate and use information, to follow a process or argument and summarise, and to synthesise and adapt what they learn from their reading. . . . 'To synthesise and adapt' – not 'to question and provide alternatives'. 'To follow a process or argument and summarise', not 'to initiate, create and pursue intriguing lines of enquiry'. 'To locate and use information', not 'to question the sources and the hidden agendas of the messages we receive'.

  They go on to quote from Steiner, who sums up this corrosive language perfectly:

  > In certain civilisations there come epochs in which syntax stiffens, in which the available resources of live perception and restatement wither. Words seem to go dead under the weight of sanctified usage; the frequency and sclerotic force of clichés, of unexamined similes, of worn tropes increases. Instead of acting as a living membrane, grammar and vocabulary become a barrier to new feeling.

  It is perhaps the paramount duty of the leader in the learning community to start that probing and questioning of the official language, to examine the dead metaphors and restricted view of what education can be about, so that the community can create a meta-language, and through that language, their *own* language, talk about the education of their students with freshness, openness, excitement. The community needs a language for life, not for an acquiescent acceptance of managerialism.
- Finally, the end point of the endeavours of such a community will be the autonomous learner – the learner who knows how to learn and wants to do so.

There are many implications arising from such a commitment to enabling learners to be both autonomous and part of a learning community, and the leader's role is crucial. However, as we discuss elsewhere in this book, there is always the need to hold firmly on to the two concepts of *a* leader and dispersed *leadership*. The former is necessary for two distinct reasons. The first is that in a complex society such as ours, there has to be a person who ultimately is accountable for the school. An important, but simple, legal necessity. The second is that a community needs a leader to articulate its vision and goals, to be the embodiment of all that is best in the community and of what it is striving for. The community needs a leader to be continuously keeping in touch with what it is doing and how its emotional health is faring, and to look to the next steps and longer-term projects. It needs a leader to enthuse and help when accidents and disasters strike, and to celebrate the triumphs and successes. Finally, the community needs the leader who demonstrates in every fibre the meaning of the idea of life-long learning; the leader is the principal learner.

Leadership, on the other hand, is something that *everyone* in the community demonstrates on a continuous basis. Let mc put that another way – if there are not possibilities for a person to demonstrate leadership, then there is no learning community, because to lead is to learn. One of the functions of the leader is to sweep away the barriers, the clutter that might hinder someone taking on a leadership role. That means first that the leader genuinely does not want to keep the levers of power in the principal's office. The comparison that Bell (1998) makes is an apt one. The leader of a learning community is playing in a jazz band, and not conducting an orchestra. Second, and it follows from this analogy, the leader has to know the strengths and development points of the community so that possibilities, opportunities to take the lead are always being opened up for each member.

On a day-to-day basis, what are the implications of this placing of learning at the core of the community? What is meant by 'the autonomous learner' that the learning community is trying to foster? And, in attempting to answer those two questions, can we at the same time tease out what the members of the community must be doing? First, we need to define the term 'autonomous learners' more exactly.

Autonomous learners know how to learn and have an eagerness to do so. Both knowing how to and wanting to are jointly essential; one without the other leads either to a mechanical response to what is offered, or to fuzzy, rushed and superficial thinking. So, from entry to school, students are encouraged and helped to acquire the questioning techniques needed to stand outside their learning and analyse it. They also need the tenacity to question and probe their own successes and mistakes. Teachers encourage students' growing self-confidence and develop in them an enquiring attitude towards their learning. Students are frequently asked: 'Do you think that is the best way of doing x? Have you thought of y? Have you asked your friend if she can help? Did you use those books in the library? Is there someone in your home community who might help?'

They are regularly asked to estimate how well they are learning. They are encouraged, by adults and peers, always to move on from the 'comfort zone' of what they know, to the next step. The adults are enthused about and committed to *their own* learning, and discuss with enthusiasm their own learning among themselves and with the students. After all, if students never see or hear that the teachers actually enjoy learning, and feel charged by it, why should they believe that 'learning is a good thing'. The classrooms are lively, with the display concentrating on provoking questions and observations. Excitement and enjoyment, as well as the need to take infinite pains, and being able to cope with frustration, are shown to be ingredients essential to learning.

The leaders throughout the school frequently meet to discuss learning, and, most importantly, to look for any impediments to learning. They will be looking for ways to improve the learning, to widen the range of learning styles and be continuously monitoring what is going on to make sure that good practice is spread as widely as possible. One important aspect is to ensure that students can recognise and pose problems. Official documents often suggest that students need to be problem solvers. However, the suggestion implicit in such a statement is that it is for others to pose the problems, which is a hierarchical way of looking at learning. The learner that I want to encourage looks for problems and can articulate their components, can identify the difficulties inherent in them, and then can initially sketch a possible solution. Also, we need to have a community which knows how to support people when they find that a problem has *no* solution; emotional intelligence manifests itself at such times.

So, autonomous learners can identify, on their own and/or with others, a problem, analyse its components and then gather the resources, human and non-human, to solve it. The students are often asked: 'What do you think the problem is? What materials do you need to solve it? Who could help you solve it?' Sometimes the group is asked: 'What problem(s) about being 15 years old do you want to study?' The problems need to be real to the students, and their brainstorming of what they want to investigate is a powerful starter to learning. The emphasis is on the process, and on the depth of that process rather than on 'covering' a range of material. Again, the leadership in the classroom steps back; the focus must be on the students' needs as they work on a problem or a project, decide whether to work on their own, or in pairs or in larger groups, and the decisions will be made according to the stage of the learning, their particular ways of learning, and the nature of the task.

They will be encouraged to cope with increasingly complex problems which demand for their solution an increasingly wide range of resources (books, ICT, peers, teacher, other adults and so on) which are not necessarily in the classroom or in the school. Indeed, for the students (from an early age) projects and extended pieces of work might well demand out-of-school research and activity. The solution is important, but getting to the solution is far more important. This emphasis on the process means that it is for the leaders to ensure that there are minimal barriers to accessing the necessary resources.

Autonomous learners are encouraged to take time to reflect on what they have learnt. Following students through a school day all too frequently points to what a harried and over-packed life they lead. Increasingly we know that there is an over-riding need to think about what is being and what has been learnt; time is needed for the new material to settle in, for connections to be made with ideas and knowledge that are already in the student's mind, and, vitally, for the student to be able to reconcile new ideas which appear to, and often actually do, conflict with previous knowledge. The average school day, divided into 40- or 60-minute segments, simply does not allow for such reflection. The further division into ten or even twelve different subject labels makes learning even more difficult.

Leaders in a number of schools have come up with a variety of solutions to the problem of timing: blocking the timetable into half days (and prior to that shift, building the capacity of the staff to make maximum use of the longer lessons); having one day a week 'off' timetable so that projects can be undertaken; having one week every two months 'off' timetable. There is no one solution, of course; each community needs to find its own solution. But the imperative is there: if we as a community know that 40- or 60-minute sessions are anathema to deep learning, then a solution *has* to be found. Not to find one would be professionally unacceptable, and unethical.

As a minimum, there needs to be built into the lesson and/or into the school day time to be reflective about what has been learnt. Once the habit of stopping and thinking and talking about what have been the high points of the day has become established, then it will be easier to move, not only into that discursive mode in which everyone in the room is jointly discussing learning, but also into the acceptance that depth of learning is infinitely more important than the amount that has been 'covered'.

One of the attributes of autonomous learners is that they can explain the processes of their learning and its outcomes with their peers and others. A learner needs to be able to be self-conscious, in the best possible way, of what is going on while involved in learning, but also s/he needs a meta-language with which to discuss, with adults and peers, that process.

Students who can articulate the processes of their learning learn more easily, and more deeply. Such articulation goes to the heart of what assessment in the learning community should look like. At present, most assessment creates and prolongs the dependency of the learner on the teacher and the system. This is not the place to go into detail as to what an assessment system for the autonomous learner should be. Those readers who want to explore this area should go to the chapter by Black and Wiliam in Davies and West-Burnham (2003) titled 'The development of formative assessment'. Also, in Chapter 9 in this book, I deal with assessment at some length. I want to put forward some headline ideas which underpin assessment *for* learning rather than assessment *of* learning. The main points are:

- as the student grows in confidence, s/he takes on self-assessment as a part of learning;
- as the individual student and the group grow in ease with and trust in each other, peer assessment will be an essential part of learning;
- assessment tasks need not be solo performances;
- one of the ways in which students demonstrate their learning will be to draw up the questions at the end of a unit of work;
- assessment tasks should, whenever possible, give students the opportunity to show their sensitivity to the whole and not merely to discrete elements;
- assessment tasks should be related to what the students will meet in the world outside, and should not be limited only to the official curriculum;
- the student(s) and the teacher(s) will agree on the mode in which the learning will be expressed – the narrow method of the written essay handicaps too many;
- performance assessment, that is students actually *doing* something (prescribing and pricing a diet for a sick elderly person; writing a play; teaching a less expert person a difficult computer skill) will be the norm;
- students will build up a portfolio of their work, and will, on 'parents' evening' take the parents and the teacher through the portfolio explaining why the entries were chosen, what they say about his/her learning, what has been difficult, and what easy, and what the next steps are to be.

In short, the student, with the teacher and sometimes peers, needs to be able to decide on how, and when, to demonstrate what has been learnt. The student, with the teacher and sometimes peers, will decide on the criteria by which the success of the learning will be judged, and the student will become increasingly at ease with those criteria being challenged so as to take him/her out of the comfort zone. The leader's task is to create the atmosphere, and build the capacity among staff and parents, in which it is accepted that when the learner and learning are put at the heart of the community, then there are certain logical outcomes, and this approach to assessment is one of them. The leader will also have to reassure both students and the larger community that this approach will *both* enable deep learning to occur *and* will ensure improving results in the public testing system.

The staff in the learning community need to ensure that students are given the time and the encouragement increasingly to take a synoptic view of what they are learning. We all learn better when we can see the whole picture, when we can, to use Forster's words, 'only connect'. If a student can make a connection between one aspect of what s/he is learning and another, then learning becomes easier and deeper. However, in the standard school day, there is no time to make those connections, and there is little help given to make them. Three extracts from research carried out in Northern Ireland by the NFER (Harland *et al.* 2000) into the Key Stage 3 cohort underline this lack of linkage:

> Pupils were generally not aware of any planned coherence in the courses offered by schools.
>
> (Ibid., p. 4)

> Teachers reported that they let cross-curricular links occur through serendipity rather than deliberately build them in.
>
> (Ibid., p. 4)

> The evidence suggested that numerous valuable learning opportunities for exploring links across the curriculum were lost to both pupils and teachers. Additionally, in the absence of any significant guidance to the contrary, the concept maps indicated that some pupils internalise images of the whole curriculum that may have deleterious effects on their learning and motivation.
>
> (Ibid., p. 5)

'Why am I learning this, at this time, and how does it fit in with all the other things I am learning?' is a legitimate question and one that requires an answer. 'Why am I teaching this, at this time, and how does it fit in with everything else that the other teachers are doing?' is a question that the reflective teacher will need to answer.

The leader of the community needs to look at the degree of coherence in the school day, and at the need for more 'custom-made' timetables for individuals. ICT has been shown to be of help in this area.

The autonomous learner knows when it is best to work alone, and when in a team. As I have said above, intelligence does not reside solely in the individual, and deep learning is promoted when work is carried out by a group. The implication is that inter- and intrapersonal intelligences need to be fostered, because such intelligences are vital to team or group work. Further, because in the adult world team work is increasingly the norm, in schools there is the need to encourage and enable students to decide what parts of coping with a topic are best fostered by solitary learning, and what parts by working in a team. Students need to be shown how to work in a team, how to gain from such work, and how to contribute to such work. As Perkins (1995: 323) puts it when discussing distributed intelligence:

> Then there is such a thing as knowing your way around working with others – how to argue fruitfully, to build on others' ideas, to provoke, to listen, to encourage.

Teachers also need to work in teams, thus not only demonstrating good practice but also enabling a wider pool of expertise to be available. Teachers need to have the opportunity to set up topics which demand teamwork and which, through being cross-curricular, demonstrate connectivity. One of the features of team work is, of course, the reduction of competition, and competition is rarely a feature of real learning. Once we get into the realm of competition, we get into the world of marks and grades, and then the focus is on the marks and not on the learning. As Kohn (1999: 21) puts it:

> This focus on results turns out to be remarkably simplistic, particularly when one considers the psychological issues involved. *A preoccupation with achievement* is not only different from, but often detrimental to, a focus on learning.
>
> (emphasis in the original)

Later, he goes on to say:

> The goal of some students is to acquire new skills, to find out about the world, to understand what they are doing. When they pick up a book, they're thinking about what they're reading, not about how well they are reading it. Paradoxically, these students who have put success out of their minds are likely to be successful. They process information more deeply, review things they didn't understand the first time, make connections between what they're doing now and what they learned earlier, and use more strategies to make sense of the ideas they're encountering. All of this has been demonstrated empirically.
>
> (Ibid., p. 31)

Undoubtedly, in creating a school which downplays the importance of marks, and stresses commenting on process instead, and which eliminates competition as an (spurious) encouragement of learning, the leader, depending on the traditions of the community, may have a deal of persuading to do. However, there is a wealth of material now available all of which points to the correctness of Kohn's position.

One of the main features of a learning community is the spirit of enquiry, or curiosity, which is palpable in the conversations between and among students and teachers, in the displays on the walls, and in the open, challenging discussions about learning that occur frequently. Perhaps the one over-riding aim of a learning community is to promote, sustain and satisfy the innate curiosity which is an integral part of being a human. Curiosity is the major driving-force to learning. Teachers need to know what makes each individual curious, and use that curiosity as the starting point for learning. But that curiosity may flag when the going gets difficult, so the teacher's role, and that of the students' peers, is to learn the basic need to stick at it. An eagerness to learn implies, *inter alia*, taking pains; the student needs to be encouraged to improve, and to be dissatisfied until the best is achieved, and then to move on to even better. The student and the teacher need to accept the untidiness and non-linearity of learning, and not be frustrated by its difficulties. The student needs to be given ample time for such painstaking work.

As I have said in Chapter 3, a learning community has to be an ethical community. Students need to grow up in a school in which the ethical imperatives are clear and in which the adults share a clear set of ethics which informs their every action. These ethics are the benchmark against which all decisions are judged. Students are helped to develop a moral sense, and they need frequently to have opportunities to judge and review their actions against a growing, increasingly sophisticated code. The leader in the community is the presence which reifies this moral code.

The leader of the community, working with the home and with the surrounding community, needs to put at the heart of all that the school does the fostering of self-esteem, for all adults and students. Without that, there can be no true learning. There needs to be a sensitive awareness of the emotional well-being of all members of the community, and opportunities for emotions to be discussed. The acceptance of difference, indeed the welcoming of diversity, needs to be central to the ethos of the community. Emotional intelligence, working within the self and with and through others, needs to be reflected on and nurtured as the essential prerequisite to anything else that happens in a school. The community needs to be outward looking; changes in the world are so rapid and all-pervasive that there cannot be any inward turning. In brief, the leader's task, working with the rest of the community, is to make the school a place to which people want to come, a community in which enjoyment, openness and caring are highly in evidence.

In conclusion, the leader of a school or college needs certain characteristics which have little in common with the charismatic, 'here's the flag, follow me' traits displayed by the hero of the action movie. The trouble is that as soon as the word 'leader' is used, there is a stereotype that is immediately assumed by most listeners. The term used by Bowring-Carr and West-Burnham (1997), which they in turn took from Senge (1990) was 'steward', and that word has the considerable advantage of not having the baggage associated with the word 'leader'. A steward has the over-riding aim of wanting to hand over the institution to the successor in the best possible shape. There is little of the possessive in the make-up of a steward.

There is much more a set of abilities which, in combination, enable and enthuse people to give of their best.

First, the steward is a facilitator, the person who, seeing a complex problem, gathers together a group of people, poses the problem and then helps the conversation to unfold and explore the complexities, and finally enables the group to articulate a conclusion. The steward does not solve the problem and then impose the solution; s/he is not in the game of demonstrating personal infallibility. Second, and as part of the first requirement, the steward understands the system and the people in it. Rather in the way that I suggested that students need to be able to identify a problem, and then bring the resources to bear in order to work towards a solution, so the steward knows the system thoroughly, which means knowing the people who work in it, and being so attuned and attentive to its workings that s/he will notice the slightest creak or missed beat, and have the emotional intelligence to know if intervention is necessary or whether the problem is self-curing.

Third, the steward needs to be continuously aware of what other people and other schools and colleges are doing and thinking. The steward is a supreme networker, someone who keeps in touch with as wide a group of fellow professionals as possible, actively seeking out new contacts, using every means of communication. From this network, the steward is open to and perceptive about new ideas, and has the ability to explain them to the community in such terms that they will see the relevance to their own system. Fourth, the steward must be continuously looking ahead five years or so to make sure that the community is not caught flat-footed by the rapid approach of a potential opportunity or disaster. The steward is the radar-scanner of the community, and as in air-traffic controlling, the radar scan cannot safely be switched off. As we explain in Chapter 5, there is an overriding necessity for the community to build capacity to meet strategic intentions, and the intentions will arise in large measure from the steward's meticulous scanning of the horizon.

Fifth, the steward has to be the guardian of the community against the arbitrary, frequently contradictory, short-term managerialism of government agencies. It is the steward who has to keep up the professional morale of the community, so that what the community knows to be the right ways to enable deep learning to occur are not stunted by, for example, an assessment system that rewards memorisation. The steward filters the deluge of official print, learning the art of constructive forgetfulness and compassionate blindness. No steward can, of course, insulate the community from all government orders, but the necessity is to ensure that the community's core message is never forgotten – that the wider and deeper the experienced curriculum, the better the students will do in any test, however silly, that is imposed on them. They will cope with such tests and do well in them, but they will also do well in other, far more meaningful demonstrations of their learning, and they will not have their experience at school curtailed by 'teaching-to-the-test'. To deny students the right to a rich, deep and inclusive range of experiences is to act unethically. One of the over-riding aims is to make sure that the deeply saddening conversations recorded by Reay and Wiliam (2001) in a primary school (class 6S) are not repeated in another community:

Lewis: I wish we did technology.
Jackie: Yeah, that would be good.
Tunde: We should do more dance. We should have dance in the SATs.
Terry: And they never teach you anything about cavemen either.
Ayse: And we don't do history any more.
Terry: All I know is because I read about it on my own.
Ayse: And we don't do geography. Only science, language and maths. Just over and over again.
Diane (R): So is the curriculum very different this term to what it was last term?
Terry: Yeah.
Jackie: Last year we done music and dance, interesting things.
Terry: The best thing we did was PE. And last week was the best session we've had in ages 'cause it was something different. And I hate football and it was football but it was the best session we done in ages.

Reay and Wiliam go on to say:

> But it was the emphasis on more individualised, competitive ways of working which were increasingly displacing the mutually supportive, collaborative group work to which the children were accustomed . . . that caused the most disquiet.
>
> (Ibid., p. 157)

The learning community must resist those outcomes at all costs.

Finally, and underpinning all that has been written above, the steward is the lead learner, showing a passionate involvement in his/her own learning, showing enjoyment in that learning, but also enthusing, encouraging everyone in the community to continue to be learners. Our students need to see how we find learning difficult, frustrating, humbling, necessitating going off at tangents, but ultimately enormously rewarding and indeed frequently fun. Our students need to hear us talking about our learning, what is proving fascinating, what insights we have gained, where such-and-such an enquiry may lead us. They need to see that learning, deep and profound learning, cannot be mandated. We need to show that we cannot *teach* anyone anything of any real importance but only through the quality of our relations with our students and adults can we motivate, guide, encourage, prod, advise, demonstrate, help our students to learn for themselves. When we have solid evidence that our learning community is learning for its own sake, and that that learning is deep, and that it involves all aspects of our humanity, then we can turn to the steward and say: 'Thank you for your stewardship, but really we have done it ourselves.' The steward will then know a feeling of real success.

9 Information for student learning – assessment for learning: the profile

Christopher Bowring-Carr

In this chapter, I am going to take the vexed question of assessment and expand its usual field of reference so that I will discuss not only assessment *for* learning, but also describe its use as an instrument which provides information that enables the leadership teams in a school to monitor whether all students are encountering, regularly, that range of situations which enables deep learning. I believe that learning is social, that learning to learn is at the heart of education, and that currently, assessment focuses on too narrow a range of memorised outcomes and simplistic information sources.

Ramsden, quoted by Willis (1993: 205), states that 'Evidence now exists to show students' interests, attitudes to studying, and approaches to academic tasks are strongly related to their experiences of teaching and assessment.'

The major problem with the assessment that Ramsden refers to is that too often it manifests itself in a number – 7 out of 10 – or a letter – B+. Such numbering or lettering is of no value, but the system of marking in this way is so ingrained in our schools that despite a very wide range of researchers on both sides of the Atlantic showing its malign effects, it still thrives. In brief, researchers have found that traditional grades are likely to lead to three separate results: 'less impressive learning, less interest in learning, and less desire to do challenging learning' (Kohn, 1999). Reay and Wiliam (2001: 150) also make the very important point that assessment can frequently seem to leave the individual child out of consideration, writing that 'children are subsumed as a means to an end within a process which is primarily an exercise in evaluating schools and their teachers'.

Current systems of assessment, put in place as a result of the National Curriculum, narrow the focus to those aspects of learning which are susceptible to simple, simplistic, numbering. Reay and Wiliam again:

> there is no doubt that such activities (teaching to the test) rob National Curriculum assessments of the power to say anything useful about what the students have learnt. The more specific the government is

> about what it is that schools have to achieve, the more likely it is to get it, but the less likely it is to mean anything.
>
> (Ibid., 160)

Darling-Hammond (1997: 240) says:

> The standards-and-sanctions approach to school reform suffers from similar shortcomings (long-term failure due to goal displacement, reduced cooperation, and inadequate attention to collective learning and problem solving). More than a decade's worth of evidence shows that simply setting test score goals and attaching sanctions to them does not result in greater learning – and sometimes produces destructive side effects (Darling-Hammond 1991; Madaus, 1991; Shepard, 1991).

Black and Wiliam (2003: 411) comment:

> The main starting point for our work on this aspect (marking and comments) was the result of research experiments that established that, while students' learning can be advanced by feedback through comments, the giving of marks does not usually help and, moreover, has a negative effect in that students ignore comments when marks are also given (see, for example, Butler 1990).

Another drawback to this emphasis on narrow numbers is that the leadership of the school will have its scope for intervention narrowed. The information that can be obtained from these numbers is information only on outcomes. The information can give no hint as to the underlying processes and how they can be improved. It is by scrutinising the processes that school improvement can occur; looking at the outcomes is, by contrast, at best a means of identifying the symptoms, but it is not a way of knowing what caused those symptoms.

In this chapter, therefore, I am going to attempt two things. The first is to give an outline of what might be put in place of marks and grades, and the second, a result of the first, is to show how the information gathered through this alternative will provide rich information to be used to go to the roots of learning and thereby improve it. I am going to attempt to move from 'assessment *of*', which is the adding to a completed piece of work some mark or letter grade (what might be termed the post-mortem approach to assessment), past 'assessment *to*', which uses both a mark or grade and a suggestion as to what the next piece of work should attempt, to 'assessment *for*'. This last type of assessment is for learning, indeed is an integral part of learning. I will be stressing that assessment is not a bolt-on, something separate from the act of learning, but must be at the heart of learning. Also, I shall be stressing that assessment needs to be in large part a commentary on the situations in which the learning did or did not take place. In order to underline that I am not discussing an improved system of marking, or a means of establishing a 'marking policy', I have sub-titled this chapter 'The profile'.

I am suggesting that when we start to analyse what we want from an effective profile system, I am, in fact, going to state what I believe effective learning and teaching are. So, let me make certain assumptions clear before I start; in no particular order of importance:

- I am putting the process of learning as opposed to outcomes at the centre of profiling, as indeed we should all put learning at the centre of all deliberations about what goes on in the school.
- Research shows that grades and marks are disincentives. Hence profiles.
- We need to recognise and exploit all intelligences.
- Any profiling system has to encompass our knowledge of the processes of what is happening when we say that this person is, or is not, learning.
- The profile reflects the belief that 'the curriculum' is the totality of what the student experiences while at school, filtered through what s/he brings to school from home and community.
- The senior leadership team will be able, having read a selection of student profiles, to obtain a very clear picture of the strengths and weaknesses of what is going on in the area of learning and teaching, and will thus have the necessary, detailed information to use in their school's improvement.

Let me try to expand on these starting points.

The first – putting learning at the centre – means that the focus of the profile is on the *processes* of the learning, with achievement comments coming as a consequence of them. I am suggesting that at the heart of the profile is a diagnosis of the strengths and weaknesses of the individual student's learning. Let me try to start building an entry to the profile. An opening comment might be:

John is relying on his memory too much. This tendency leads him to rush to a response without thinking through if it is reliable. However, when he does slow down, and is encouraged to burrow into the text, his emotional maturity enables him to understand the characters' motivation.

That is just a start but it does suggest what will be aimed at. How can that starting point be built on? Our knowledge of what constitutes effective learning is growing by the day. We know of a number of attributes and assumptions that are connected with deep learning. One set of assumptions is that intelligence is not fixed, is not singular and is not located solely in the individual's being. Intelligence can be increased, can grow, if the social and physical circumstances are right. We do not have a single intelligence, but, as Gardner (1983, 1999) has shown, we have multiple intelligences. We are enabled to be more intelligent if we are in a social setting which encourages, fosters and celebrates our collective intelligences. Perkins (1995: 322) states that intelligence is *distributed* in three ways:

> Physical. We rely on physical artefacts as simple as note pads and as complex as computer-aided design systems and beyond to do various kinds of remembering and computing for us.
>
> Social. We do not typically think solo but in teams in which different people bring different abilities to the mix, and patterns of collaboration move the general enterprise along.
>
> Symbolic. We do not think in bare thoughts but thoughts clothed in symbol systems, including natural languages with their rich vocabulary of thinking-oriented terms and a variety of notational and graphic symbol systems.

He goes on to ask us to try to imagine the totally solo thinker. No pencil or calculator, no friend or partner, no linguistic or other symbolic resources, no terms and concepts like option or reason. How impaired such a person would be.

Putnam and Borko (2000) in their work quoted in the OU course E843 state that 'First – cognition is situated.' This means that the physical and social contexts in which an activity takes place are integral to the learning process. Our learning is not an individual event, but arises from the interaction with other people, materials and representational systems. 'Second, cognition is social', so that what we take as knowledge and how we think and express ideas are the results of interactions among people over time. Third, we should now give importance to the idea that 'cognition is distributed'. Knowledge and learning are often and effectively created by groups with the individuals in them bringing different skills and expertise to bear on common tasks. The profile, therefore, has to reflect both the individual's progress in learning, and also that individual's part in the group's learning – the part s/he plays in the learning of the group, and the learning s/he takes from the group.

The aim of this chapter, as I said above, is to show that a profile is not an inert bolt-on merely recording what is happening. It is, in fact, a vital part of the learning and teaching process. It both reflects that process, and, more importantly, it is a continual reminder of good practice, a stimulant to look for a multitude of ways to enable learning to take place. It is a leadership tool of the greatest importance as profiling goes to the heart of what a school is about – enabling deep learning to take place.

If the school staff considers, in the traditional way, what intelligence is, there is a tendency to look inwards, to the individual and to ways of training/developing individual minds of various kinds in various ways.

As a result, and this is an important point when considering profiles, undue attention is paid to the individual and what strengths and weaknesses he/she displays, with the suggestion (sometimes much more than a suggestion) that if learning has not taken place or cannot be displayed, then it is the individual's fault. If, however, 'distributed intelligence' and 'social learning' are taken into account, then the school has to pay heed to the physical, social and symbolic settings. Such a change of view is vital to the success of a school. The implication is that there is a contract between the student and the school. It is not the old contract: 'You behave yourself and work hard, and we will teach you and help you pass the examinations.' The contract now is rather: 'We will try our hardest to put in place all the circumstances which we know will enable you to learn at a deep level, and you will take advantage of all these settings and resources, and from this combination you will be able to expand your intelligences and learn profoundly and meaningfully.' That contract means that the school's part in providing the range of settings to increase the individual's intelligence needs to be monitored continuously, and only from a careful reading of many profiles can such monitoring be possible.

Perkins (1995: 323) writes:

> To put this in terms of realm theory; there is such a thing as knowing your way around the use of various physical support systems for thinking from pencil and paper to spreadsheets to word processors to decision-analysis systems. . . . Then there is knowing your way around working with others – how to argue fruitfully, to build on others' contribution, to provoke, to listen, to stimulate. Finally, there is knowing your way around symbolic resources, such as the language of thinking with its reservoirs of terms like decision, option, reason, evidence, consequence.

He goes on to suggest that if we want to enable our students to extend their distributed intelligence, then the place in which they study needs to be as conducive to supporting intelligent behaviour as a good kitchen is conducive to good, healthy cooking. Such a place would have the computer-driven means of enabling real-time video contacts and asynchronous communication; programs which build concept maps and contrast lists, many spaces to write on, and 'easy connectivity with those who might work with you, through electronic mail but also real-time video communication'. The human side of the equation is equally important. We have all sat through committee meetings which achieved little because people do not know or use the language needed – meanings and decisions blur. Students (and some adults) need to learn the language of intelligent and purposeful discourse, and of collaborative thinking and communicating. (Ibid., pp. 323–4, adapted.)

There are other factors that impinge on the student's ability to learn. Diet plays a vital part, as do sleep, physical exercise and emotional security. There is little we can do to influence the average student's dietary or sedentary habits – but we can point out the consequences, and do so with some vigour. We can also start to inform the parents, from entry year onwards, about the close connection between physical well-being and mental health and agility. We can, as far as possible, ensure that the physical and emotional areas which the student inhabits are as fear-free as possible; no threats, no implied dire consequences as to what will happen if something is done, or is not done.

Let us return to the start of a profile and see, at this stage, what needs to be added.

John is relying on his memory too much. This tendency leads him to rush to a response without thinking through if it is reliable. However, when he does slow down, and is encouraged to burrow into the text, his emotional maturity enables him to understand the characters' motivation. Although there is a wealth of computer software to help sift through the many approaches to the complex interaction between characters and environments, John does not take advantage of them and is therefore coming to less tenable and less well constructed theories than his colleagues. He is good in discussions and helps promote and steer focused arguments. He needs to take better care of his physical needs; too often he is losing concentration and appears tired early in the day.

Briefly, it is important to stress that learning is made easier and deeper not only through an individualistic approach but by working collectively. Although the profile will focus on the individual, it must not constrain us into thinking that effective learning is individual; it is very frequently collective, occurring through the interplay of discussion, argument and group exploration. Ways need to be found of incorporating the collective experience into the individual's profile.

There is still another area to look at. A reminder of Gardner's (1999) multiple intelligences (MI) is necessary, namely: linguistic, musical, spatial, logical-mathematical, bodily kinaesthetic, interpersonal, intrapersonal, naturalist. I am assuming that there is a general acceptance of the existence of MI. If this assumption is correct, then the implications of such acceptance are very clear. To ignore MI is to say that all students are more or less the same and can be taught in the same way, will learn in the same way, and can be assessed in the same way. That is not a stance that is acceptable.

Therefore, teachers have to know their students' main intelligence(s), and play to that/those strength(s). In exactly the same way as teachers need to provide the human and physical surroundings for distributed intelligence to thrive, so there is a need to provide opportunities for the student who is, for example, spatially very sharp, to use, inter alia, mind-maps and spider-grams to help him/her learn, but also use them to display the results of learning. It appears to be fairly well established by educational research that the student who is enabled to develop the main intelligences gains in self-esteem and develops other intelligences also.

The profile might be developing along these lines:

John is relying on his memory too much. This tendency leads him to rush to a response without thinking through if it is reliable. However, when he does slow down, and is encouraged to burrow into the text, his emotional maturity enables him to understand the characters' motivation. Although there is a wealth of computer software to help sift through the many approaches to the complex interaction between characters and environments, John does not take advantage of them and is therefore coming to less tenable and well constructed theories than his colleagues. However, he is good in discussions and helps promote and steer focused arguments. He needs to take better care of his physical needs; too often he is losing concentration and appears tired early in the day.

He worked with two other students on providing a musical background to a scene in the play that his group is studying. It was outstanding. The texture of sounds added to the understanding by all in the group of the tensions in the scene. They were very warmly congratulated on this work; their stature in the group has been immeasurably heightened.

There are some further matters to be considered. The first is the area of ethics. I deal with this topic in detail in Chapter 3, but it is necessary to summarise some of the main points. It is a truism to say that a school has to be an ethical place; indeed there are few decisions made in a school which are not rooted in a strong and clearly stated set of ethics. However, it is not as clear that we sufficiently and *overtly* help students to develop their own reflected-upon and argued-through set of values and from those values be encouraged to establish an ethical code. Perhaps it is assumed that if the community's ways of dealing with each other on a day-to-day basis are informed and guided by an ethical stance, then it will in some way rub off on the students. This is not a convincing argument. Ethics is not something that can be caught by propinquity. The question of how best students can not only learn about ethics but learn to live by an overt ethical code is closely bound up with the concept of 'student voice'.

In very brief terms, the idea of 'student voice' relates to the degree to which students take a responsibility *for*, and a sharing in the governance *of* the school. This is not the time to discuss in any detail the ideas behind 'the learning community' – this is a topic dealt with in Chapter 8 – but one of the features of a learning community is that it is (in the proper sense of the word) self-conscious and is explicit about the values, the ethics, which drive and guide it. Stemming from that idea, one can say that it is only through taking an active and reflective part in the community's governance that students can build an ethical frame, test it, refine it, and see its pertinence to their day-to-day life.

Another visit to the profile:

John is relying on his memory too much. This tendency leads him to rush to a response without thinking through if it is reliable. However, when he does slow down, and is encouraged to burrow into the text, his emotional maturity enables him to understand the character's motivation. Although there is a wealth of computer software to help sift through the many approaches to the complex interaction between characters and environments, John does not take advantage of them and is therefore coming to less tenable and well constructed theories than his colleagues. He is good in discussions and helps promote and steer focused arguments. He needs to take better care of his physical needs; too often he is losing concentration and appears tired early in the day.

He worked with two other students on providing a musical background to a scene in the play that his group is studying. It was outstanding. The texture of sounds added to the understanding by all in the group of the tensions in the scene. They were very warmly congratulated on this work; their stature in the group has been immeasurably heightened.

His membership of the Community Council has become increasingly important to him. He is discussing with me (as tutor) and with his group more and more how to make decisions which on the surface are fairly straightforward, but are actually complex, fit in with the community's ethical stance. He is realising the complexity of being part of our community's way of running things.

The next two elements are closely linked – connectivity and application. It is accepted that once learners can see the connections between aspects of what is being learnt, then learning becomes easier and more profound. Also, when knowledge learnt in one situation can be applied in a situation different from that in which it was learnt, then the knowledge is internalised and becomes more readily accessible. Too often in schools, particularly in the first few years of secondary school, there is little that connects one subject to another, and rarely is there any chance of applying new knowledge to help embed it. For the sixth-form student, the subject of the profile that is growing in this chapter, there is a need for his teachers and his tutor to ensure that he is making connections across the normal subject boundaries, and how, perhaps in school, perhaps in work outside school, he is applying that knowledge. If he is not doing either, or if he is making the connections only in one situation, then ways of enabling those processes to take place both in and out of the classroom must be found.

Two final points need to be made on the topic of the adults' input to the profile. (Of course, a number of 'adults', and not all of them necessarily teachers, will contribute to the profile, though the tutor/learning manager will be responsible for writing up the profile.) The first has been alluded to above. The profile needs to include comment on any work being done out of school. It might be no more than a bald statement that the student works in Tesco all weekend, and such work is not helping his school work at all. It might be that the work is connected with what is being studied, and then the applicability can be underlined.

The profile might also carry some indication of what home life is like, with the permission of the student, and within the constraints of data protection legislation. The point to be made is that as the human and physical helps to learning need to be recorded and their influences noted, so those events which hinder learning need to be known about by the staff involved. It is the question of how and if those events are recorded that needs to be addressed by each school.

There is one further point to be made. Much of work outside schools is organised around teams. Too little work inside schools, except on the sports field, is so organised. There is a need to encourage and enable teamwork by both teachers and students. There is also a need to enable work to be carried out which crosses the traditional subject boundaries; I referred to connectivity above. I suggest that part of the curriculum should involve a group of students carrying out a project which involves sustained work over time, using a range of different disciplines. This concept comes from the Coalition of Essential Schools in the United States. One of the imperatives that a school signs up to if it wants to join the Coalition is the idea that a 'demonstration' or 'exhibition' of a cross-disciplinary project carried out by a team of students is a requirement for graduation. As increasingly employers in all walks of life are asking that employees work in teams, there is a need to build such work into the curriculum, and, of course, such work must be reported in the profile. Apart from anything else, such a project can lead to connectivity, applicability and a growth in inter-personal intelligence.

Two further points need to be made, one a major and the other a minor. As I have said, there is an overwhelming amount of research which shows beyond any doubt that giving marks out of ten, or allocating letter grades, are disincentives to learning. It is a commentary on the *process* of the work that is necessary; how the work could be improved, what the next piece of work should be about, whether the resources (human and/or material) used were the right ones, or if there were untapped but available resources, and so on. As students are enabled to acquire and use a metalanguage to become self-conscious and articulate about the process of their learning, so teachers' written and spoken comments will be focused on the process, and will point to the Zone of Proximal Development rather than be irrelevant asides on past work.

Finally, I suggest that there needs to be a parallel profile, this one written by the student. The student would write a journal that was a distillation of the comments and discussions that s/he has regularly with the teachers and tutor. It would highlight what had been easy, what difficult, what had excited or bored – in short it would be a written form of the metalanguage used in the day-to-day conversations about learning that all students carry on. Over time, patterns emerge, which help both student and tutor steer the learning opportunities. In an MEd course that I am tutoring, some of the students have been writing papers on how they used pupil-generated journals to help their pupils analyse their strengths and weaknesses in mathematics, and also to comment on the teaching styles which were being used. Unanimously, the MEd students showed in their assignments that such journals were very useful in helping their students to learn, and also helped the teachers adapt their teaching styles to meet the needs of the pupils.

So, it is suggested that the profiles that will be kept for students need to run in parallel to the ones that they, the students, are keeping. It is, of course, a skill that does not develop unaided. The idea of the journal needs to be introduced quite early – precisely when is up to each individual school. Perhaps for the two years leading up to GCSE students could, in some subjects if not all, start the process of learning how to write journals. Staff, too, will have to accept the possibility that not all students like all the teaching strategies employed, but such acceptance is a necessary part of their being a member of a learning community. Journals add powerfully to that absolute bedrock of a learning community – the establishment of a metalanguage with which all can talk professionally about the core activity.

So, what might the profile look like when those latter points have been added in?

John is relying on his memory too much. This tendency leads him to rush to a response without thinking through if it is reliable. However, when he does slow down, and is encouraged to burrow into the text, his emotional maturity enables him to understand the character's motivation. Although there is a wealth of computer software to help sift through the many approaches to the complex interaction between characters and environments, John does not take advantage of them and is therefore coming to less tenable and well constructed theories than his colleagues. He is good in discussions and helps promote and steer focused arguments. He needs to take better care of his physical needs; too often he is losing concentration and appears tired early in the day.

He worked with two other students on providing a musical background to a scene in the play that his group is studying. It was outstanding. The texture of sounds added to the understanding by all in the group of the tensions in the scene. They were so warmly congratulated on this work; their stature in the group has been immeasurably heightened.

His membership of the Community Council has become increasingly important to him. He is discussing with me (as tutor) and with his group more and more how to make decisions which on the surface are fairly straightforward, but are actually complex, fit in with the community's ethical stance. He is realising the complexity of being part of our community's way of running things.

Through discussions that I helped establish with his class, John is beginning to understand the theme that any technological advance has its benefits and drawbacks. He is using his A-level history of Europe in the nineteenth century, and his A-level Economics to explore the topic, and bring to it some illuminations from each discipline. His essays have improved as a result. However, he has not taken the opportunities offered through studying his part-time work placement to see how that business puts some of the economic theories he is learning into practice.

He is beginning to come out of the shock and depression that he felt when his father left home. His first term in the sixth-form was badly affected by this loss. The counselling that we recommended has appeared to help.

He has joined a group of eight other students to carry out a long-term project on the amenities and community services needed in the housing estate being planned on the south-east of town. They have lined up a really impressive list of sub-topics and people to interview, and background research to be done. The knowledge that there is a six-month time limit has sharpened their approach.

At the beginning of the chapter, I said that an assessment system that focused on the processes would also give rich information to the leadership team to analyse in order to see the extent to which the school is providing the resources, human and material, the settings and the ethos which together make for real learning. If we look at the profile above, in its completed form, we can begin to see what an extensive fund of information is here. In very brief form:

- Memory is seen not to be all-important.
- Quick responses are not rewarded.
- Emotional intelligence is fostered and monitored.
- Computer resources are available.
- Discussion is valuable and encouraged. The individual is not learning on his/her own.
- The link between physical well-being and learning is established.
- All the intelligences are encouraged and celebrated.
- Self-esteem is fostered.
- There is a Community Council – learning about democracy and its ethical underpinnings can occur only in a school in which there is democracy.
- Ethics are at the heart of the process.
- Connectivity is understood as vital to learning.
- Application of knowledge is seen to be important.
- Emotional security is recognised as important.
- Team learning is essential.

Were the leadership team to read, regularly, twenty or thirty such profiles, it would be very easy to see where the learning processes were being well cared for, and where neglected. Remediation, which focuses on processes and not outcomes, stands a far greater chance of success.

Let me end the chapter with some caveats and questions.

The first is that a very fine line has to be steered between, on the one hand knowing enough to help the students learn, collectively and individually, and on the other, becoming obsessive collectors of minutiae. The profile needs to be an aid, not an intrusion.

The second is that such profile writing takes time, but if a school is serious about enabling autonomous learning, and puts in place the ICT needed to extend learning, then there will not be as much up-front teaching as there is now. It is to be hoped that the profile, and the student's parallel journal, will become an essential part of the learning process. It will be a dialogic commentary for learning.

Third, the desire to present a profile that is coherent may lead to thinking that learning is linear and neat. It is not. The art will be in writing coherently about a process that is frequently incoherent.

Fourth, there is the question as to whether the profile should be written in the third person, as in this chapter, or whether it should be in the second person, so that in time a dialogue builds between student and tutor, with the student's journal being one side of the 'conversation', and the tutor's profile the other.

Fifth, if learning is frequently collective, as we are sure it is, how can the profile reflect and comment on the collective? The journal could have such statements as: 'I joined with Sean and Ilsa in . . . and we managed. . . . There were times when Sean's comments really helped me to understand . . .'. In the examples of the profile above, there is a hint as to how the tutor might reflect such work.

Sixth, can a space always be found to record that Eureka moment, that moment when a real breakthrough has been achieved, when learning has resulted in a real change in the student's perception of the world and her/his place in it? And of course, that moment may have nothing to do with the official curriculum.

Seventh, and vitally important, the community as a whole has to have come to a collective and agreed understanding as to the meaning of 'worthwhile learning', of what the processes of such learning are, and what constitutes an expression of that learning.

There is one last query. Can we use the technology that is available to enable teachers to include video clips of the students going about their work – showing the art work they have done, showing a discussion, the Community Council at work, the music they have composed, and so on and on? If only paper profiles are used, then much of the richness of a student's life in school will be lost, and because unrecorded, undervalued.

There have been two parallel aims in this chapter. The first is to suggest ways in which the leadership of a school or college can acquire information needed to ensure that the school is continuously aware of how it is fostering learning and improving the range of ways in which people learn. The second is to suggest a tool which goes to the heart of improving the process of learning, turning away from the mere accretion of superficial, and ultimately meaningless, marks. For the individual student and for the teachers the second aim is probably the more important. For the school as a whole, the profile is the more important as it gives, possibly for the first time, a detailed way of maintaining a steady look at the core activity.

10 Information for organisational learning – establishing a coherent, rigorous and workable system of self-evaluation

Peter Smith

INTRODUCTION

Whole school self-evaluation was not the first thing on everyone's mind when we started the development of a workable system a few years ago. Today it has become something which is central to the leadership and management of school improvement. It is an increasingly important element of OfSTED Inspections and of local Advisory and Inspection 'health checks'.

I believe that this is a good thing. It returns a degree of control to us as professional educators, something which only a few years ago seemed to be lost for ever. It provides the opportunity to prove our expertise and our worth. Ultimately, it could enable schools to set their own agenda for improvement, an agenda that dismisses schools as a standardised factory for information cramming but moves them towards being centres of learning and a reflection of the finest achievements of human endeavour.

In this chapter, I propose a system of collating information for school self-evaluation which the reader can adapt. The essence of this chapter is probably best summed up by considering the following questions posed by OfSTED:

How does your school rate against the following statements?

1. *Standards in our school are higher than average and higher than our previous best and better than in most other schools serving similar pupils.*
2. *Progress of most pupils is better than expected from their previous results or their attainment on entry to the school.*
3. *The school knows whether any groups of pupils have results which are lower than those of the rest, for reasons other than prior attainment, and is targeting and monitoring these groups.*
4. *The school knows which subjects and teaching groups, relatively, reflect the highest and lowest standards and which elements within subjects are the strongest and weakest.*

> The school that knows and understands itself is well on the way to solving any problems it has. The school that is ignorant of its weaknesses, or will not, or cannot, face up to them is not well-managed.
> (Office for Standards in Education 2000)

In order to simplify matters I have not entered into all the steps taken over more than ten years. This chapter has not been written in the form of a logically unfolding master plan which you can copy. Indeed our actual plans often changed to accommodate some new piece of legislation or a new national initiative. Instead it explains ideas and gives sources of information. It also presents some formats for information gathering and analysis which you might adapt to your own situation. None of this would be of any use if the information gleaned was not used to improve the education we were giving to our children. Discovering and instigating such improvements should naturally follow on as the end product of self-evaluation. The methods of doing this would form a whole new chapter and, therefore, only have implicit references in this text. There has also been a degree of poetic licence in an attempt to make the whole readable and understandable but I do not believe that this has compromised the integrity of our work.

FIRST STEPS

The mother of invention

Reading through notes and school documentation in preparation for this chapter, I was reminded of how relentless the pace of change has been in our schools since the education acts of the 1980s. Those who were teaching in the 1990s will remember the almost weekly (daily?) deluge of instructions from on high, consultations with too short a time scale and the seemingly constant carping by sections of the press and many other people who should have known better. The introduction of the National Curriculum was a mammoth task in itself, while the prospect of the end of key stage tests and the unknown quantity of a tough inspection regime made many people question why they had chosen to teach in the first place.

Heads who had been appointed well before any of the above started, suddenly found themselves, as it were, having to play a new game. Unfortunately, in this game, the rules seemed to change constantly while the pitch was re-marked in a different pattern almost every day. The scoreboard showed we were losing, even when we thought we were at least drawing, while the referee was definitely biased. At least that is the way it felt to me. Despite all of this, I knew my school was performing well. Local inspectors had said so and had even written it, parents had confirmed it and all my experience said we were achieving a great deal with relatively poor resources. I believed our development planning addressed all the issues and was built on the expertise and judgment of a first-rate set of professionals. But I soon discovered that we were moving into a new era when our experience and knowledge would not be enough.

It was at about this juncture that I was asked one of the most significant questions of my career. A visiting LEA inspector, unofficially wearing his OfSTED hat, asked me who was the best teacher on my staff. I answered using my personal knowledge and experience going back over nearly 30 years in primary education. His reply, 'but *how* do you know?' actually left me lost for words. I knew because I knew because I knew. I couldn't back up my thoughts with any performance indicators or comparative data. I had nothing in writing, no empirical measures, just personal experience and a degree of self-belief. Now I was a lamb going to ritual slaughter by a dangerous beast unless I could find protection. Necessity is, they say, the mother of invention. It was, therefore, this rather defensive posture that led me towards systems of self-evaluation.

Making a start

But where to start? To many people the words 'self-evaluation' immediately conjure up visions of the statistical analysis of SATs and other tests, of classroom observation and feedback and possibly long essays justifying the school's performance. It did not take long for us to realise that:

- we had been self-evaluating all along but in a much less formal and rigorous way than would be required;
- self-evaluation is actually a proactive tool which can lead to greater competency and even win us back some of the right to professional judgement that we perceive has been taken away by the recent reforms;
- factors influencing raising standards of achievement were more than just teaching and learning in the classroom.

The implication of this last point was that some official documents at this time were wrong. We believed that while teaching and learning were the core purpose of the school, excellence could not be achieved by concentrating solely on classroom practice. Any self-evaluation system would need to examine the whole organisation and management of the school; its systems, its ethos and its vision. Take, for example, relationships and leadership. If the school has a climate of trust, a 'no blame' culture attached to innovation and change, a mutual respect of individual strengths and capabilities, how much easier it is to introduce new ideas for teaching or classroom monitoring. If school leadership provides opportunities for individuals to take charge, and therefore responsibility, or if it can successfully ensure that the vision for the school is shared and owned by all staff, how much easier to adopt or adapt all the changes being introduced. Get such matters as these right and a virtuous circle of improvement is created with obvious implications for pupil achievement.

Looking back, the systems we created or borrowed then were very good for the time but probably would not stand up today. They did, however, do the job we wanted at the time. The school was inspected and the result justified our efforts as we were judged to be a very good school with four areas of curriculum excellence. Overall the teaching was judged very good with no unsatisfactory lessons. Data analysis/ evaluation was said to be a strength. Relationships and pupil behaviour were graded very good and exemplary. Such a report in the climate of the time could be a cause for complacency. However, no sooner had we read the report than members of staff were asking how we might become an 'excellent' school with no weaknesses. In our opinion, the answer lay in taking self-evaluation to new heights and introducing systems that were so efficient that any weakness could be identified and acted upon. Quite a challenge, but one to which we were keen to respond.

What actually happened over the next seven years was a process of evolution which resulted from a growing awareness of possibilities, a widening of personal knowledge and expertise, and a reaction to new demands made by initiatives such as the numeracy and literacy strategies. Despite the last phrase, it also gave us a greater feeling of being in charge of our own destiny and not constantly feeling overwhelmed by events.

Cracking the code

At about this time OfSTED had circulated a pamphlet to schools entitled *School Evaluation Matters* (Office for Standards in Education 1998). Perhaps one of the best documents ever produced for schools, this not only gave a breakdown of a system which would evaluate school performance, but related it to the inspection framework. The publication is no longer available but some of what follows is an interpretation of the text and a summary of sections that we adopted. The core of our efforts at this stage was a School Improvement File (SIF). This was not intended to be a replacement or substitute for the School Development Plan (SDP) which remained central to whole school strategies for improvement/management. Indeed the making of this file of information formed part of a priority in the SDP pertaining to school improvement. The purpose of this new file was to provide a central theme, shape and order in our efforts towards school improvement by:

1. holding some original documents which monitor, evaluate and draw conclusions about school improvement;

2. cross-referencing supportive evidence in other documents, policies and practice in order to provide a coherent picture about all that was taking place and would take place in the school;
3. provide a resource to inform SDP priorities or short-term fixes.

OUR FIRST SYSTEM

The basics of our first system: the collection and analysis of data

Seven methods of collecting and analysing data were listed in School Evaluation Matters. Most were already in use and nearly all could be undertaken by staff in the normal time available for curriculum development or administrative work. All could be undertaken as part of some other project, thereby maximising the use of time and easing workload. All would provide important information which could be co-ordinated and acted upon. Table 10.1 tabulates the information about the seven methods as shown in the introduction to our SIF. Note that some of the nomenclature is now outdated but has been left for the purpose of this illustration.

The basics of our first system: methodology

School Evaluation Matters (OfSTED 1998) stressed the importance of establishing a climate of understanding the methodology of self evaluation so that it would become embedded in the school culture. This involves the activities of monitoring, analysing, evaluating, planning and acting as discussed below.

1. *Monitor* performance at all levels in the school.

   This is attained by effective school monitoring/evaluation policies and good inter-staff relations. It can be applied across the school as shown in the Monitoring and Evaluation Matrix (Table 10.3).

2. *Analyse* where the standards are high enough throughout the school and compare with data for similar schools.

   An example is shown in Section 4 of our SIF on page 155. In addition to an individual school's PANDA, there will be local data such as a local tracking project and LEA analysis.

3. *Evaluate* the quality of teaching and learning and other aspects of the school's provision against national criteria, to diagnose strengths and weaknesses.

   Published criteria, benchmarks or performance indicators from national and local sources can be used e.g. OfSTED Inspection Framework. Such

Table 10.1 Methods of collecting and analysing data

Method	*Activity*	*Comment*
Checklist approach	The staff carry out an audit against a long list of questions generated by the school or by the LEA	Often used prior to embarking on a new initiative, e.g., audits for Literacy and Numeracy Strategies, National Grid for Learning
Ballot approach and SWOT analysis	Staff identify the wide range of influences on their work or proposed initiative. They consider more productive approaches, systematic analysis of strengths, owning up to weaknesses, identifying opportunities and assessing threats/problems.	Used in staff meetings when planning the approach to a problem or topic. Led by subject co-ordinators or senior staff. Good for clearing the air and dispelling irrational fears (if handled properly)
Curriculum-led approach	An approach where one or two areas of the curriculum are reviewed each year, usually on a rotational basis. Weakness – that curriculum review is normally undertaken in the context of the coverage and design of the curriculum rather than its effectiveness in developing knowledge, understanding and skills, with a focus on raising standards.	Originally used by us in the early Management Plans as a systematic way of completing curriculum review and improvement but then largely swept aside by a myriad Government initiatives. We had not adhered to a strict order but had frequently adapted to school needs.
Appraisal approach	Strategies for the appraisal of teachers and headteachers concentrates the focus of evaluation closer to our core purpose: teaching and learning.	We strongly believe that the essence of a high-quality evaluation of teaching and learning is a system of trust and mutual respect between professionals who can communicate hard lessons and recognise success in all its guises. The present performance management system, if underpinned by the above, can form an effective method of developing individual competencies within the context of the whole school.
Client-centred approach	Involves the school in surveying the views and attitudes to the school of parents, pupils and other interested parties.	Will inevitably throw up something you did not know and give the opportunity to improve or put things right. Essential to remain objective in the face of seemingly groundless criticism.

Table 10.1 continued

Method	*Activity*	*Comment*
The quality mark approach	Used by us and other schools seeking external recognition of their success, e.g., School Curriculum Awards, Charter Mark, Investors in People.	School Evaluation Matters says, 'Effective self-evaluation does not rely solely on such endorsements, none of which focuses explicitly on teaching and learning and raising educational standards.' This is true but such endorsements can highlight particular successes which support teaching and learning e.g. Investors in People shows a strength in staff development which in turn influences personal performance. Such areas must contribute to the raising of standards.
Self-evaluation (i.e., of pupil performance data and classroom monitoring)	Self-evaluation as distinct from review must be able to: • take an objective look at pupils' achievements; • pinpoint areas of underachievement; • account for results by identifying strengths and weaknesses and the quality of effectiveness of any part of the school's work, particularly teaching and learning; • provide information for the school improvement plan which will in future be a vehicle for raising standards and improving quality	The basis of what we were trying to achieve, the data from which we collated our SIF and which would enable us to reach our goal of whole school excellence.

sources as the national standards for entry to the teaching profession, the Hay McBer work on excellence in teaching and in leadership, Investors in People indicators etc have all become available, and provide a rich source for constructing evaluation formats.

4. *Plan* what needs to be done to overcome weaknesses and set clear objectives and targets for improvement.

   This is usually accomplished through development plans and target-setting (official and unofficial). Plans are useless unless they are put into action so this needs the wholehearted commitment of all, ownership throughout and a shared vision.

5. *Act* on the findings of monitoring, evaluation and diagnosis to promote more effective teaching and learning through support and training.

   There needs to be a recognition that the twin constraints of time and money inevitably impinge on all we do. Our experience showed that prioritising and delegation were the keys to action whilst, once again, commitment, ownership and vision were also essential.

In summary, therefore, any system which is devised must:

- have the support of staff;
- use monitoring of results to focus evaluation on raising standards;
- evaluate the quality of teaching and learning against criteria using a range of evidence;
- involve all staff, particularly those having curricular responsibilities and ensure that teachers have the opportunity, not only for self-evaluation, but for seeing the work of others;
- provide performance feedback and an agenda for improvement;
- ensure that evaluation leads to action, support and development.

Our first system: collating the data

Having established a climate for school improvement through self-evaluation, we were making a good start. All data concerned with self-evaluation and analysis were now collated in the School Improvement File (see Tables 10.2 and 10.3). Where there was cause for concern and a need for action, plans were made and became part of the School Development Plan (later called the School Improvement Plan) or, if it was something which could be dealt with quickly, a note was made and action taken.

Table 10.2 shows an overview of the SIF structure and content; some of the questions posed will be very familiar! The structure is entirely based on School Evaluation Matters. Pages 148 to 157 (Table 10.3) then provide an explanation of the various sections which make up the system's structure, with illustrations of data collection methods.

Table 10.2 The contents of the School Improvement File

Introduction What is school evaluation ?

Section 1: Action Planning, review and outcomes following OfSTED

1a	Whole school issues from recent OfSTED report
1b	Co-ordinator's analysis of progress made in each individual subject
1c	Implementation of the Post-OfSTED Action Plan

Table 10.2 continued

Section 2: External Perspective and Review

2a PANDA/Autumn Package: Analysis of PANDA

2b School Improvement Report (SIR)

Section 3: Internal Data and Review

What are our strengths and weaknesses? Where shall we start?

3a (i) How can we evaluate teaching?

3a (ii) How can we evaluate other areas which may impact on standards?

3b Fulfilling the aims of the school

3c Development Plan priorities and targets

3d Monitoring by HT and co-ordinators, record and outcomes (where appropriate)

3e Self-review summary using the OfSTED Framework for Inspection

Section 4: Statistical Evidence of Progress and Improvement

How good is our school?

4a How good is our school?

4b Are standards improving?

4c (i) SATs for last 4 years

'Are standards as high as they should be?'
'Do pupils make the expected progress or better?'
'Are results better in some subjects than others?'

4c (ii) Internally administered tests to present cohorts

'Are standards as high as they should be?'
'Do pupils make the expected progress or better?'
'Are results better in some subjects than others?'

4d Progress and gender: 'Are some groups doing better than others?'

4e Analysis of tracking project long-term data

4f Special Needs

4g 'How can we monitor other types of achievement?'

Section 5: Target Setting/Our Capacity for Improvement

Annual Target Setting Process

What must we do to improve? **Have we got what it takes?**

Table 10.3 The School Improvement File

Section 1: Action Planning, review and outcomes following OfSTED

1a Whole school issues from recent OfSTED report.

Completed by HT in consultation with staff.

What to do

- Take each section of your last OfSTED report which relate to whole school issues.
- Use highlighter pens to draw attention to strengths (green) and weaknesses (red).
- Reference these S1, S2, etc for strengths/good practice and W1, W2, etc for weaknesses/concerns
- Enter these on a chart, stating present position and explaining plans for development/improvement.
- Complete summative statement and future action sections as appropriate.

Why you should do it

- Provides a framework to review a particular aspect of the school
- Provides an on-going assessment of progress and a base for further improvement
- Useful as a basis for Form S4 or similar, School Improvement Plan/Strategic Planning, dialogue with link inspectors , updates to Governors' Committees
- If done honestly, provides OfSTED Inspectors with an in-depth assessment of school progress.
- Shows that you know what's going on!

When you should do it

- As often as you like, but certainly before an OfSTED Inspection.
- Bear in mind that changes in staff, imposed initiatives and circumstances beyond your control, may radically alter particular levels of efficiency in the school.

1b Co-ordinator's analysis of progress made in each individual subject

The same format as above but concentrating on individual subjects. Usually conducted by co-ordinators.

1c Implementation of the Post-OfSTED Action Plan

Completed by HT following consultation with staff and drawing from Development Plan, reports to governors etc.

What to do
A record of the progress of your Post-OfSTED Action Plan.
Include the original plan with any updates.
Include all written reports by you to the Governors

Why you should do it
A convenience to you, Governors and Inspectors.
Brings together all aspects of the work undertaken to implement the plan and thereby provide a coherent record of progress so far.
Feeds reports to Governors and Link Inspectors etc.
A confirmation that you are dealing with points raised by a rigorous evaluation from outside the school.

When you should do it
On-going from one OfSTED inspection to the next, provides a summary at the end of each year.

Example

School's Response to OfSTED report
Implementation of the Post Inspection Plan

(Insert the time report completed in relation to the Inspection)

Key Issue 1:
Actual wording of the Key Issue.

Overview
Your commentary on the relevance of the issue and its place in the development of the school

What we have done	Impact of action	Evidence
A succinct list of actions	The impact of each action on the school and its place in raising standards	Clear reference to documentation, statistical evidence which proves actions and improvements.

Summary judgement:
Your assessment of the work so far and its overall impact

continued

Section 2:
External Perspective and Review

2a PANDA/Autumn Package: Analysis of PANDA

What to do
Analyse and pick out key issues from PANDA/Autumn Package
Place in file for ease of access when completing reports, action plans etc. May be cross-referenced to other sections if necessary

Why you should do it
Condenses complex messages from an enormous amount of data

When you should do it
This section to be changed each year following publication of PANDA. Earlier reports filed and available.

2b School Improvement Report (SIR)

This may be a termly LEA Inspector's Report (or local equivalent).

An annotated copy of any external written report would be placed in the file and may be used as evidence in earlier sections or as a springboard for further action.

Section 3:
Internal Data and Review

What are our strengths and weaknesses ? Where shall we start?

3a (i) How can we evaluate teaching?

Pointers to effective evaluation of teaching.

What to do
This section is intended as a summary of the school's philosophy and policies for evaluating teaching. It should make reference to any publications that the school has found useful and also refer to school policies on classroom monitoring and appraisal. It may form the introduction to a school policy. Its content should be known and agreed by all staff.

Why you should do it

Explains school procedures/ethos on evaluation of teaching and supports and makes public a uniform approach.

When you should do it

Now. Review as necessary.

3a (ii) How can we evaluate other areas which may impact on standards?

Taken from OfSTED School Evaluation Matters and showing how the school has inaugurated systems which enable the evaluation of other areas (e.g. non-teaching) which impact on standards.

What to do

- Take each statement from School Evaluation Matters (see A to D below) and consider how the school addresses the matter.
- Make responses by cross-referencing to supportive remarks in the last OfSTED, SIR, school documents, governors'/parental comments, etc. If the response is negative cross reference to SIP/SDP or suitable initiative.

Why you should do it

- Provides a thorough assessment of the area for development or foundation for future success
- Gives a strong indication of the school's ethos and its success in achieving its stated Aims

When you should do it

- As required. Update to take account of changes, particularly if initial negative response requires action.

Example for 3a (ii)

(School's response shown in boxes on first two of A only)

A. Evaluation of the curriculum and assessment is concerned with how the school plans for, provides and assesses the full range of learning experiences **in order to promote higher standards.** You should evaluate how far the curriculum:

is balanced and broadly based;

See: OfSTED 33, Aims of the school, planning documentation

continued

promotes pupils' intellectual, physical and personal development and prepares pupils for the next stage of education, training or employment;

See: Aims of the school, OfSTED 2, Reports to Governors and parents

meets statutory requirements to teach the subjects of the national curriculum, religious education and sex education, where these apply;

etc.

provides equality of access and opportunity for pupils to learn;

meets the curriculum requirements for all pupils with special educational needs;

is planned effectively, provides continuity and progression of learning;

is enriched by curriculum provision, including sport.

B. Pupils' spiritual, moral, social and cultural development. These aspects also reflect the ethos of the school. They should be judged by the extent to which the school:

provides its pupils with knowledge and insight into values and beliefs and enables them to reflect on their experiences in a way which develops their spiritual awareness and self knowledge;

teaches the principles which distinguish right from wrong;

encourages pupils to relate positively to others, take responsibility, participate fully in the community, and develop an understanding of citizenship;

teaches pupils to appreciate their own cultural traditions and diversity and richness of cultures.

C. Support, guidance and pupils' welfare. These areas should be evaluated in terms of the extent to which the school:

provides effective support and advice for its pupils, informed by monitoring of their academic progress, personal development, behaviour and attendance;

has effective measures to promote discipline and good behaviour; and illuminate oppressive behaviour, including all forms of harassment and bullying;

has effective child protection measures;

is successful in promoting the health, safety and general well-being of its pupils.

D. Partnership with parents and community. Evaluation should consider the extent to which:

links with parents (home/school contracts), contribute to pupils' learning including information to parents and reporting on pupils' progress.

3b Fulfilling the aims of the school

An analysis of the aims and how we try to achieve them. Also cross-referenced with OfSTED and other external documents as supporting evidence. It is particularly important that supporting evidence is accurate and up to date in this section, referring as it does to a fundamental of the school.

What to do

- State the aims of the school and comment on how these have been/are/will be achieved.
- Cross reference to OfSTED Reports, LEA inspector reports, school documentation, visiting governors' reports, events etc.

Why you should do it

- Provides a good indication to you and others of how successful the school is in terms of achieving its aims.
- Shows how successful you are in producing a shared vision with which all can identify.

When you should do it?

- At least every year.

3c Development Plan priorities and targets

3d Monitoring by HT and co-ordinators, record and outcomes (where appropriate)

3e Self-review summary using the OfSTED Framework for Inspection

Each of the above, 3c, 3d and 3e to be completed with specific reference to your school.

Section 4: Statistical Evidence of Progress and Improvement

Background information on Section 4

The availability of performance data in a range of formats has improved beyond all measure since we devised this section. Originally we had to invent our methods of presenting data in an understandable and accurate form using Microsoft Excel. This task has now largely

continued

been completed for us through the county tracking project and the annual PANDA. The introduction of benchmark groups, value added and a points system were all to come. However, the rationale behind what we did and why we did it remains largely intact. Extracts from the SIF are given below. Today it may only be necessary to take data from sources available rather than starting from scratch.

The use of testing and analysis of data was already well established by the mid-1990s and, indeed, was described as a strength of the school. By using our test results databases built up over a number of years, it was even then, possible to track progress, target individual needs and adopt suitable corrective strategies in teaching. Since then, however, several important developments enabled us to improve our systems even further.

What we have done

Sources now provide us with comparative data which enables us to:

- compare our performance with national results and national data groups (PANDA);
- compare our performance with all local schools and local benchmark groups (using LEA data and tracking projects);
- compare the performance of cohorts against national standardised results in English, Maths and general potential (NFER);
- compare the performance of individual children in SATs with their performance in standardised national tests by NFER in English and Maths;
- use subject performance indicators to examine a child's long-term performance as against that 'on the day'.

Each layer of the above gives a truer reflection of performance finishing, as it does, with the potential of performance of the individual child. When we devised this system, great emphasis was being placed on the aggregated performance of schools. We felt that such information did not truly reflect performance; indeed it could obscure excellent teaching and individual success. By using the data provided by the tracking project, we have been able to examine the potential and progress of individual pupils and relate this to targets and performance at national and local level.

Additionally, we have been able to take into account very real differences in our intake, differences which could totally mask any trends and true levels of achievement. By aggregating this data we have also been able to monitor trends, revise teaching strategies and check our own 'gut' feelings as to how well we are doing as educators. We believe that this aspect of school self-assessment has given us a much more accurate picture, relating as it does to the individual.

The content of Section 4 is set out opposite.

Section 4:
Statistical Evidence of Progress and Improvement

4a How good is our school?

We felt that success measured as an end of Key Stage percentage against a national curriculum level was an extremely misleading measure of school and pupil achievement. We therefore developed an average level measure which reflected the achievement of all children. A similar system based on points is now to be found in PANDA reports. Both systems give credit to schools which manage, for example, to achieve a high proportion of level 5 at KS2. Furthermore such a system does not ignore the achievement of children who strive to attain levels below 4.

4b Are standards improving?

Statistical records by individual subject or all core subjects which show yearly results of the SATs average (points scores). Best shown as a histogram. A commentary is essential.

4c (i) SATs for the last x (decide) years answering the following questions:

'Are standards as high as they should be?'

School results compared with local and national results and targets in English, Maths and Science. Comparison with benchmark group and full national results.

'Do pupils make the expected progress or better?'

A look at end of Key Stage results compared with school-based assessments/tests. LEAs will probably conduct a tracking project such as that based on NFER maths 7–11, Progress in English (PiE) and Non Verbal Reasoning Quotient. Standardised test results give a good indication of progress and ability over time which can then be combined with SATs to answer the above question.

'Are results better in some subjects than others?'

Comparison of average or points scores in core subject SATs over the chosen time scale. Similar figures available from PANDA. Analysis of data used in curriculum development and adjustments to teaching strategies.

4c (ii) Internally administered tests to present cohorts

Present cohorts' progress in English, Reading and Maths using Neale Analysis of Reading and NFER PiE and Maths 7–11. Comment and analysis of yearly results answering the same three questions as in 4c (i) above.

'Are standards as high as they should be?'

'Do pupils make the expected progress or better?'

'Are results better in some subjects than others?'

continued

4d Progress and gender

'Are some groups doing better than others?'

Comparison of average or points scores of boys and girls in all core subjects using tracking project and PANDA data. County Tracking Project also gives evidence of social class and achievement.

4e Analysis of tracking project long-term data

Some current references but rest held over in Data File.

4f Special Needs.

Additional answer to the question,

'Are some groups doing better than others?'

How the children on the Special Needs Register are achieving success which represents individual challenge and school-based targets.

4g 'How can we monitor other types of achievement'?

This question may be answered by using the system described in 1a and 1b. As much inevitably depends on subjective judgements, the observations of those outside the day-to-day life of the school are probably of most use. These include Governors, Inspectors, parents and a range of visitors.

In relation to this wider analysis, School Evaluation Matters says:

'You may consider pupils' attitudes, behaviour and personal development in terms of the extent to which pupils:

- show interest in their work, sustain concentration, develop their capacity for personal study;
- behave well in and around the school, are courteous and trustworthy and show respect for property;
- form constructive relationships with each other, teachers and other adults;
- work collaboratively when required;
- show respect for people's backgrounds, feelings, values and beliefs;
- show initiative and are willing to take responsibility;
- attend well and come to school and lessons on time'.

Section 5:
Target Setting/Our Capacity for Improvement

Annual Target Setting Process.

Cross-refers to a separate file on this.

These final questions from School Evaluation Matters are ones which are best answered by schools on an individual basis.

'What must we do to improve.'

'Have we got what it takes?'

EARLY VISITORS

Once we had started work to build our self-evaluation system, over the following two years we applied the method described above to fine tune, improve or reconstruct perceived weaknesses. Not such an arduous task as one might think. For example, Section One completed by subject co-ordinators not only enabled them to monitor their subject, but provided the basis for reports to Governors or dialogues with the LEA inspectorate.

At the same time as we were developing and using our system, we were having to adapt our methods to cope with a new OfSTED framework, new national strategies, changes to the National Curriculum and a host of other initiatives and requirements. Within two years of starting we were entering another chapter in the whirlwind of change we had come to expect.

We commenced work towards the Investor in People award, in itself an excellent means of self-evaluating the development and management of a school's most expensive and important resource, its staff. Two of us were about to embark on the OfSTED School Self-evaluation course, a useful tool in our continuing work with classroom monitoring. We had discovered the useful publication *The Numbers Game*[1] which confirmed much of our approach to the analysis of test results.

It was about this time that we also discovered the Scottish schools' system of self-evaluation, based on the European Foundation for Quality Management Framework (EQFM).[2] Here was a ready-made system that used an established framework, gave performance indicators and also provided a comprehensive list of actions and relevant documentation needed for analysis. It also covered the entire spectrum of school organisation and management in a rigorous but user-friendly way. It was already becoming obvious that self-evaluation would play an increasing role in future OfSTED inspection and so it was decided to trial some of the indicators in parallel with, or instead of, the formats we had devised.

Table 10.4 Our first system: overview: monitoring and evaluation matrix

This matrix provides an overview and guide to our systems of monitoring and evaluation which contribute data to our School Improvement File and thereby inform whole school improvement. Each school will have a different text in columns A–F which reflect local arrangements

Focus/evaluation questions	*A Criteria for judgement*	*B Sources of evidence available*	*C Method of information/evidence collection*	*D Roles/ responsibilities*	*E Frequency of occurrence and timeline*	*F Summative evaluation: format and destination of outcome*
1 School aims	See report in SIF. Do aims reflect true picture of the school ethos? Do all members of the school community identify with them?	1 Feedback from visiting governors. 2 Parental survey. 3 Teacher observations. 4 Quality of work and evident school ethos.	1 Written report. 2 Survey of statistical analysis. 3 Discussion, informal/formal. 4 Levelling and other work examination.	See Management Responsibilities list. Developed by all staff and members of school community.	1 Termly. 2 Alternate years. 3 On-going. 4 Yearly or more frequently if requested.	Aspects of aims figure in HT report to governors. See also SIF.
2 Pupil achievement	1 Improvements set against national figures and chronological age. 2 Figures analysed by LEA and school in Tracking Project report and SIF. 3 National comparisons by PANDA etc.	1 Reading tests. 2 NFER tests. 3 SATs tests. 4 Previous reports. 5 Pupil records. 6 Subject assessments.	1 Individual children read to Headteacher. 2 Conducted as per test rules. 3 Conducted as national rules. 4 Compiled by class teacher, copy sent to new class. 5 Compiled by class teacher. 6 Agreed by all staff.	See Management Responsibilities list. Data co-ordinated by Headteacher / Deputy Headteacher. Subject co-ordinators lead specific discussions. Class teachers 2, 3, 4, 5	1 Entry, then yearly. 2 Yearly, spring term. 3 Yearly, summer term (end KS2). 4 Others, yearly by arrangement. 4 and 5 Ongoing. 6 See whole school plan.	Data available to staff in class lists. Data converted to charts etc. for summative records, report to governors, etc. Scores available to parents.

3 Budget	Mostly outcomes set against projected expenditure. Final outcome set against budget plan. Efficiency of resource provision/ payment etc.	School – mainframe printouts. Departments – mainframe printouts.	See Financial Procedures file. Office computer system linked to LEA.	See Management Res. list. Secretary obtains report. Headteacher reports to Finance Committee. Chair of Finance Committee reports to governors. Gov. Annual Report to Parents.	Monthly printout to Finance Committee. Bi- or tri-termly meeting. Report to monthly governors' meeting.	All reports printed and distributed as detailed left. LEA figures published annually
4 Teaching	Based on OfSTED criteria, policy contains breakdown.	Classroom 1 Visit by subject co-ordinators. 2 Visits by Headteacher. 3 Visits by local inspectors.	1 and 2 See Classroom monitoring policy. 3 Inspector agrees sessions with Headteacher.	1 Co-ordinator with reference to Development Plan agreed focus 2 HT / DHT Curric. overview + mediation if necessary 3 As above but not limited to single subject. + NQT mentor. (LEA-trained)	On-going but see monitoring policy for details. Usual limit 1 session per half-term. Exceptions NQT, weaknesses	1 Co-ordinators, summary in SIF file. 2 Headteacher, as above. 3 Feedback to staff, usually verbal. 4 Report to governors, number, type, main outcomes only.

continued

Table 10.4 continued

Focus/evaluation questions	*A Criteria for judgement*	*B Sources of evidence available*	*C Method of information/evidence collection*	*D Roles/ responsibilities*	*E Frequency of occurrence and timeline*	*F Summative evaluation: format and destination of outcome*
5 Pupil support	NVRQ scores against NFER Maths/PiE scores. Targets set individually in IEP. Policy aim to help all children achieve Level 3 or above.	1 Yearly progress tests as in 2 Pupil Achievement. 2 Year 6 SATs outcomes against SEN Policy. 3 Parent/teacher interview.	Data, see SIF file, Data file. Support record in SEN file, see also 2 left. Other pupil records.	SEN Co-ordinator, feedback from staff and assistants, leading to development of 'next step' strategy. HT analysis and publication of outcome data.	Ongoing assessment, usually half-termly, IEPs. Other tests as in 2, Pupil achievement.	1 Data available as in 2, Pupil Achievement. 2 SATs/SEN policy report to governors' and parents' annual report. 3 Individual pupils: annual/special reports.
6 Staff development	Completion of courses. Relevance to SDP of feedback. One-to-one and group discussions. Raising of pupil achievements/ staff expertise and confidence.	Staff Development – Appendix to Development Plan	Recording course details with explicit intro to Development Plan and school aims. Use of IiP criteria as performance indicators.	See Staff Development Policy. DHT co-ordinates. HT overall within school Dev Plan.	On-going recording of needs/course attendance. Yearly summary in Development Plan. Annual. HT/teacher dialogue.	Termly report to governors and section in annual report. Record kept of courses attended and outcomes in Development Plan. See also teacher appraisals.
7 Communication	1 Do parents have a coherent view of their place in their child's education?	Questionnaires to parents/staff/ governors etc.	Periodic questionnaires with opportunities for follow up and feedback to respondents.	All staff to be involved.	As necessary, main questionnaire at least every year.	Information gathered to be used to inform next development plan or change present one.

	2 Do all members of the school community clearly understand systems of organisation and management? 3 Is there a clearly stated philosophy of education and vision which all staff support and own? 4 Are there explicit systems for the above?	Other written responses e.g. parents' letters, report comments. Informal verbal feedback from the school community. Feedback and discussions at Governors' meeting. LEA inspectors.	Compile responses to discover patterns or widely held beliefs which can then be used to make changes where necessary. Governors can play an important role in ensuring open and constructive debate.	HT has important role in establishing a 'no blame' culture which will support development.		Information requiring immediate action should be dealt with, and seen to be dealt with, as soon as possible.
8 Efficiency	1 Do a range of procedures exist for all contingencies? 2 Are procedures revised and renewed as necessary? 3 Are documents circulated to correct audience and then available for later examination?	1 Feedback from parental survey/ OfSTED. 2 Informal/formal staff discussions. 3 School documentation and procedures.	1 Part of Development Plan. 2 Publication and availability of documents paramount.	See Management Responsibilities List. Ultimately Headteacher.	1 Alternate years, see Development Plan. 2 Annual internal organisation review. 3 Review of documentation, usually every 2 years.	Written reports to governors on procedural changes. Relevant documents circulated to governing body committees as part of consultation progress.
9 Curriculum	For curriculum, monitoring and evaluation system – see classroom monitoring reports in SIF					

This work had barely begun when we received notification of an OfSTED inspection to take place three years and three months after our first. Although we had not completed all the targets in the School Improvement Plan (formerly School Development Plan) relating to self-evaluation, we had reached a fairly advanced stage. Tasks such as updating Form S4 were completed in record time, largely because we had the majority of information to hand, information that was based on the solid analysis of data.

Our inspection was one of the first 'short' inspections awarded to schools that had had a good first round inspection. The final report stated that the school had made 'excellent improvement' since the last inspection, 66 per cent of teaching was judged to be very good or excellent, all four areas of leadership and management were graded excellent, relationships were said to be a strength of the school whilst the system of self-evaluation was described as rigorous. Later we were named as an 'outstanding school' by HMCIS and awarded Beacon status by the DfES. Two of our Beacon areas were self-evaluation and the use of data.

WHERE NEXT?

The non-existence of a post-OfSTED action plan or key points for improvement was a liberating professional experience. For the first time in perhaps ten years, I felt that my professional integrity was unchallenged and that I was actually being trusted to run the school without outside interference. I also felt that it was necessary to continue the development of our self-evaluation systems, not only to maintain and perhaps even improve our performance still further, but also to justify the faith that had been put in us.

Following the inspection and the award of Beacon status, I explored the Scottish system and its EFQM framework to a greater depth. I had also acquired a Lloyds TSB CD-rom entitled *Quality in Education* which supported the process of self-assessment against the EFQM Excellence Model. The CD contained quality tools, best practice resources and school/LEA generated exemplars to support improvement activities.

We had already started to use parts of the Excellence Model in our normal on-going evaluations and it now seemed a good idea to examine the possibilities more widely. Business Link Nottinghamshire was providing EFQM Assessor Training Courses and following discussions with their representative, we assembled several local heads, deputies and other school leaders into an initial group of self-evaluation enthusiasts. About a dozen schools were represented and, following the successful completion of the course, the group continued meeting on a regular basis as a quality network. We were able to run these meetings as a Beacon activity with the attendant advantages of financial support. Business Link Nottinghamshire also provided us with the services of one of their business advisers and Wyn Williams, an acknowledged expert on EFQM and an excellent facilitator for our deliberations.

Additionally, we made contact with André Haynes, the person responsible for the development of the Lloyds TSB CD-rom. Consequently, we were kept informed of further changes resulting from the continuous review of the Excellence Model which was making it of even more use to schools. Latest versions provide a section on change management, the evaluation of inclusion/diversity and a school-based case study which can be used for training purposes. An electronic filing cabinet provides a flexible system of accessing and cross-referencing school documentation. A second group of local headteachers has committed to undertake training with this updated resource and will also take part in a follow-up quality circle.

Did all of this mean that we had wasted our time developing our own system? The answer is 'no' on two main counts. First, at the time, there was no published system that completely fitted our needs. Second, the framework we had developed was based on sound principles which taught us valuable lessons. These lessons could and would be applied no matter which underlying system we used. The five main sections of our SIF could still form a core of questions that would always need to be answered.

Later I invested some time investigating a range of other benchmark or performance indicator systems. These enabled a pick and mix or best fit method of assessing almost any area of school life. As well as the systems above, I examined the West Sussex Model of Self-review, The Charter Mark criteria, Investors in People, the Hay McBer Models of Excellence and, of course, the OfSTED Framework for Inspection. A matrix showing their application over a range of areas of school management/organisation was drawn up using general headings such as community, governors, assessment. While it is not suggested that all of these be applied in school at once, they do provide a ready-made series of formats for use by the person(s) charged with conducting self-evaluation in any area of school life. For example, they have particular uses in assisting with performance management or reports to governors. School data or personal self-review information may be compared with indicators that give strong evidence of success or otherwise.

CONCLUSION

And finally

. . . a return to School Evaluation Matters. How do you evaluate your evaluation method? Whatever system you devise or use, whether it's a mix and match or 'off-the-peg', the following qualities should be present. If they are, congratulations, you've made a start.

To monitor and analyse standards you need to:

- collect all available reliable data on attainment and progress with any other aspects of pupil development which the school values;
- analyse these achievements regularly and systematically, looking for: trends; relative levels of attainment between subjects, groups and individuals; highlights; areas of concerns;
- compare data about your school with those of similar schools and with local and national averages;
- devise and adopt indicators for other important aspects such as behaviour and pupils' attitudes to school and seek parents' and pupils' views on the school's strengths and weaknesses.

NOTES

A list of useful resources appears at the end of the book (pages 215–16).

1 Using Assessment Data in Primary Schools, Hedger & Jesson, Shropshire County Council

2 Some readers will also know EFQM by the name of the 'Excellence model' referred to in a NAHT Primary Leadership Paper or through the first Lloyds TSB CD-Rom *Quality in Education*.

11 Resourcing learning

Mick Brookes

INTRODUCTION

In the beginning was the word, and the word was with the Local Education Authority (LEA) officers and those in their favour were blessed. Nowadays, there are many in leadership roles in schools who do not remember the times before delegated budgets, when headteachers were freer to be head*teachers*, but funds to support the learning process were allocated on an apparently irrational basis. In contrast, today, the leadership and management of the school budget is a major role for senior staff and impacts on the roles of all in the school. Leaders need to be able to make significant decisions which determine the effectiveness of the school in meeting its aims. This requires strategic and ethical leadership and it links to the other chapters of this book.

In this main part of the chapter, I will consider two aspects. The first part will look at the funding of schools and the second at some aspects of good practice in the leadership and management of those funds. Those who are unfamiliar with developments in school finance which have led to the current responsibilities may wish to turn to the Appendix to this chapter which charts the journey from the 1980s to the election of the Labour Government in 1997.

THE FUNDING OF SCHOOLS

In order to understand and to challenge the levels of funding to schools and the mechanisms which are employed, leaders need to look more widely and to be aware of the policy context in which the schools operate.

The current Government was elected on the promise of 'education, education, education', suggesting that spending on this vital area of the social fabric would improve. It was hoped that such a focus would end the huge inequalities in the funding of education across the country and the subsequent inequalities of class sizes and facilities which appeared to depend on a postcode lottery. It was also hoped that any new system would provide greater transparency as there remained a lack of clarity about where the money was going. In some cases there was considerable leakage between the funding allocated to education and the final amount ending up in schools, leading to perennial rows between central government and the LEAs about where the money had gone. The LEAs blamed the Government and the Government blamed the LEAs. The schools lost.

This debate sharpened the political situation. An obvious answer to the funding debate was to distribute money directly to schools on a formula basis. This was greeted with a chorus of disapproval from the Local Government Association who saw that losing control over education funding (the largest 'purse' in the local treasury) would strip them of a power. The compromise that followed, and still exists, resulted in some funding being allocated directly to schools (the Standards Grant) and some being allocated to schools via the LEA (the Standards Fund). In addition there grew numerous separate funding streams that could be bid into. Alongside this were strict guidelines on the distribution of the general funding to schools so that LEAs were increasingly being cut back to a smaller and smaller share of the budget. We now have discrete budgets for LEA and school funding.

However, there was still some room for 'sleight of hand' under these rules. In one LEA where schools' funding was particularly dire, it was apparent that money had been diverted from the education budget and into the social services budget. When challenged, a local Councillor responded, 'Don't think you're getting your hands on the money we use to run our women's refuge!' This remark brings into sharp focus the problem for schools and the competing demands at national and local level for a limited pot of gold. Demand for high cost services (education, health, social services, crime prevention) will always outstrip supply. High taxation is one of the hurdles on which 'socialist' governments will fall. It is arguable that low taxation and worsening public services present a hurdle to trip up a 'conservative' administration. This funding pipeline is illustrated in Figure 11.1.

The determination to ensure that funding should go directly to schools persuaded the DfES to design a new formula for funding schools. This formula intends that the funding allocated to schools should be 'passported' by the LEA directly to schools. Fairly stringent checks are made to ensure that LEAs pass on the designated funding to schools (the Individual Schools Budget, ISB) and the Secretary of State has powers to ensure that this is the case. He/she may direct an LEA to spend allocated funding on schools.

Some local authorities spend more on education than the government allocates. This situation will usually lead to higher local taxation . . . and so the national funding dilemma (higher spending = higher taxation) is replicated at a local level.

The new formula was devised by the DfES and implemented in April 2003.

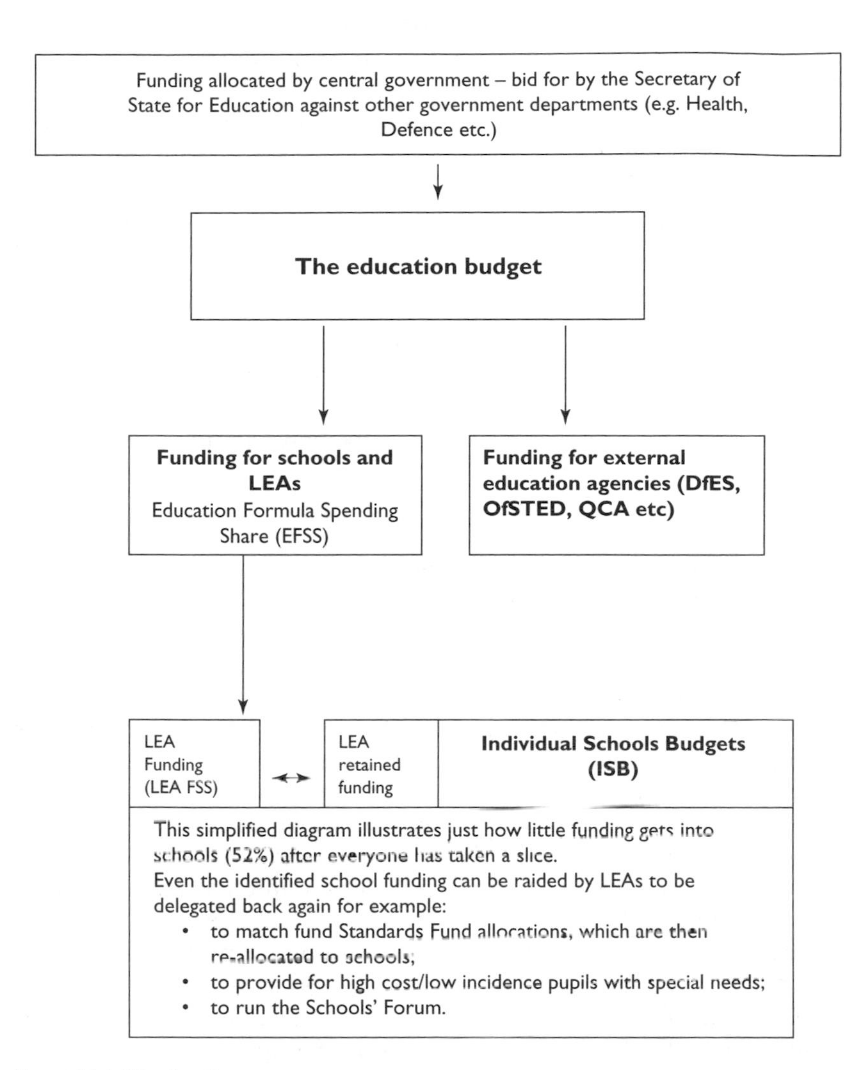

Figure 11.1 The funding stream

The new formula was intended to distribute funding to schools so that the postcode lottery of a child's entitlement to equality of education was fair, wherever the child lived. To illustrate how this has worked, it is easier to confine the situation to the funding of schools in England. Scotland, Wales and Northern Ireland all have significantly different funding systems.

Inequalities of funding were twofold:

- differences of funding between geographical areas;
- differences of funding between phases of education (Key Stages).

The new system of funding has largely failed to address these fundamental differences in funding. There are *still* huge differences. For instance, at the time of writing, a primary pupil living in Leicestershire receives on average £360 per annum less than a primary pupil in Leicester City. Year 6 pupils (primary) are still funded at about 66 per cent of the average Year 7 (secondary) pupil. This can mean that a Y6 pupil is funded at £2,083 per year in July and at £3,075 six weeks later in September of the same year.

How can this possibly have happened when the new formula was supposed to be based on a notion of fair funding so that, no matter where you live, the base unit of funding should be the same? In order to explore this we need to take a detailed look at how the new formula operates. The formula comprises four components:

- basic entitlement
- additional educational needs (AEN)
- area cost adjustment (ACA)
- sparsity (primary only).

The basic entitlement certainly conforms to the requirements of the fair funding lobby. Wherever you are in England (2003), all Early Years pupils under 5 have the same entitlement, £2,549; all primary pupils have £2,006; and all secondary pupils have £2,659.

These figures illustrate that while the intention to fund fairly across England is a clear part of the formula, the opportunity to address the historic inequality of funding across Key Stages has been missed. Add to this the class size requirement in Key Stage 1 schools (no more than thirty in a class) and it becomes obvious that the notional funding for primary education is drawn out of Key Stage 2 and into Key Stage 1 to enable schools to adhere to the Government's class size promise. Key Stage 2 in the shire counties has thus become the Cinderella of the funding regime.

However, while it looks as though the geographical issue has been resolved, the formula confounds this belief through the application of the additional educational needs (AEN) factor.

The additional educational needs factor is computed by the following components:

- income support (working families' tax credit);
- English as an additional language (primary);
- ethnicity (secondary);

- High Cost Pupils, calculated by income support plus low birth weight (research shows that babies with a low birth weight do significantly less well at school and are more prone to ill-health).

This AEN factor adds a huge top-up to the basic entitlement (for instance Leicestershire pupils receive on average, £14 per pupil while their near neighbours in Leicester City receive on average £447 per pupil). The distortion of pupils' entitlement caused by this factor must be questioned. Few would argue that additional resources are required in the toughest socio-economic areas, but a difference of £433 seems to be overdoing it, particularly when there are pockets of extreme deprivation in the shire counties, and considering also all the problems of rural deprivation.

The *area cost adjustment* has a less profound effect, and used to favour the Greater London area, but is now more widespread. The 'Earnings Survey' is used to calculate this and gives a geographic index for all LEAs. There are 51 LEAs out of 148 that receive no area cost adjustment.

The net effect of any formula change is that there will be winners and losers, and there *have* been winners and losers across the country. Therefore a transition was put in over two years so that LEAs moving to higher budget shares would receive two tranches of additional funding, while LEAs that were moving downwards lost funding over two years. Even so, in 2003 the introduction of this formula produced a funding and political disaster that threatened to destabilise the Government's main policy – 'education, education, education'. The problems encountered by schools in 2003 were complex and compound, and are summarised as follows:

1 Although the LEAs that were losing funds had an historically larger slice of national funds, schools had quite properly spent up to the limits set. The effect of greater funding can be most keenly felt in advantageous levels of staffing, better classroom resources and better support for a wider curriculum. It is always difficult to adjust down, whatever one's income. This is as true in schools as it is in the domestic situation. This led to an outcry from the 'South' that the 'North' had grabbed their money. This is only partly true; the winners and losers were scattered across the country. However the reduction in the amount of the Area Cost Adjustment (largely a Home Counties benefit) did have an effect.

2 At the same time as changing the formula, huge increases hit schools in the form of:

   - increases in the employers' rate of 'on-costs' (National Insurance and teachers' pensions);
   - increases caused by the compression of the teachers' pay scale;
   - insufficient funding of the performance pay scheme;

- a continuous stream of government initiatives that are either unfunded or partially funded. (e.g. inclusion of pupils with moderate or severe learning difficulties into the mainstream setting, and workload reduction).

This severely damaged schools' budgets and caused widespread job losses, prevented in some areas only by the use of contingency reserves. While, for the first time, spending in England's schools was in mid-table relative to our European neighbours (OECD 2003), cost pressures in schools had risen by more than the extra funding put in. This amounts to an embarrassment as the tenets of creating a new funding system were to:

- create greater clarity about funding streams;
- even up the disparities in funding between geographical areas;
- create budget stability over three years.

Only the first of these was successful.

There are still wide disparities in levels of funding. *Some* disparity is unavoidable. It *does* cost more to support the disadvantaged in our schools. The question is – how much more? It appears that the 'basic entitlement' aspect of the funding formula is at too low a value, while the AEN factor has too high a weighting. The solution is obvious – *freeze the additional factors and put increase into the basic entitlement*. However, the *political* expedient for a Labour government is to pour money into areas of deprivation – so no change is expected!

In summary, the net negative effect on schools was that they were hit by all of the cost pressures above, in addition to the school-based factor of falling rolls across the primary sector. This left some schools in dire financial straits, and destabilised budgets.

However, before we put all the lights out, there is no doubt that greater funding over the past few years has led to real benefits in schools:

- more employed staff;
- unprecedented levels of ICT equipment and software;
- gradually improving buildings and facilities;
- standards of literacy in the primary sector that are the envy of the world (Ogle *et al*. 2003) and some good rankings in the PISA study (OECD 2002) as discussed in Chapter 12.

It is now time to turn the focus to the management of funding in schools and the leadership opportunities in the deployment of school-based budgets.

LEADERSHIP AND MANAGEMENT OF FUNDING IN SCHOOLS

It would be a mistake to think that dealing with the financial resource is simply a management function. The entrepreneurial ability of school leaders has been remarkable over the past decade. The new Workload and Standards initiative from the DfES has already produced innovative solutions to the challenge of providing a reduction in workload and the introduction of quality reflective time for teachers across the country. This is discussed further later in this chapter. However, effective leadership can only happen within a context of sound management.

A useful differentiation between leadership and management can be demonstrated in the analogy of planning a journey. Leadership requires the vision of destination. Effective management will provide the resources to realise the vision. The vision without the management will result in a mere dream, while management without vision will stultify and stagnate. In a churchyard in West Sussex, England, there is a useful summary of this condition.

> A task without a vision is drudgery
> Vision without a task is a mere dream
> A vision and a task are the hope of the world.
>
> *Anon.*

So, the task is to set an effective context within the school. Badly managed, this can result in an over-bureaucratic monolith that stultifies growth and the creative use of resources. In diagrammatic form the continuum of management would appear as follows:

Tight systems	Loose systems
• Over bureaucratic • Excessive control • Insufficient flexibility • Constant meetings and checks • Blocking the flow of funding	• Thin policy direction • Insufficient control • Dangerous flexibility • Lack of structured meetings and checks • Free flow of funding without agreed limits

A generality would be to claim that the larger the school organisation, the tighter the bureaucratic structure and control; the smaller the organisation, the lighter that structure needs to be. Larger organisations also have a greater capacity to delegate control functions. The danger of systems that are too loose is the possibility of the accusation of financial impropriety. (Sadly this is the subject of too many disciplinary actions involving budget managers.)

Adopting a robust system of financial control is not difficult. OfSTED, the Audit Commission, LEAs and private organisations all have guidelines and advice to assist. Schools must consider the following if they are to operate within a sensible construct of financial probity and control and to satisfy the demands of OfSTED and the LEA finance department.

Schools should

- plan the future;
- access external funding;
- set balanced budgets;
- operate effective and efficient systems;
- benchmark spending against other schools;
- operate within a 'best value' policy;
- provide 'value for money';
- have well-thought-out financial planning cycles;
- be clear about roles, responsibilities and accountabilities.

Aspects of thinking and planning strategically have already been covered in earlier chapters. I will focus here on developing the ideas in the last four points above.

'Best value' policy

The word 'policy' is misleading here. The word conjures up the vision of a dusty tome hidden on a shelf. A true best value policy should permeate the operation of the school management systems in an active and continuous state. Best value requires that the school will constantly *compare* its spending decisions with other schools, *consult* with appropriate personnel, *challenge* orthodoxies and *compete* with similar schools in terms of effective management.

A good working policy will guide the provision of goods and services to a school. It is wrong to think that best value is another term for 'cheapest'. In life, as well as in school, the cheapest option does not necessarily represent the best value. Conversely the most expensive option will not necessarily provide the best quality.

One illustration of the most difficult area of achieving best value is in the provision of computer hardware to schools. There are numerous disaster stories up and down the country of schools that have gone for a cheap option, only to find that machines do not have the capacity to perform properly and therefore require replacement or costly upgrades. This situation has not been helped by some LEAs providing heavy-handed coercion to the purchase of 'recommended' systems that are very expensive, and it has also suffered from a lack of guidance from Becta, the national committee responsible for the oversight of ICT provision. (Until recently

Becta did not have an efficient system of checking with schools whether ICT products worked well.)

Likewise the selection of plumbers, electricians, gasfitters and boiler maintenance personnel is fraught with the probability of shoddy service or exorbitant costs. All this takes time to administer, and can be time taken away from the 'teacher' part of headteacher. This is particularly true in small primary schools. Sadly some LEA provision of domestic services (which would be an asset to schools) is still riddled with shoddy workmanship and work done at times not convenient to the effective operation of schools. Most heads will have stories of work neglected over the summer closure, only to be started in September when the pupils return.

The services of known and trusted local firms can greatly reduce costs, expenditure and precious time. Even so, occasional challenges as to the competitiveness of your trusted friend should be made. The use of local providers also raises the necessity to be scrupulous in the declaration of interest, and avoidance of falling into legal difficulties of taxation. In short, everything is required to be 'above board'.

'Best value' represents the culture in which modern schools exist – the checks and balances applied to external providers are also applied to schools themselves. OfSTED must report on whether schools provide value for money. The next section will examine what this means.

'Value for money'

Currently OfSTED 'measures' schools according to a set of criteria that seek to give a definition of value for money. Inspectors will look at the school's effectiveness (standards, leadership/management, etc.), contextual factors (the school and its pupils in the local environment), and unit costs. This will give a definition of 'Value for money' which is best illustrated by two extremes in Figure 11.2. School A has high standards, unfavourable contextual factors and low unit costs. Such a school would be judged to give excellent value for money. School B might have poor effectiveness (low standards, weak leadership/management), favourable contextual factors and high unit costs. Such a school would be considered to give poor value for money.

This is really quite a crude measure for several reasons.

Effectiveness as measured by league table status will depend on the context of the school. It is a truism that children from privileged backgrounds outperform children from deprived backgrounds.

For *contextual* factors, OfSTED has chosen to use the narrow measure of free school meals (income support). This is only one element of the school's contextual factors and may give a very misleading view. An unemployed barrister will probably have children better equipped to do well at school than an unemployed manual worker. This does not condemn the deprived,

Effectiveness	Excellent	A	B	Poor
Contextual factors	Favourable	B	A	Poor
Unit costs	High	B	A	Low
resulting in a judgement of				
Value for money	Excellent	A	B	Poor

Figure 11.2 OfSTED judgement on value for money for schools A and B

but merely represents common sense. Other factors, such as the percentage of higher education qualifications in the community or the occupation of parents, could be more significant contextual factors, but are largely ignored.

Unit costs will favour large schools in the worst funded areas with the worst funded Key Stage. (A two-form entry junior (Key Stage 2) school in a shire county is likely to have very low unit costs.) On the other hand, a small (50 place) primary school may have very high unit costs and thus be at a disadvantage.

However, whatever the fairness of the system, it is up to the school leadership team to ensure that funding is properly expended and that the school does not (for instance) have large unexplained balances. (A surprising number of governors think that having £110,000 in reserves shows good financial management.)

OfSTED will also examine whether clear financial management supports educational priorities. This requires that the School Improvement Plan be properly costed. There should be a clear audit trail that links the provision for expenditure on a specific priority to the impact that the expenditure has on the effectiveness of the school. However, it would be easy to get into a 'measuring the marigolds' frame of mind here. Sometimes it is not easy to measure impact, particularly when (for instance) applied to professional development. Funding aimed at a 'tips for teachers' course may have an immediate, but limited, impact whereas funding for a school leadership course may have a less measurable impact, but the *behavioural* change may be far more significant.

One aspect more closely investigated by OfSTED is whether specific grants have been used for specific purposes. The provision of 'hypothecated' funding may be seen as a good way of ensuring that schools use funding for specific purposes, but it does rather militate against the ideal of delegated budgets whereby schools operate within their local context and know what best suits their needs. For instance, a school in good structural repair may not need to use its Capital Funding grant for that purpose, but, because the use of that funding is strictly limited to the fabric (renovation, repair or new build) of the building, it is a contravention of the rules to use it for any other purpose. While there was a need to ensure that the fabric of our schools was improved, the maintenance of tight control means that schools will either waste precious resources on structural expenditure that is not entirely necessary or risk losing the funding. It is also absurd that capital funding can be used to install new windows, but cannot (for instance) be used to paint (and therefore maintain) existing windows. There are numerous other examples of such bureaucratic short-sightedness.

A valuable aspect of OfSTED scrutiny is financial benchmarking (as shown in Table 11.1) which compares the use of resources, in this case in two-form entry junior schools. This information is useful in that it provides a direct comparison between similar 'types' of school.

Table 11.1 Financial benchmarking

Category	*School P*	*Average*	*Highest*	*Lowest*
Employees	86.03%	81.97%	86.03%	74.50%
Premises	3.54%	6.00%	7.96%	3.54%
Supplies	7.88%	7.54%	11.18%	4.23%

The importance of this information is not that it varies from school to school, but that the differences can be explained. Comparatively, therefore, it looks as though School P's expenditure on staffing is excessively high. The reality is that this school decided to directly employ its grounds and premises staff. This factor explains the above average expenditure on direct employee costs, and shows why that the premises costs are the lowest. The other schools have their 'bought' premises services shown in this category. However, the school's expenditure on supplies looks about average.

OfSTED will visit only once every few years, and as long as the school's own systems of information gathering and review are firmly in place, it has nothing to fear from external scrutiny. Nevertheless, external inspection is an important part of the guarantee that public money is being properly managed.

The financial planning cycle

There is a cyclical nature to the planning of school expenditure that is an essential tool for ensuring that the impact of falling or rising revenue is properly predicted. A calendar of events may look as below. For this example, a financial year cycle has been used, but one of the anomalies of the administration of finance in school is that we deal with two or possibly three years – financial, academic and calendar. It is important to time meetings to take place a few days after the end of the financial 'quarter' as the full month's quota of payments will not be known until then. This keeps the 'pending' column manageable.

April – new budgets begin. Consultations with Finance Committee and consent to present the budget to the full governing body (mandatory regulation) need to be given. April may seem a little late to external eyes, but as many schools may have received budget allocations only shortly before this date it represents a reasonable timescale.

July – review with the Finance Committee the performance of the budget against the first quarter of the budget set for the beginning of the year. An expectation of 25 per cent expenditure may be misleading for two reasons. First, incremental rises in teacher's pay do not impact until September, so the profile will probably be lower than 24 per cent. Second, expenditure on school resources (books, pencils, equipment etc.) is normally made at the beginning of the year and so the profile may look much higher than 25 per cent. This period of time is sufficient to be certain that no major mistakes have been made in the budget setting exercise. This is also the time for finalising the School Improvement Plan (SIP) for September of the new academic year. The current budget will have to support 7/12 of the envisaged expenditure, i.e. September to March.

October – half way through the school year. If things are going badly off track, schools will know by now! The SIP should have been agreed by the full governing body, or at least presented to the appropriate curriculum committee. This is not too early to begin planning for the following financial year. The school's main internal factor, the numbers of pupils on roll, will be known. The pupil driven factor will amount to approximately 80 per cent of the school's total budget. What is less clear for many schools at this stage is the number of new pupils to be enrolled the following September. This will have a significant effect on the school's future funding, and so can make the budget prediction exercise a far more risky business.

January – predicting out-turn values for the current year's budget should be possible at this stage. Higher than expected income, or unexpected expenditure, should be known by now. Early warning of budget difficulties makes it possible for the school to operate without using crisis management. If job losses look likely, this is not too early to warn staff about the possibility of redundancies. The period between the finance meeting in January and the budget agreement meeting in April is a busy one. New shapes and dimensions and initiatives will need to be 'felt out' without absolute certainty about the capacity to fund.

Roles and responsibilities

The Senior Leadership Team (a committee of one in very small schools!) should consider consultation with Governors, school staff, pupils, parents and the LEA as key stakeholders.

Governors

They *must* approve the budget and *should* be kept regularly informed about budget progress and planning. The Finance Committee will require a greater level of detail than the governing body as a whole, who should just receive agreed 'headlines'. It is not an efficient use of time to debate budget detail in two committees. If the governing body is delegating power, it must trust the sub-committee. The governing body is a curious beast: it can either be a source of support and guidance for the beleaguered head, or it can be a millstone that interferes with the day-to-day management of the school. These dimensions are illustrated below.

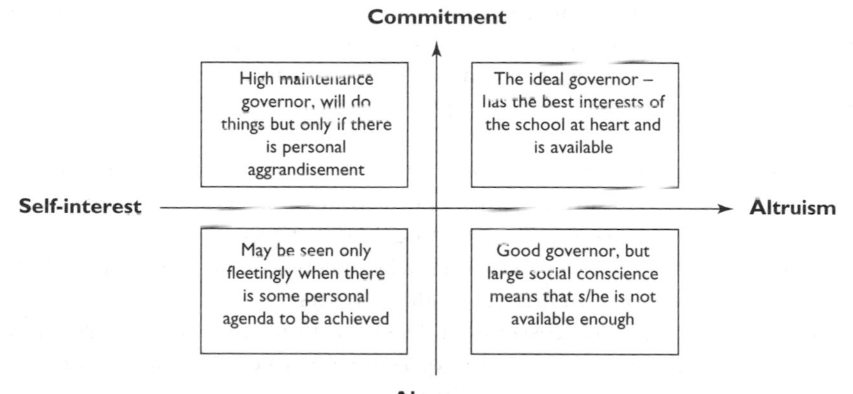

Figure 11.3 Dimensions of governance

School staff

All the members of staff (not just teachers) have a real vested interest in the effective management of the budget. Their jobs depend on it. Therefore they should be kept regularly informed. The whole staff should have the opportunity to contribute to the SIP. It is good practice and good leadership and management development to delegate funding to post-holders. Some budget information (e.g. salary details) is confidential and should not be open to general view.

Pupils

All pupils can be involved but the extent varies according to age. Many schools give School Councils a delegated sum to use to fund their own initiatives.

Parents and carers

Parents and carers have a right to see the summary school expenditure (provided in the Annual Governors' Report), and may be kept informed about budget progress either as representatives on the governing body or as part of the PTA. The group may want to contribute to the school budget share.

The LEA

The LEA has a statutory duty to ensure that school budgets are properly maintained and will require to be regularly informed. This duty still gives LEAs some considerable power which is exercised to the benefit or detriment of schools, according to the prevailing LEA culture. The implementation of 'Consistent financial reporting' means that LEAs are required to receive and report budget income and expenditure in a particular format that enables comparisons to be made from school to school and from LEA to LEA.

The wider the involvement and consultation on the budget has been, the more likely it is that the whole school community will take ownership of responsibility. However, strong ethical leadership needs to be demonstrated if funding is not to be pulled into projects that do not contribute to the school's agreed vision and its strategic focus.

In addition to roles and responsibilities of individual stakeholders, there are levels of working to be considered. To be effective and efficient, finance in school should be dealt with on three levels:

1 *Administration* – dealing with the day-to-day maintenance of ordering, paying invoices, completing staffing returns and obtaining budget summary information. All schools should have the capacity to operate at this level without the direct involvement of the headteacher or senior staff.

2 *Management* – checking that budgets are running on track, getting quotations for works costing more than £1,000, preparing information for the Finance Committee, managing virements within permitted parameters. If schools have a competent person to operate at this level, it frees up the headteacher to be head*teacher*! However there should be regular (monthly) collaboration at this level between the senior leadership team and the budget manager/bursar. Those who lead very small schools will find that it is at this level that frustrations are felt as all roles fall on the headteacher.
3 *Leadership and strategic development* – this is the realm that requires vision, a strategic focus for the school and entrepreneurial skill. If s/he is not officially part of the Senior Leadership Team, the budget manager should be included in these discussions, not least so that vision can be grounded in reality.

CONCLUSION: STRATEGIC LEADERSHIP AND MANAGEMENT OF THE BUDGETARY PROCESS

The degree to which there is scope to operate visionary leadership is governed to some extent by the capacity of the budget. Tight budgets, and little room for change within the school, mean that there is little scope to manoeuvre once the essentials (staffing, utilities, books and paper, etc.) have been paid for. But even with tight budgets it is possible to free up funding that can make a difference in the classroom. For instance, when teaching staff leave, decisions can be made about replacement by a newly qualified teacher (NQT), or even the employment of teaching assistants (TAs). The difference in cost between an NQT and a member of staff on the top of the scale can be as much as £15,000. While some of that funding will be needed to support the teacher, funds can also be used to provide additional high cost equipment, schemes of work, or to fund field trips. Care must be taken, however, not to commit the additional funding to items (such as staffing) that do not take into account the rising cost of employing an NQT on an incremental basis each year.

A true test of leadership and creative management is already challenging schools across the country. The workload and raising standards initiative is challenging school management and fundamental tenets of the profession in the role of the TA. There is clear division between those willing to expand the role of the TA to the borders (and beyond?) of the kingdom of the teacher, and those who adamantly oppose this concept. Visionary leadership can be exciting, but it can also be risky. Partnership between key players in the school can ensure that vision is properly planned and channelled into new reality.

We live in interesting times. They have been interesting for the past decade. We are getting closer to a funding system that is fit for the twenty-first century; the clarity of the formula is there, but it needs to be fine-tuned. But, however good the formula, if it does not have the quantum of cash to drive it, it will lead to failure. A change in central government priorities, an expensive war, a costly disaster or a change of government may all affect the way in which schools are funded.

The school of the future may be a lonely place. If external support is cut away to allow greater funding to be aimed at the classroom, we must ask ourselves, 'who cares for the carers?'. There can be no replacement for the excellent teacher who motivates, and builds hopes and dreams in his/her children. The principal use of funding of schools is very simple. It was, is and always will be to enable that person to be the gateway to new futures for our children.

APPENDIX

School finance in England: a recent history

Before the Education Reform Act (1988) the funding of schools from the school's point of view was a very simple matter. All they received was a virtual pittance in order to buy the basic tools of the classroom: books, pencils, paper and wax crayons. This did not amount to much – the equivalent, according to a pressure group in Lincolnshire, the FEN (For Education Now) Group of a Mars Bar a day. The LEA, rather than the schools, controlled staffing, building maintenance, minor works and so on. There was no clarity about where the funding had gone, what method had been used to distribute that funding or what accountability there was for that distribution. This is, of course, the prevailing situation in many countries.

However, it did mean that headteachers were freer to be head*teachers*, and that clerical support was exactly that. No need then for bursars and office managers. But the random distribution of the allocation of resources was all too evident in the first round of budget distribution to schools on a formula basis.

Local Management of Schools (LMS), introduced by the Education Reform Act (DES 1988), has dramatically taken power away from the Area Office of the LEA (many are now closed). At its extreme, grant-maintained schools removed themselves completely from the local structure, and were autonomous within a framework of control directed by the Department for Education and Science.

This is an important historical turning point, and began a furious struggle for survival by the local council against a strong move towards centralisation promoted by the Conservative Government of the time. This power struggle still exists today, between the current Labour Government and the champions of local democracy led by the Local Government Association (LGA). This group has political power because it represents many of the local party members (in all political parties) who are relied upon to rally the troops at election time.

The introduction of school based finance in the 1990s caused, respectively, widespread uproar or glee among the favoured or the neglected of the previous baronial rule. The neglected found that budgets allocated by formula for the first time, aimed at distributing funding on a more equable basis, meant that they received funding that was *above* their current allocation of staffing and resources. On the other hand, those who had been in favour in the previous regime were outraged that their generous allocation of funding and resources was not matched by their formula funding allocation. Opprobrium followed. Transitional arrangements were put in that enabled those losing funding to manage staff reductions, while those moving to a higher base had to wait three years to receive the full benefit of the new funding regime. Interesting times . . . but things were to get much worse!

The delegation of funding to schools and the vast new powers extended to Governing Bodies meant that accountability was firmly placed within the school, and allowed the government of the early 1990s to make swingeing cuts in the education budget. Because the effect of these cuts was not felt so much at the LEA, the outcry came from 24,000 individual schools without a collective voice. The effect of these cuts became a national scandal. Funding of education in England was one of the worst in any developed country (OECD 1994) and class sizes were beginning to look as though schools had returned to Victorian times. Indeed, 'victorian' politicians of the time thought that this was 'a jolly good thing'. They reasoned that a good teacher 'could teach 40 children in a bus shelter'. Some of us were beginning to think that we might have to, as the fabric of school buildings had deteriorated to the extent that they were uninhabitable in wet weather! Such was the furore over the plight of schools that a report commissioned by the National Association of Headteachers, and conducted by Nottingham University 'The Class Size Report' (Day *et al.* 1996), severely embarrassed the Secretary of State who, supported by the Chief Inspector of Schools, issued a statement claiming that 'class size did not matter, it was the quality of teaching that counted'. This was greeted with such incredulity by the general public, not least by the 'elite' who were paying to send their children to private schools to benefit from small class sizes, that the subsequent election defeat was not much of a surprise, so far had the government moved away from the reality of the state school classroom.

Things improved very little under the early years of the new Government (1997), despite the promise of 'education, education, education'. Most of the previous Government's systems were retained but with the abolition of grant-maintained status. As reported earlier in this chapter, we are now beginning to see a focus on funding and several changes to the system, largely as a result of an outcry from schools which attracted media attention.

ACKNOWLEDGEMENTS

My grateful thanks to Peter Downes (ex Headteacher of Hinchingbrooke School and one of the fathers of school-based funding), and George Phipson. Their commitment to school funding has been instrumental in leading the agenda for change. Thanks also to the NAHT 'think tank' on funding that has contributed to the funding debate.

Part IV

Leading transformation

12 The transformation of schools in the twenty-first century

Brian J. Caldwell

INTRODUCTION

My approach to this exploration of transformation is to adopt an international perspective. A study of education in other countries is important for several reasons. First, to the extent that systems of education have common aspirations, strategies that have led to success in other places may be adopted or adapted in the local setting, and strategies that have proved unsuccessful elsewhere may be set aside in the search for solutions. Second, problems that appear intractable in the local setting may be the subject of fresh enquiry leading to possible resolution when approaches in other countries are critically examined. Third, knowledge of approaches in other places may suggest possibilities for critical scrutiny in the search for alternatives. Fourth, local policy and practice can be affirmed with knowledge that others have adopted similar approaches and have achieved success. In each instance it is acknowledged that a country should not adopt an approach from another setting in the absence of evidence that it suits the local scene. The insights in this chapter thus draw from my knowledge of what is occurring in many countries. I hope that the outcome will add value to each of us as we seek to lead the transformation of schools in the twenty-first century.

THE CASE FOR TRANSFORMATION

It is necessary at the outset to establish the case for transformation. After all, some may argue that there has been enough transformation and that too many changes are being foisted or foreshadowed. Surely this is a time for consolidation. Not so!

There are four reasons why further transformation in desirable as well as inevitable. First, the performance of significant numbers of students falls short of expectations. Second, every scenario suggests that further change is inevitable if the institution of 'school' is to survive in the years ahead. Third, the technologies of learning are changing in irresistible and irreversible ways. Fourth, each of the first three calls for new associations between schools and other human services in the public and private sectors – the school as a stand-alone institution cannot and should not survive.

In relation to performance, we can look at the UK where the achievements of the schools are a cause for celebration, according to some media reports. The students are among the very best in the world judging by the performance of 15-year-olds in tests of their capacity to apply knowledge and skills in reading, mathematics and scientific literacy to real life problems. A total of 265,000 students from 32 countries participated in the landmark Program for International Student Assessment (PISA) conducted by the OECD (OECD 2002). The UK ranked seventh behind Finland, Canada, New Zealand, Australia, Ireland and South Korea in reading; eighth behind Japan, South Korea, New Zealand, Finland, Australia, Canada and Switzerland in mathematics; and fourth behind South Korea, Japan and Finland in science. However, a more sombre mood takes hold when deeper analysis reveals that the disparities among different groups of students are wider in the UK, along with Australia and New Zealand, than in 29 of the 32 countries. No government will rest on these achievements or be satisfied with these disparities. The case for transformation can stand on this fact alone.

There is evidence that these and other disparities are becoming greater. Is such a trend sustainable? Not so, according to some scenarios, as illustrated in two of the three outlined below. Each scenario is written as if in the future, describing an outcome in 2010 if certain events come to pass. It must be stressed that these are not the only scenarios, but they are examples of credible constructions that commence with current circumstances.

Scenario 1: public schools are safety net schools

It is 2010. The disparities among schools in terms of outcomes and resources that were evident in 2002 have widened, especially but not exclusively at the secondary level. About 60 per cent of secondary students attend private schools, reflecting a steady increase over recent years. Parents became increasingly dissatisfied with education offered by schools owned by public authorities. They left the system, prepared to invest ever-larger proportions of personal resources to assure their children success in a knowledge society, with access to the individual care and attention and the increasingly rich range of technologies necessary to achieve these ends. Most public schools are now simply safety net schools.

Scenario 2: the decline of schools

It is 2010. Schools are rapidly disappearing. A range of educational, technological and social developments overtook the institution that dominated the twentieth century. Schools became increasingly dangerous places to be, a perception fuelled by media accounts of frequent violence and the prevalence of drugs. Combined with advances in information and communications technology, home schooling gathered momentum in the early years of the century. Support for secondary schools, in particular, fell dramatically when traditional approaches to curriculum, teaching, learning and organisation proved impervious to change. Innovative learning centres steadily replaced them, with many operated in public–private partnerships as government, parents and the wider community lost patience with the existing system.

Scenario 3: the transformation of schools

It is 2010. The disparities among schools in terms of outcomes and resources that were evident in 2002 have narrowed. There is agreement on expectations for schools and the values that should underpin the endeavour. Governments concentrate their efforts on creating a climate in which the whole community provides resources to support schools, with a demanding regime of accountability in the use of a steadily increasing pool of public funds. There is a range of innovative approaches in community-based learning centres and in the use of information and communications technology. There is still a place called school, but that place has been transformed after a decade of creative leadership.

Scenarios along these lines are not the daydreams of an idle academic. A conference on 'Schooling for tomorrow' in Rotterdam in November 2000 led to the presentation in April 2001 to OECD Ministers of Education of a set of six scenarios (OECD 2001). Two were described as 'status quo' ('bureaucratic school systems continue', 'teacher exodus – meltdown'); two were described as 're-schooling' ('schools as core social centres', 'schools as focused learning organisations'); and two were described as 'de-schooling' ('learning networks and the network society', 'extending the market model'). That the OECD is prepared to contemplate such a range of scenarios is evidence that education, especially public education, has reached a watershed, and that transformation is inevitable if expectations are to be realised. The blueprint for leadership presented here is designed to bring about Scenario 3 ('the transformation of schools'). It is offered as the starting point for 'a decade of creative leadership'.

The third reason why transformation is irresistible and irreversible is derived from change in pedagogy, energised in part by advances in information and communications technology (ICT). Expressed simply, people can now learn anywhere and anytime. Learners have been empowered as never before. Schools must accommodate these developments as surely as they accommodated the advent of the printing press. More broadly, however, our knowledge about what works and why in approaches to learning and teaching is better than it has ever been. Accommodation along these lines is part of Scenario 3 ('the transformation of schools').

The fourth reason is connected to the other three and, indeed, underpins them if expectations for schools are to be realised. Schools will not survive as free-standing isolated institutions unless there is change of another kind. The call for 'joined-up solutions to joined-up problems' applies more to schools than to most other organisations if the disparities in student achievement are to be addressed. The concept of full-service schools where a range of public and private sector services is located at or near the school is one manifestation of what is required. The concept of a 'whole-of-government' approach to dealing with particular services is another manifestation. Michael Barber's role in the UK as Chief Advisor to the Prime Minister on Delivery is concerned with the links between services such as education health, law enforcement and transformation. To achieve these links, at national or local levels, calls for a dramatic change in culture – a transformation.

THE BLUEPRINT

The blueprint which I propose comprises one vision, three tracks, six values, four dimensions, five domains and one integrating theme, as shown in Table 12.1. The vision refers to the desired outcome of the global transformation that is under way and the emerging consensus on expectations for schools. The tracks refer to the broad directions of change in schools and school systems. The values are those that underpin a sense of the public good in education. The dimensions refer to major classifications of approaches to leadership that should be evident in practice. The domains refer to areas in which leaders should concentrate their efforts. The integrating theme is the capacity that must be developed to ensure success in transformation.

Table 12.1 One vision: the blueprint

Component		*Description*
Vision	1	Emerging global consensus on expectations for schools
Tracks	3	Broad directions for change in schools and school systems
Values	6	Defining the public good in education
Dimensions	4	Major classifications of approaches to the practice of leadership
Domains	5	Areas in which leaders should concentrate their efforts
Integrating theme	1	Capacity that must be developed to ensure success in transformation

I have refined and presented the blueprint over time in Australia, England, Hong Kong, India, Japan, Taiwan and Thailand, in each instance drawing on developments in the different national settings. Responses in these seven countries suggest it is relatively robust.

One vision

Agreement is emerging on expectations for schools, if documents from key international institutions, such as UNESCO and OECD, and the espoused policies of governments, are taken as a guide (Barber 1999; Chapman 1997; Chapman and Aspin 1997; Delors 1996). This agreement amounts to a global consensus on expectations for schools and it may be summarised in these words:

> All students in every setting should be literate and numerate and should acquire a capacity for life-long learning, leading to success and satisfaction as good citizens and productive workers in a knowledge society.

It is important to stress that this is an emerging *consensus*. Different countries, schools systems and schools will, of course, have their own special expectations.

Embracing this vision forms part of what Fullan (2001) calls 'moral purpose' in leadership. If we cannot embrace the vision of 'all students in every setting' we do not need transformation, and Britain can rest on its laurels in PISA.

Three tracks

A blueprint for successful leadership at all levels calls for a vision of education along the lines suggested above. It also calls for recognition that movement in this direction is occurring at different rates in different settings but in the same broad directions. There seem to be three such directions or tracks for change in education (Caldwell and Spinks 1998):

Track 1 Building systems of self-managing schools
Track 2 Unrelenting focus on learning outcomes
Track 3 Creating schools for the knowledge society

In Track 1, the building of systems of self-managing schools, more authority and responsibility are being decentralised to the local level within a framework of centrally determined goals, priorities, frameworks, standards and accountabilities. Track 2 is an unrelenting focus on learning outcomes for students where there is unprecedented concern for the monitoring of student achievement, with international benchmarking now gathering momentum (as illustrated in PISA). In Track 3, the creation of schools for the knowledge society, ICT is a powerful force for change. A defining characteristic of the knowledge society is that the largest group in the work-force comprises knowledge workers, being those who solve problems, manage information, or create new knowledge, products and services.

In relation to self-managing schools (Track 1), it seems that Victoria in Australia continues to set the pace, with 94 per cent of the state's recurrent budget for schools decentralised to the local level, an even higher level than the 90 per cent under New Labour in England. There are, however, some important aspects of the concept of self-management that need to be affirmed at this time. I refer here to the concept as Jim Spinks and I employed it in three books over ten years (Caldwell and Spinks 1988, 1992 and 1998).

> A self-managing school is a school in a system of education to which there has been decentralised a significant amount of authority and responsibility to make decisions related to the allocation of resources within a centrally-determined framework of goals, policies, standards, and accountabilities. Resources are defined broadly to include knowledge, technology, power, material, people, time, assessment, information and finance.
>
> (Caldwell and Spinks 1998: 4–5)

We stressed that 'a self-managing school is not an autonomous school nor is it a self-governing school, for each of these kinds of schools involve a degree of independence that is not provided in a centrally determined framework' (Caldwell and Spinks 1998: 5).

Evidence that a balance of centralisation and decentralisation is required comes from recent analysis of student achievement in 39 countries. The Third International Mathematics and Science Study (TIMSS) was the largest international comparative study of student achievement ever undertaken. As part of the project, information was gathered on a range of factors, including student and family characteristics, resources and teacher characteristics, and institutional settings. Analysis of the performance of more than 260,000 students from 39 countries was undertaken at Kiel University in Germany and reported by Woessmann (2001). Among the policy settings that are favourable to student performance are the following:

- central examinations;
- centralised control mechanisms in curricular and budgetary affairs;
- school autonomy in process and personnel decisions;
- an intermediate level of administration performing administrative tasks and providing educational funding;

- individual teachers having both incentives and powers to select appropriate teaching methods;
- scrutiny of students' educational performance; and
- encouragement of parents to take an interest in teaching matters.

It is important to note that 'centralised control mechanisms in curricular and budgetary affairs' refers to centrally determined frameworks, not to the manner of implementation at the school level. In the case of budgets, this refers to the existence of a funding mechanism that specifies how funds shall be allocated to schools, but schools then determine how these funds are deployed at the local level.

The connection between self-management and improved student learning is becoming clear, with research at the University of Melbourne by Wee (1999) mapping the links. Indeed, there is now a relatively robust 'theory of learning' in self-managing schools (Caldwell 2000; Caldwell and Spinks 1998). Interest in self-management is now extending to developing countries, with a UNESCO forum in February 2001 sharing international experience of success with strategies that link self-management, enhanced professional development for teachers, community support for schools, and making learning for students more active and enjoyable.

Themes from Tracks 2 and 3 are followed up in the discussion of the other components of the blueprint below.

Six values

Strategies for leadership should be shaped by a set of values, and six values in public education are proposed in the blueprint, as follows:

- choice
- equity
- access
- efficiency
- economic growth
- harmony.

It is suggested that these should provide the basis for a test of 'the public good' for leadership at all levels in a system of schools.

- *Choice* reflects the right of parents and students to choose a school that meets their needs and aspirations.
- *Equity* provides assurance that those students with similar needs and aspirations will be treated in the same manner in the course of their education.

- *Access* ensures that all students will have an education that matches their needs and aspirations.
- *Efficiency* optimises outcomes, given the resources available.
- *Economic growth* generates resources that are adequate to the task.
- *Harmony* ensures commitment among all stakeholders in efforts to realise high expectations for schools.

The first five are drawn from a classification proposed by Swanson and King (1997). Three are based on the classic trio of liberty (choice), equality (equity) and fraternity (access). Efficiency and economic growth are important if these three values are to be realised in practice. Educators are now coming to terms with the need for economic growth to fund the rapidly escalating costs of schooling, given the high expectations as far as outcomes are concerned.

Four dimensions

Four major dimensions are included in the blueprint for leadership for sustainable improvement. These dimensions are: strategic, educational, responsive and cultural (Caldwell and Spinks 1992).

Strategic leadership

School leadership is strategic when it involves:

- Keeping abreast of trends and issues, threats and opportunities in the educational environment and in society at large, nationally and internationally; discerning the 'megatrends' and anticipating their impact on education generally and on the school in particular;
- Sharing such knowledge with others in the school community and encouraging other leaders within the organisation to do the same in their areas of responsibility;
- Establishing structures and processes which enable the school to set priorities and formulate strategies which take account of likely and/or preferred futures, and being a key source of expertise as these occur;
- Ensuring that the attention of the school community is focused on matters of strategic importance;
- Monitoring the implementation of strategies as well as emerging strategic issues in the wider environment, and facilitating an ongoing process of review.

A capacity for strategic leadership has special priority at this time. Higher expectations for schools present challenges that have no counterpart in the history of education if they are to be brought to realisation. It requires every leader at every level to do the things listed above. It is no longer sufficient for a single minister, or head, or president of a professional association, to be out in front saying these things. It is a 'whole-of-government' or 'whole-of-enterprise' approach, with every minister, every school leader and all officials in professional associations having a capacity for strategic leadership in the specific meaning of that term: seeing 'the big picture', discerning the 'megatrends', understanding the implications, ensuring that others can do the same, establishing structures and processes to bring the vision to realisation, and monitoring the outcomes.

Educational leadership

Educational leadership refers to a capacity to nurture a learning community, again defined broadly to include a country, state, school system, but especially a school. This is explained in more detail in one of the domains for leadership (see page 200), but there is a 'hard edge' to the concept. A 'learning community' or a 'learning organisation' sounds a very comfortable place in which to work, but the stakes are high if the consensus on expectations for schools is to be realised.

With the wide range of learning needs in schools, these and other strategies to achieve targets call for teachers to have state-of-the-art knowledge about what works for each and every student. It calls for leaders who themselves will have much of this knowledge, but will certainly be able to manage learning and teaching so that knowledge is acquired and successfully brought to bear. Once again, this extends to all levels, including government, as well as applying to leaders in the local school setting.

Responsive leadership

There is an implication here that leaders will respond to the expectations for schools and will be comfortable in collecting, analysing and acting on data that let them know how well things are going (as outlined in Chapter 10). Responsive leaders accept that there are many stakeholders who have a 'right to know'. As with the other three dimensions, this acceptance extends to all levels of leadership.

The importance of this dimension is reflected in current interest in 'evidence-based leadership'. It is good to see that people are now examining ways in which school leaders can gather data as a basis for making good judgements and good strategic leadership decisions.

Cultural leadership

Each of the above indicates that there will be dramatic change to 'the way we do things around here', at the national, local and school levels. Successful leaders will have a capacity to change the culture. This is no easy task, given that the scale of the change and the seriousness of the endeavour are still not broadly understood, let alone accepted, in many settings.

Five domains

Five domains for action are proposed for those who seek to lead the transformation of schools in the twenty-first century. These domains of practice in the exercise of leadership are:

- school design
- boundary spanning
- curriculum
- pedagogy
- professionalism.

Some lie squarely in the field of education while others span the fields of education, health, and a range of other institutions and agencies in the public and private sectors across the community, reflecting the view that we cannot close the gap between current achievement and higher expectations unless we can, quite literally, 'span the boundaries'.

The integrating concept here is change. Drucker (1999: 73) contends that the only ones who will survive in a period when change is the norm will be the change leaders, for 'to be a successful change leader an enterprise has to have a policy of systematic innovation' (Drucker 1999: 84). For this reason, each domain for leadership is considered to be a field of innovation.

School design

The first domain, school design, is a comprehensive one, for it integrates all the work of a school in a comprehensive and coherent whole. Hill and Crévola (1999) refer to a 'whole school design' and propose eight elements:

- standards and targets;
- monitoring and assessment;
- classroom teaching programs;
- professional learning teams;
- school and class organisation;
- intervention and special assistance;
- home, school and community partnerships; with all
- underpinned and centred on beliefs and understandings.

(Hill and Crévola 1999: 123)

A design for the third track for change introduced on page 189 ('creating schools for the knowledge society') may be illustrated in a *gestalt* – a perceived organised whole that is more than the sum of its parts – as in Figure 12.1. The factors shown in the figure are explored below.

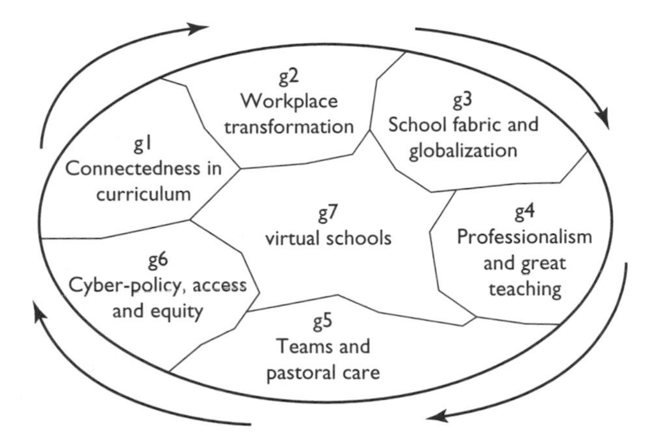

Figure 12.1 A *gestalt* design for creating schools for the knowledge society
Source: Caldwell and Spinks 1998: 160

Dramatic change in approaches to learning and teaching is in store as electronic networking allows 'cutting across and so challenging the very idea of subject boundaries' and 'changing the emphasis from impersonal curriculum to excited live exploration' (Papert 1993: 39). At risk is the balkanised curriculum that has done much to alienate children from schooling, especially following the transition from primary to secondary (represented by g1 Connectedness in curriculum in Figure 12.1).

Schools as workplaces are transformed in every dimension, including the scheduling of time for learning and approaches to human resource management, rendering obsolete most approaches that derive from an industrial age, including the concept of 'industrial relations' (g2 Workplace transformation).

The fabric of schooling is similarly rendered obsolete by electronic networking. Everything from building design to the size, shape, alignment, and furnishing of space for the 'knowledge worker' in the school is transformed. In one sense, of course, the school has no walls, for there are global learning networks, and much of the learning that calls for the student to be located at school occurs in many places, at home and, at the upper years of secondary schooling and for lifelong learning, in the work place. (g3 School fabric and globalization).

A wide range of professionals and para-professionals support learning in an educational parallel to the diversity of support that may be found in modern health care. The role of teacher is elevated, for it demands wisdom, judgement, and a facility to manage learning in modes more complex and varied than ever. While the matter of intellectual capital must be resolved, teachers are freed from the impossible task of designing from their own resources learning experiences to challenge every student: the resources of the world's great teachers will be at hand (g4 Professionalism and great teaching). (The Department for Education and Skills in the UK has published on its website more than a thousand evaluated lesson plans in most key learning areas (see http://www.teachernet.gov.uk and then look for lesson plans).)

A capacity to work in teams is more evident in approaches to learning, given the primacy of the work team in every formulation of the workplace in the knowledge society. This, of course, will confound those who see electronic networking in an outdated stereotype of the loner with the laptop. The concept of 'pastoral care' of students is as important as ever for learning in this mode, and in schools that quite literally have no boundaries (g5 Teams and pastoral care).

The formulation of 'cyber-policy of the future' (Spender 1995) is a priority. The issues of access and equity will drive public debate until such time as prices fall to make electronic networks as common as the telephone or radio, and that may soon be a reality, given trends in networked computers (g6 Cyber-policy, access and equity).

The concept of the virtual organisation or the learning network organisation is a reality in the knowledge society. Schools take on many of the characteristics of such organisations, given that learning occurs in so many modes and from so many sources, all networked electronically (g7 Virtual schools).

The challenge for leaders is to work with others to create a design that suits the setting. Is there a design for your school that can be described and illustrated along the lines proposed by Hill and Crévola (1999) or Caldwell and Spinks (1998)? What changes should be made on the basis of what is learned here? What processes should be set in train to create a design or change a design?

Boundary spanning

The second domain lies in organisational arrangements to design, deliver or in other ways drive the effort. We have had a century or more of largely successful effort in the public sector with responsibility in the hands of discrete government departments, each reporting to a particular minister. What happens at a government or public school is largely a matter for the department and a responsible minister. Yet the problems to be addressed in closing the gap are complex and demanding of attention of those who work in different departments, or elsewhere, outside government and in the private sector.

While inter-department cooperation and freewheeling boundary spanning have been evident, it is only in recent times that signs of a major shift in culture that fosters even higher levels have been seen. That shift has resulted from a backward-mapping approach, starting from a focus on people and a problem, then selecting a strategy to address the problem, then designing and delivering a constellation of services and resources, without consideration of organisational boundaries except where the public good test is not satisfied. This linear process is made more complex because there is rarely a single problem to address and rarely a single solution. Governments that have taken this approach now speak of 'joined-up solutions to joined-up problems' and advocate breaking down organisational boundaries. They use the metaphor of a silo to describe the isolation of a government department. I should hasten to add that the same metaphor has been adopted to describe different faculties in universities.

One attempt at boundary spanning appears to have met with limited success. Despite several significant achievements, the Blair Government will not continue with EAZs beyond the statutory lifetime of five years from the date of their establishment. More than 2,000 schools have joined an EAZ. Links have been made with more than 1,000 businesses. Additional cash and in-kind support is likely to exceed £300 million over the course of the project. However, the impact on learning outcomes has been mixed. School standards Minister Stephen Timms reported that:

> The most significant impact has been made in primary schools, where achievement continues to rise faster than the national rate. The challenge for zones now is to bring about comparable improvements at secondary level. Some zones are matching or outpacing the national improvement rate, but considerable work remains to be done, particularly at Key Stage 3 [age 14–16] where the rate of improvement is still not matching the national figures.
>
> (cited in Department for Education and Skills, 2001)

Does your school seek 'joined-up solutions to joined-up problems'? Can you map the relationships with organisations and agencies outside the school, and outside education that reflect the importance of 'boundary spanning'? To what extent does the metaphor of 'silo' apply to your school?

Curriculum

The emerging global consensus on expectations for schools is commendable, but many would argue that the range of outcomes and their measures are much too narrow. The idea of 'multiple intelligences', based on Gardner's *Frames of Mind* (Gardner 1983), is a helpful starting point. He included logical mathematical, linguistic, spatial, musical, bodily kinaesthetic, interpersonal, existentialist, intrapersonal and naturalist.

Handy provides a more accessible classification, suggesting that three intelligences – factual intelligence, analytical intelligence and numerate intelligence – 'will get you through most tests and entitle you to be called clever' (Handy 1997: 211). He suggests eight more: linguistic intelligence, spatial intelligence, athletic intelligence, intuitive intelligence, emotional intelligence, practical intelligence, interpersonal intelligence and musical intelligence (Handy 1997: 212–13).

Leadbeater suggests that 'the curriculum needs to encourage creativity, problem solving, team building, as well as literacy and numeracy' (Leadbeater 1999: vi) while Beck sets a similar curriculum in the context of globalisation:

> One of the main political responses to globalisation is . . . to build and develop the education and knowledge society; to make training longer rather than shorter; to loosen or do away with its link to a particular job or occupation. This should not only be a matter of 'flexibility' or 'lifelong learning', but of such things as social competence, the ability to work in a team, conflict resolution, understanding of other cultures, integrated thinking and a capacity to handle the uncertainties and paradoxes of the second modernity. Here and there, people are beginning to realise that something like a transnationalism of university education and curricula will be necessary.
>
> (Beck 1999: 27)

To do all of this will require the abandonment of much of the existing curriculum. Writing for the UK setting, Seltzer contends that 'we can't just keep piling new expectations and structures on to old ones. Something has to give. We should aim to have reduced the national curriculum by half by 2010 in order to make room for new approaches' (Seltzer 1999: xxi).

It is clear that school leaders will be actively engaged in this domain over the next decade.

Pedagogy

The revolution in ICT and the advent of exciting, pedagogically sound approaches to inter-active multi-media learning mean that it is possible to learn anytime, anywhere. A revolution is clearly under way. Kenichi Ohmae has captured the new reality in *The Invisible Continent* (Ohmae 2000). Compared with continents that have clearly defined boundaries, geography that is visible, governments that hold power, and societies that celebrate unique cultures, the invisible continent has these characteristics.

1 It is 'cyber-enabled'. The new continent 'easily moves information across all kinds of borders, both national and corporate'.
2 As 'a continent without land, the new continent is easy to enter, but only for those who are willing to give up their old ways of thinking'.
3 'No nation holds a monopoly on entrance to it. Any nation, any company, any race, any ethnic group, or any individual may enter.'
4 The new continent draws on 'highly individualistic values. Communities and families, or old-style establishment connections, do not determine worth in this world.'

(Ohmae 2000: 16–20)

Ohmae is in no doubt about the place of education. He states that 'The most fundamental lever for success in the new continent is education' and 'education is the first and foremost priority for any nation'. Preparing youngsters to comprehend the invisible continent and compete in its endeavours and explorations is the best investment that a government (or parents, for that matter) can make. (Ohmae 2000: 227–9)

More fundamentally, and linked to the domain of innovation in curriculum, is how learning occurs. The challenge is to provide balance. To what extent does the following commentary on developments in the United States apply to students in other countries?

> They are extremely good at manipulating symbols and working on computers, they are verbally fluent and extremely good at asking questions, but they don't really know anything in depth and they haven't really read anything. The high school curriculum is so chopped up into tiny bits and pieces that the integrating power of a liberal education is somewhat lost.
>
> (Sheridan 1999: 274)

Henry Kissinger said that 'the present generation has the power to tap into astonishing amounts of knowledge on any subject but no ability to integrate it into a knowledge of the past and no ability therefore to project it meaningfully into the future' (cited by Sheridan 1999: 274).

School leaders will be at the centre of many discussions and debates on pedagogy in the decade ahead. The use of ICT is just one strand of these deliberations. The wider issue will be to bring about a high degree of alignment of curriculum, pedagogy and assessment. These three will shape the more comprehensive school design, described and illustrated in domain 1, on pages 194–6.

More generally, however, is the issue of knowledge about pedagogy, and what works and why for different students in every setting. It is my view that this knowledge base is stronger than it has ever been, and the challenge for leaders is to ensure that this knowledge is created, shared and managed in the local setting. An illustration of the strength of that knowledge base is in Carolyn Orange's user-friendly summary of practices, programmes, policies and philosophies associated with different innovations (Orange 2002).

Professionalism

The unrelenting focus on learning outcomes in the emerging consensus on expectations for schools suggests 'innovation in professionalism', in that teachers' work will be research-based, outcomes-oriented, data-driven, and team-focused, with lifelong professional learning the norm as it is for medical specialists.

A wonderfully rich professionalism is evident in the 'intelligent school' proposed by MacGilchrist, Myers and Reed (1997). This is the organisational counterpart of an individual with 'multiple intelligences'. Professionals in an 'intelligent school' will have contextual intelligence, strategic intelligence, academic intelligence, reflective intelligence, pedagogical intelligence, collegial intelligence, emotional intelligence, spiritual intelligence and ethical intelligence.

Leaders will be actively engaged in the promotion of this kind of professionalism in the decade ahead. There has been impressive achievement in recent times, as evidenced by the acquisition of knowledge and skill in the areas of literacy and numeracy. The challenge is to ensure that this applies for all teachers in every area of their professional work. A starting point for appreciating the size of this domain is the taxonomy of educational innovations prepared by Orange (2002).

There is also the challenge of how to attract and keep in the profession the best of our young people and the wisest of our mature people. There are implications for governments and the wider community as well as for schools and, in universities, there is a need to re-design programmes in teacher education.

The numbers of people seeking to enter the profession are increasing. On the other hand, the numbers who leave are increasing. Internationally, at least in most Western countries, there is a crisis in these matters, and a failure to resolve it is one of the six OECD scenarios referred to earlier ('teacher exodus – meltdown') (OECD 2001). In the United States, there is evidence that the nature of teachers' work is at the root of the problem. The data show 'that the amount of turnover accounted for by retirement is relatively minor when compared to that associated with other factors, such as teacher job dissatisfaction and teachers pursuing other jobs' (Ingersoll 2001: 499).

Integrating theme

You may already have detected the integrating theme in the blueprint. Expressed simply, there is an unprecedented large body of knowledge relevant to the work of leaders that has to be managed. Knowledge management includes knowledge creation, dissemination and utilisation for the purposes of improved learning and teaching and to guide decision-making and priority setting in every domain of professional practice. Knowledge management is not just a fad that will pass or a piece of jargon to describe what has always been a requirement in the organisation.

According to Bukowitz and Williams (1999: 2), 'knowledge management is the process by which the organisation generates wealth from its intellectual or knowledge-based assets'. In the case of school education, 'knowledge management is the process by which a school achieves the highest levels of student learning that are possible from its intellectual or knowledge-based assets'. Successful knowledge management is consistent with the image of 'the intelligent school' (MacGilchrist, Myers and Reed 1997) and the concept of 'intellectual capital' (Stewart 1997).

Knowledge management calls for a school to develop a deep capacity among its entire staff to be at the forefront of knowledge and skill in learning and teaching and in the support of learning and teaching. This is more than occasional in-service training or professional development. This is a systematic, continuous and purposeful approach that starts with knowing what people know, don't know and ought to know. It assumes an innovative professionalism, as already described, and includes a range of functions such as selection, placement, development, appraisal, reward, succession planning, contracting of services and ensuring that every aspect of the workplace is conducive to efficient, effective and satisfying work for all concerned.

It is important to conceptualise the process of knowledge generation and utilisation in knowledge management. Burgoyne (cited by Bahra, 2001, pp. 155) offers the following:

Data are collected, stored and processed to create
↓
Information that is reflected on to produce
↓
Knowledge that is the basis for
↓
Action
↓
Reflection on which may lead to *wisdom*.

Leadership for the transformation of schools calls for the design of a system of knowledge management. A starting point is to conduct an audit of existing capacity. Rajan (as cited by Bahra 2001: 110–14) has developed a tool for self-assessment that can be used for this purpose.

Competitive intelligence, a capacity for school leaders to work in an environment of competition and choice is necessary, with knowledge management a key component of the role. The analysis of TIMSS data by Woessmann (2001) reported above included 'competition from private educational institutions' as a factor associated with high student achievement. A key issue is defined by the question: 'Is competition helpful or harmful in efforts to improve learning outcomes for students?' Recent studies in Britain suggest that there are benefits for students in communities where there is competition among schools. A study of competition among secondary schools in Britain in the late 1990s (Levačić 2001) found that schools perform better, as indicated by the proportion of students achieving high grades in the GCSE examinations, in communities where there are a number of perceived competitors. It appears that this outcome is not determined by unfair 'rivalrous' conduct but by the greater stimulus to improve and maintain the school's position and by the taking up of opportunities for cooperation in matters that may improve outcomes for students.

A number of writers (see review by Bahra 2001: 202–3) distinguish between knowledge management and competitive intelligence, and advocate that organisations need to combine the two in an 'intelligence pyramid'. Knowledge management (KM) forms the base, with three layers: data, information and knowledge. In this view:

> Knowledge management facilitates 'the now' – knowledge, information and data collection and sharing. It emphasises the people, culture and process.
>
> (Bahra 2001: 203)

Competitive intelligence (CI) forms the apex, with two layers: intelligence and actionable intelligence. In this view:

> Competitive intelligence focuses on 'the future' – likelihood and possibility, influencing future events and decisions. It emphasises trends, patterns and what is currently unknown.
>
> (adapted from Bahra 2001: 203)

The completed 'intelligence pyramid', as illustrated in Figure 12.2, that combines knowledge management (KM) with competitive intelligence (CI), should inform decisions and lead to action, in this instance, to guide the transformation of the school in a competitive environment. The challenge for leaders is to build the intelligence pyramid.

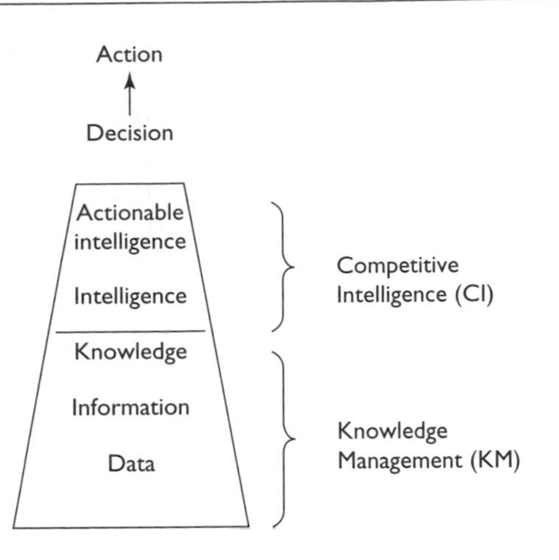

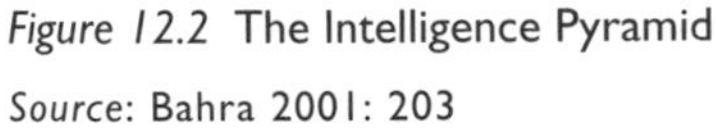

Figure 12.2 The Intelligence Pyramid

Source: Bahra 2001: 203

Levačić's finding in relation to cooperation in a competitive environment is interesting, suggesting that competition and cooperation are not mutually exclusive. The creation of 'knowledge networks' (Networked Learning Communities) around England by the National College for School Leadership is consistent with this view. The challenge is to transform the culture in education to enable such networks to be created and sustained. Jackson (2002) draws attention to the currently weak culture compared with that in medicine (moderate) and in the high technology industry (high).

If the integrating theme among the domains of leadership is innovation, and if there is not to be an accretion of new tasks on old, it follows that a capacity for systematic abandonment is as important as a capacity for systematic innovation. Effective knowledge management should enable the school to engage in systematic abandonment, something the culture has not allowed to this point. The outcome has been a clearly over-worked profession.

Drucker (1999) calls for 'organised abandonment' for products, services, markets or processes:

- which were designed in the past and which were highly successful, even to the present, but which would not be designed in the same way if we were starting afresh today, knowing the terrain ahead;
- which are currently successful, and likely to remain so, but only up to, say, five years – in other words, they have a limited 'shelf life'; or
- which may continue to succeed, but which through budget commitments, are inhibiting more promising approaches that will ensure success well into the future.

Virtually every domain of leadership calls for abandonment of one kind or another, regardless of the scenario.

The five domains call for abandonment of a range of approaches. Innovation in design will certainly require abandonment of standard class sizes for all students at every level in facilities built like a collection of boxes, lined end to end or stacked one upon the other. Innovation in boundary spanning calls for abandonment of the silo metaphor and abandonment of the view that problems occur in simple clusters and can be addressed by networking of services in a single sector. Innovation in curriculum requires abandonment of some learning areas that have been painstakingly constructed over the past decade. Pedagogy is a domain fraught with dilemmas, but ripe for abandonment of approaches that do not yield outcomes consistent with expectations for world-class schools. Innovation in professionalism challenges the modest levels of knowledge and skill that sufficed in the past with a vision for values-centred, research-based, outcomes-oriented, data-driven and team-focused approaches that matches or exceeds that of the best of medical practice.

CONCLUSION

This completes the blueprint for successful leadership in an era of globalisation of learning. The different components are brought together in Table 12.2. It cannot, of course, tell us all about the requirements for successful leadership, but a capacity to grasp the vision and work along the tracks in each of the domains, exercising leadership in several dimensions, underpinned by a commitment to a set of public values, will surely go a long way to bringing the vision to realisation.

A recent study in England by Hay McBer (Forde, Hobby and Lees, 2000) suggests that headteachers have a much wider range of skills than they are often given credit for, and on some dimensions they outperform leaders in business. The sample comprised 200 headteachers and 200 senior managers and directors in multinational companies. In each instance, five members of staff were asked to describe and rate leadership according to a set of common criteria.

> The results leave us in no doubt that headteachers have much to offer their counterparts in business. While business leaders are more adept at strategy and vision, headteachers' strengths lie in raising capability.
>
> (Forde, Hobby and Lees 2000: 4)

There is now a growing literature on the transformation of schools and perhaps the best in recent times is a book by Hedley Beare (2001). He is one of Australia's most experienced leaders in public education and a

Table 12.2 Blueprint for leadership in the transformation of schools

Component	*Element*	
Vision	1	Global consensus on expectations for schools.
Tracks for change	1	Building systems of self-managing schools
	2	Unrelenting focus on learning outcomes
	3	Creating schools for the knowledge society
Values defining the public good	1	Choice
	2	Equity
	3	Access
	4	Efficiency
	5	Economic growth
	6	Harmony
Dimensions of leadership	1	Strategic
	2	Educational
	3	Responsive
	4	Cultural
Domains of practice	1	School design
	2	Boundary spanning
	3	Curriculum
	4	Pedagogy
	5	Professionalism
Integrating theme	1	Knowledge management

distinguished scholar with an exceptional capacity to see the pathways from past to present to future. He concludes an uplifting chapter about teachers for the school of the future with these words:

> This terrain is *not* for the immature, the shallow, the unworthy, the unformed, or the uninformed, and society needs to be very careful about what people it commissions for this task.
>
> (Beare 2001: 185)

References and further reading

Adair, J. (1986) *Effective Teambuilding*, London: Pan.

Adair, J. (2002) *Effective Strategic Leadership*, London: Macmillan.

Adams, J., Hayes, J. and Hopson, B. (eds) (1976) *Transition: Understanding and Managing Personal Change*, London: Martin Robertson.

Argyris, C. and Schön, D. (1978) *Organisational Learning*, Reading, MA: Addison-Wesley.

Aspinwall, K. (1998) *Leading the Learning School*, London: Lemos and Crane.

Aspinwall, K., Simkins, T., Wilkinson, J. and McAuley, M. J. (1992) *Managing Evaluation in Education*, London: Routledge.

Bahra, N. (2001) *Competitive Knowledge Management*, Basingstoke: Palgrave.

Barber, M. (1999) *A World Class School System for the 21st Century: The Blair Government's Education Reform Strategy*, No. 90 in a Seminar Series of the Incorporated Association of Registered Teachers of Victoria (IARTV), December (reprint of a paper presented at the Skol Tema Conference in Stockholm in September 1999).

Barker, G. (2003) 'Case study 1: Reengineering teaching and learning in the primary school' in Davies, B. and West-Burnham, J. (eds) *Handbook of Educational Leadership and Management*, London: Pearson.

Barth, R. (1990) *Improving Schools from Within*, San Francisco, CA: Jossey-Bass.

Bartunek, J.M. and Necochea, R. (2000) 'Old insights and new times: Kairos, Inca cosmology and their contributions to contemporary management inquiry', *Journal of Management Inquiry*, 9(2): 103–13.

Bass, B. M. (1985) *Leadership and Performance beyond Expectations*, New York: Free Press.

Beare, H. (2001) *Creating the Future School*, London: RoutledgeFalmer.

Beck, U. (1999) 'Beyond the nation state', *New Statesman*, 6 December, pp. 25–7.

Belbin, M. (1981) *Management Teams: Why They Succeed or Fail*, London: Heinemann.

Belbin, M. (1985) *Management Teams: Why They Succeed or Fail*, London: Heinemann.

Belbin, M. (1993) *Team Roles at Work*, Oxford: Butterworth-Heinemann.

Bell, L. (1998) 'From symphony to jazz: the concept of strategy in education', *School Leadership and Management*, 18 (4) pp 449–460.

Bennett, D. (2000) *The School of the Future*, National College for School Leadership, Leadership evidence base, NCSL: Nottingham.

Bennett, N., Wise, C., Woods, P. and Harvey, J. A. (2003) *Distributed Leadership*, Nottingham: NCSL.

Bennis, W. and Nanus, W. (1985) *Leaders*, New York: Harper and Row.

Berman, P. (1980) 'Thinking about programmed and adaptive implementation: Matching strategies to situations', in Ingram, H. and Mann, D. (eds) *Why Policies Succeed or Fail*, Beverley Hills, CA: Sage.

Black, J.A. and Boal, K.B. (1996) 'Assessing the organizational capacity to change', in Heene, A. and Sanchez, R., eds. *Competence-based Strategic Management*, Chichester: John Wiley.

Black, P. and Wiliam, D. (2003) 'The development of formative assessment', in Davies, B. and West-Burnham, J. (eds) *Handbook of Educational Leadership and Management*, London: Pearson.

Boal, K. B. and Bryson, J. M. (1988) 'Charismatic leadership: A phenomenological and structural approach', in Hunt, J. G., Baliga, B. R., Dachler, H. P. and Schriesheim, C. A. (eds) *Emerging leadership vistas*, New York: Lexington.

Boal, K. B. and Hooijberg R. (2001) 'Strategic leadership research: Moving on', *Leadership Quarterly*, 11(4): 515–49.

Boisot, M. (1998) *Knowledge Assets: Securing Competitive Advantage in the Information Economy*, Oxford: Oxford University Press.

Boisot, M. (2003) 'Preparing for turbulence', in Garratt, B. (ed.) *Developing Strategic Thought*, London: McGraw-Hill.

Bowring-Carr, C. and West-Burnham, J. (1997) *Effective Learning in Schools*, London: FT Pitman Publishing.

Buckingham, M. and Clifton, D. O. (2001) *Now, Discover Your Strengths*, New York: Free Press.

Bukowitz, W. R. and Williams, R. L. (1999) *The Knowledge Management Fieldbook*, London: Financial Times Prentice Hall.

Buley, A. L. (1998) 'A vision of learning', in Kakabadse, A., Nortier, F. and Abramovici, N-B. *Success in Sight*, London: International Thomson Business Press.

Burgleman, R.A. and Grove, A.S. (1996) 'Strategic dissonance', *Californian Management Review*, 38(2): 8–28.

Bush, T. and Glover, D. (2003) *School Leadership: Concepts and Evidence*, Nottingham: NCSL.

Butler, H. (1990) *Grandmother and Wolfe Tone*, Dublin: Lilliput Press.

Caldwell, B. J. (2000) 'Local management and learning outcomes: Mapping the links in three generations of international research', in Coleman, M. and Anderson, L. (eds) *Managing Finance and Resources in Education*, London: Paul Chapman Publishing.

Caldwell, B.J. and Carter, E.M. (1993) *The Return of the Mentor*, London: Falmer.

Caldwell, B. J. and Spinks, J. M. (1988) *The Self-managing School*, London: Falmer Press.

Caldwell, B. J. and Spinks, J. M. (1992) *Leading the Self-managing School*, London: Falmer Press.

Caldwell, B. J. and Spinks, J. M. (1998) *Beyond the Self-managing School*, London: Falmer Press.

Carmichael, L. (1993) 'The management paradigm shift', unpublished presentation to the National Project on the Quality of Teaching and Learning, Adelaide.

Chaleff, I. (1995) 'All hail the brave follower', *The QANTAS Club*, November.

Chapman, J. (1997) 'Leading the learning community', *Leading & Managing*, 3(3): 151–70.

Chapman, J. and Aspin, D. (1997) *The School, the Community and Lifelong Learning*, London: Cassell.

Cheng, Y. C. (2002) 'Leadership and strategy', in Bush, T. and Bell, L. (eds) *The Principles and Practice of Educational Management*, London: PCP.

Clarke, L. (1994) *The Essence of Change*, Hemel Hempstead: Prentice-Hall International.

Cohen, W. M. and Levinthal, D. A. (1990) 'Absorptive capacity: A new perspective on learning and innovation', *Administrative Science Quarterly*, 35: 128–52.

Collins, J. (2001) *Good to Great*, London: Random House.

Constable, J. and McCormick, R. (1987) *The Making of British Managers*, London: NEDO.

Covey, S. (1989) *The Seven Habits of Highly Effective People*, New York: Simon & Schuster.

Craig, E. (ed.) *The Concise Encyclopedia of Philosophy* (2000), London: Routledge.

Cuban, L. (1988) 'A fundamental puzzle of school reform', *Phi Delta Kappan*, 70 (5): 341–4.

Dalin, P. (1978) *Limits to Educational Change*, London: Macmillan.

Darling-Hammond, L. (1991) 'The implications of testing policy for educational quality and equality', *Phi Delta Kappan*, 73, 220–5.

Darling-Hammond, L. (1997) *The Right to Learn*, San Francisco, CA: Jossey-Bass.

Davies, B. (2002) 'Rethinking schools and school leadership for the 21st century: Changes and challenges', *International Journal of Educational Management*, 16(4): 196–206.

Davies, B. (2003) 'Rethinking strategy and strategic leadership in schools', *Education Management & Administration*, 31(3): 295–312.

Davies, B. (2004) 'Developing the strategically focused school', *School Leadership and Management*, 24(1): 29–38.

Davies, B. and Davies, B. J. (2003) 'Strategy and planning in schools', in Davies B. and West-Burnham, J. (eds), *Handbook of Educational Leadership and Management*, London: Pearson.

Davies, B. and Ellison, L. (2003) *The New Strategic Direction and Development of the School*, London: RoutledgeFalmer.

Davies, B. and West-Burnham, J. (2003) *Handbook of Educational Leadership and Management*, London: Pearson.

Davies, B. J. (2003) *Washingborough Foundation Primary School Planning for 2003/4*, Washingborough, Lincolnshire.

Day, C., Tolley, H., Hadfield, M., Parkin, E. and Watling, R. (1996) *Class Size Research and the Quality of Education: A Survey of the Literature Related to Class Size and the Quality of Teaching and Learning*, London: National Association of Headteachers.

Delors, J. (ed.) (1996) *Learning: The Treasure Within*, Paris: UNESCO.

Department for Education and Skills (2001) 'Continued Support for Education Action Zone Schools', Report of School Standards Minister's Address to seventh EAZ Conference, 14 November.

DePree, M. (1990) *Leadership is an Art*, New York: Currency Doubleday.

DePree, M. (1993) *Leadership Jazz*, New York: Dell.

DES (1988) *Education Reform Act*, London: HMSO.

DES (1990) *Developing School Management: The Way Forward (Report of the School Management Task Force)*, London: HMSO.

DfES (2004) *The National Standards for Headteachers*, London: DfES.

Drucker, P. F. (1999) *Leadership Challenges for the 21st Century*, Oxford: Butterworth Heinemann.

Education Training and Inspectorate (2000) *Report of a Survey of Provision for Education for Mutual Understanding in Post-primary Schools*, Bangor, Northern Ireland: Department of Education.

Esp, D. (1993) *Competences for School Managers*, London: Kogan Page.

Fiedler, F. E. (1967) *A Theory of Leadership Effectiveness*, New York: McGraw Hill.

Flecknoe, M. (2001) 'ICT doing different things, rather than doing them differently', *Management in Education*, 16 (1): 26–30.

Forde, R., Hobby, A. and Lees, A. (2000) *The Lessons of Leadership*, London: Hay Management Consultants.

Forster, E. M. (1969) *Howard's End*, London: Penguin.

Fullan, M. (1993) *Change Forces: Probing the Depths of Educational Reform*, London: Falmer Press.

Fullan, M. (2001) *Leading in a Culture of Change*, San Francisco: Jossey Bass.

Fullan, M. (2003) *Change Forces with a Vengeance*, London and New York: RoutledgeFalmer.

Gardner, H. (1983) *Frames of Mind*, London: Heinemann.

Gardner, H. (1985) *The Mind's New Science: A History of the Cognitive Revolution*, New York: Basic Books.

Gardner, H. (1999) *Intelligence Reframed*, New York: Basic Books.

Garratt, B. (2003) *Developing Strategic Thought*, London: McGraw-Hill.

Georgiades, N. (1990) *The Service Organisation Profile*, Chorleywood, Hertfordshire: NGA Organisation Consultants.

Gioia, D. A. and Thomas, J. G .(1996) 'Identity, image, and issue interpretation: Sensemaking during strategic change in academia', *Administrative Science Quarterly*, 41: 370–403.

Goleman, D. (1998) 'What makes a leader?', *Harvard Business Review*, November–December: 93–102.

Goleman, D. (2000) 'Leadership that gets results', *Harvard Business Review*, March–April: 78–90.

Gratton, L. (2000) *Living Strategy: Putting People at the Heart of Corporate Purpose*, London: Financial Times–Prentice Hall.

Grundy, T. (1998) *Harnessing Strategic Behaviour*, London: Financial Times–Pitman Publishing.

Hambrick, D. C. (1989) 'Guest editor's introduction: Putting top managers back in the strategy picture', *Strategic Management Journal*, 10: 5–15.

Hamel, G. and Heene, A. (eds.) (1994) *Competence Based Competition*, New York: John Wiley.

Hamel, G. and Prahalad, C. K. (1994) *Competing for the Future*, Boston, MA: Harvard Business School Press.

Handy, C. (1987) *The Making of Managers*, London: British Institute of Management.

Handy, C. (1996) 'The New Language of Organizing and its Implications for Leaders', in Hesselbein F., Goldsmith, M. and Beckhard, R. *The Leader of the Future*, San Francisco, CA: Jossey-Bass.

Handy, C. (1997) *The Hungry Spirit*, London: Hutchinson.

Hargreaves, A. (1994) *Changing Teaching, Changing Times: Teachers' Work and Culture in the Postmodern Age*, New York: Teachers' College Press.

Hargreaves, A. and Fullan, M. (1998) *What's Worth Fighting for out There? Guidelines for Principals*, Toronto: OISE.

Harland, J., Moor, H., Kinder, K. and Ashworth, M. (2000) *Is the Curriculum Working? The Key Stage 3 Phase of the Northern Ireland Curriculum (Summary)*, Slough: National Foundation for Educational Research.

Harris, A. (2002) *School Improvement: What's in it for Schools?*, London: RoutledgeFalmer

Hayes, M. (1984) Lecture, 'Why can't they be more like us?' Belfast: John Malone Memorial Committee.

Hayes, M. (1990) Lecture, Conference on Education for Mutual Understanding, Bangor: Department of Education, Northern Ireland.

HayGroup (2000) *Raising Achievement in our Schools: Models of Excellence for Headteachers in Different Settings*. Boston, MA: Hay Resources Direct.

HayGroup (2001) *The Manager Competency Model*. Boston, MA: Hay Resources Direct.

HayGroup (2003a) *Leadership Competency Inventory* http://www.hayresourcesdirect.haygroup.com/Competency/Assessments_Surveys/Leadership_Competency_Inventory/Overview.asp accessed 10 Nov. 2003.

HayGroup (2003b) *Managerial Competency Questionnaire* http://www.hayresourcesdirect.haygroup.com/Competency/Assessments_Surveys/Managerial_Competency_Questionnaire/Overview.asp accessed 10 Nov. 2003.

Heifetz, R. and Linsky, M. (2002) *Leadership on the Line: Staying Alive through the Dangers of Leading*, Boston, MA: Harvard Business School Press.

Hersey, P. (1990) *Mentoring and Coaching: A Development Program for Educational Leaders*, Reston, VA: NASSP.

Hersey, P. and Blanchard, K. (1982) *Management of Organizational Behaviour: Utilizing Human Resources*, fourth edition, Englewood Cliffs, NJ: Prentice-Hall.

Hill, P. and Crévola, C. (1999) 'The role of standards in educational reform for the 21st century', in Marsh, D. (ed.) *Preparing our Schools for the 21st Century*, ASCD Yearbook 1999, Alexandria, VA: ASCD.

Hirschhorn, L. (1997) *Re-working Authority: Leading and Authority in the Post-modern Organisation*, Cambridge, MA: MIT Press.

Hitt, M. A., Keats, B. W. and DeMarie, S. M. (1998) 'Navigating in the new competitive landscape: Building strategic flexibility and competitive advantage in the 21st century', *Academy of Management Executive*, 12: 22–41.

Hopson, B., Scally, M. and Stafford, K. (1992) *Transitions: The Challenge of Change*, London: Mercury Books.

Ingersoll, R. M. (2001) 'Teacher turnover and teacher shortages: An organizational analysis', *American Educational Research Journal*, 38 (3): 499–534.

Jackson, D. (2002) 'The creation of knowledge networks', Paper presented at the CERI/UNESCO/DfES/QCA/ESRC Forum on Knowledge Management and Learning, 18–19 March, Oxford.

Jaeger, R.M. (1991) 'Legislative perspectives on state-wide testing', *Phi Delta Kappan*, 73: 239–42.

Javidon, M. (1991) 'Leading a high-commitment, high-performance organisation', *Long Range Planning*, 24(2): 28–36.

Kakabadse, A., Nortier, F. and Abramovici, N-B. (1998) *Success in Sight*, London: International Thomson Business Press.

Kaplan, R. S. and Norton, D. P. (1996) *The Balanced Scorecard*, Boston, MA: HBS Press.

Kaplan, R. S. and Norton, D. P. (2001) *The Strategy-focused Organization*, Boston, MA: Harvard Business School Publishing Corporation.

Klein, G. (2003) *Intuition at Work*, New York: Doubleday.

Kohn, A. (1999) *The Schools our Children Deserve*, New York: Houghton Mifflin.

Korac-Kakabadse, N. and Kakabadse, A. (1998) 'Vision, visionary leadership and the visioning process: An overview', in Kakabadse, A., Nortier, F. and Abramovici, N-B. *Success in Sight*, London: International Thomson Business Press.

Kotter, J. P. (1990) *A Force for Change: How Leadership Differs from Management*, New York: The Free Press.

Leadbeater, C. (1999) 'It's not the economy, stupid', *New Statesman*, special supplement on the theme Knowledge is Power! 27 September, pp. iv–vi.

Levačić, R. (2001) *An Analysis of Competition and its Impact on Secondary School Examination Performance in England*, Occasional Paper No. 34, National Centre for the Study of Privatisation in Education, Teachers College, Columbia University, September.

Louis, K. and Miles, M. (1990) *Improving the Urban High School: What Works and Why*, New York: Teachers College Press.

MacGilchrist, B., Myers, K. and Reed, J. (1997) *The Intelligent School*, London: Paul Chapman.

Madaus, G.F. (1991) 'The effects of important tests on students: Implications for a national examination system', *Phi Delta Kappan*, 73: 226–31.

Manz, C. & Sims, H. (1994) *Superleadership*, New York: Berkeley.

Marris, P. (1975) *Loss and Change*, New York: Anchor Press/Doubleday.

Marsh, D. (2000) 'Educational leadership for the twenty-first century: Integrating three essential perspectives', in *The Jossey-Bass Reader on Educational Leadership*, San Francisco, CA: Jossey-Bass.

Martin and D'Agostino (2003) 'Having a field day: managerialism, educational discourse and the fifth province of Ireland', paper presented at Conference: Discourse Power Resistance, New Directions, New Moves, University of Plymouth.

McClelland, D.C. (1988) *Human Motivation*, Cambridge: Cambridge University Press.

Mintzberg, H. (2003) 'Strategic thinking as seeing', in Garratt, B. (ed.), *Developing Strategic Thought*, London: McGraw-Hill.

Mintzberg, H., Ahlstrand, B. and Lampel, J. (1998) *Strategy Safari: A Guided Tour through The Wilds of Strategic Management*, San Francisco, CA: Prentice Hall.

Morgan, G. (1993) *Imaginization: The Art of Creative Management*, London: Sage.

Moses, J. (1990) 'High performance leadership', unpublished paper presented to the Twenty-first International Congress on the Use of the Assessment Centre Method, Anaheim, California.

MSC (2004) *Development of World Class National Occupation Standards for Management and Leadership*. www.managers.org.uk/msu2001/review.htm.

National College for School Leadership (2001) *Report of the Think Tank to the Governing Council*, Nottingham: NCSL.

NCSL (2003) *Consultation on the National Standards for Headteachers*, Nottingham: NCSL.

Niven, P. R. (2002) *Balanced Scorecard Step-by-Step*, New York: John Wiley.
OECD (1994) *Education at a Glance: OECD Indicators*, Paris: OECD.
OECD (2001) *What Schools for the Future?* Paris: OECD, Chapter 3 'Scenarios for the Future of Schooling'.
OECD (2002) *Knowledge and Skills for Life: First Results from PISA 2000*, Executive Summary, Paris: OECD (data underlying PISA available on www.pisa.oecd.org).
OECD (2003) *Education at a Glance 2003*, Paris: OECD.
Office for Standards in Education (1998) *School Evaluation Matters*, London OfSTED.
Office for Standards in Education (2000) *Handbook for Inspection*, London OfSTED.
OfSTED (2002) *Inspection Report on Cheddington Combined School*, Leighton Buzzard, Hertfordshire.
Ogle, L. T., Sen, A., Pahlke, E., Jocelyn, L., Kastberg, D., Roey, S. and Williams, T. (2003) International Comparisons in Fourth Grade Reading Literacy: Findings from the Progress in International Reading Literacy (PIRLS) of 2001 on line from National Center for Education Statistics nces.ed.gov/surveys/pirls.
Ohmae, K. (2000) *The Invisible Continent: Four Strategic Imperatives of the New Economy*, London: Nicholas Brealey.
Orange, C. (2002) *The Quick Reference Guide to Educational Innovations*, Thousand Oaks, CA: Corwin Press.
Papert, S. (1993) *The Children's Machine: Rethinking School in the Age of the Computer*, New York: Basic Books.
Parikh, J. (1994) *Intuition: The New Frontier of Management*, Oxford: Blackwell.
Pascale, R. (1990) *Managing on the Edge*, London: Penguin.
Pedler, M. (1996) *Action Learning for Managers*, London: Lemos and Crane.
PDI (1995) *The Principal Development Inventory*. Fadden, Australian Capital Territory: Sawatzki Consulting Group International.
Perkins, D. (1995) *Outsmarting IQ – The Emerging Science of Learnable Intelligence*, New York: Free Press.
Pietersen, W. (2002) *Reinventing Strategy: Using Strategic Learning to Create and Sustain Breakthrough Performance*, New York: John Wiley.
Plant, R. (1987) *Managing Change and Making it Stick*, London: Fontana.
Postman, N. (1996) *The End of Education*, New York: Vintage.
Prahalad, C.K. and Hamel, G. (1990) 'The core competence of the corporation', *Harvard Business Review*, 68: 79–93.
Pugh, D. (1993) 'Understanding and managing organisational change', in Mabey, C. and Mayon-White, B. (eds) *Managing Change*, second edition London: Paul Chapman/Open University.
Putnam, R.T. and Borko, H. (2000) 'What do new views of knowledge and thinking have to say about research on teacher learning?', Moon, B., Butcher, J. and Bird, E. (eds) *Leading Professional Development in Education*, London: RoutledgeFalmer with the Open University.
Reay, D. and Wiliam, D. (2001) 'I'll be a nothing': Structure, agency and the construction of identity through assessment', in Collins, J. and Cook, D. (eds) *Understanding Learning*, London: Paul Chapman Publishing with the Open University.
Revans, R.W. (1983) *ABC of Action Learning*, Bromley, Kent: Chartwell-Bratt.
Rittel, H. and Webber, M. (1973) 'Dilemmas in a general theory of planning', *Policy Sciences*, 4: 155–69.

Sanders, T. I. (1998) *Strategic Thinking and the New Science*, New York: Free Press.
Schwenk, C. R. (1997) 'The case for "weaker leadership"', *Business Strategy Review*, 8(1): 4–9.
Scottish Executive (2003) *Standards for Headship*. www./scotland.gov.uk/library5/education/shss.pdf
Seltzer, K. (1999) 'A whole new way of learning', *New Statesman*, special supplement on the theme Knowledge is Power! 27 September, pp. xvii–xix.
Selznick, P. (1984) *Leadership in Administration: A Sociological Interpretation*, Berkeley: University of California Press.
Senge, P.M. (1990) *The Fifth Discipline: The Art and Practice of the Learning Organisation*, New York: Doubleday.
Sergiovanni, T. (1992) *Moral Leadership*, San Francisco, CA: Jossey-Bass.
Sergiovanni, T. (1996) *Leadership for the School House*, San Francisco, CA: Jossey-Bass.
Sharpe, F.G. (1995) 'Educational leadership for the twenty-first century', *The Practising Administrator*, 2.
Shepard, L.A. (1991) 'Will national tests improve learning', *Phi Delta Kappan*, 73: 232–8.
Sheridan, G. (1999) *Asian Values, Western Dreams*, St Leonards, Sussex: Allen & Unwin.
Spender, D. (1995) *Nattering on the Net: Women, Power and Cyberspace*, North Melbourne: Spinifex.
Stacey, R. D. (1992) *Managing the Unknowable: Strategic Boundaries between Order and Chaos in Organisations*, San Francisco, CA: Jossey-Bass.
Stalk, G., Evans, P. and Schulman, L. (1992) 'Competing on capabilities: the new rules of corporate strategy', *Harvard Business Review*, 70(2): 57–69.
Sternberg, R. J. (2002) 'Wisdom, schooling and society', keynote presentation to the 2002 International Thinking Skills Conference, Harrogate, UK.
Stewart, T. A. (1997) *Intellectual Capital: The New Wealth of Organisations*, London: Nicholas Brealey.
Stoll, L., Fink, D. and Earl, L. (2002) *It's about Learning (and it's about Time)*, London: RoutledgeFalmer.
Stoll, L. and Myers, K. (1998) *No Quick Fixes: Perspectives on Schools in Difficulty*, London: RoutledgeFalmer.
Swanson, A. D. and King, R. A. (1997) *School Finance: Its Economics and Politics*, second edition, New York: Longman.
Tichy, T. and Sharman, S. (1993) *Control Your Destiny or Someone Else Will*, New York: Doubleday.
TTA (1997) *National Standards for Headteachers*. London: HMSO.
TTA (1998a) *National Standards for Subject Leaders*. London: HMSO.
TTA (1998b) *National Standards for Special Needs Co-ordinators*. London: HMSO.
TTA (2003a) *Qualifying to teach*. www.tta.gov.uk/qts standards/index.htm
TTA (2003b) *Induction Standards for Newly Qualified Teachers*, London: TTA.
Tuckman, B. (1965) 'Developmental sequence in small groups', *Psychological Bulletin*, 63: 384–399.
van der Heijden, K. (1996) *Scenarios: The Art of Strategic Conversation*, New York: John Wiley.
Volberda, H. W. and Elfring, T. (2001) *Rethinking Strategy*, London: Sage.
Wee, J. (1999) 'Improved student learning and leadership in self-managed schools',

Unpublished thesis for the degree of Doctor of Education, University of Melbourne.

Whitbourn S, *et al.* (2000) *What is the LEA for?* Emie, NfER.

Whittington R. (2001) *What is Strategy – and Does it Matter?* (second edition), London: Thomson Learning.

Willis, D. (1993) 'Learning and assessment: Exposing the inconsistencies of theory and practice', *Oxford Review of Education*, 19(3): 383–402.

Wilson, D. (1992) *A Strategy of Change: Concepts and Controversies in the Management of Change*, London: Routledge.

Wilson, J. M., George, J., Wellins, R.S. and Byham, W.C. (1994) *Leadership Trapeze: Strategies for Leadership in Team-based Organizations*, San Francisco, CA: Jossey-Bass.

Wise, D. (2003) 'Case study 2: Reengineering teaching and learning in the secondary school', in Davies B. and West-Burnham, J. (eds) *Handbook of Educational Leadership and Management*. London: Pearson.

Woessmann, L. (2001) 'School resources, educational institutions, and student performance: The international evidence', Kiel Institute of World Economics, University of Kiel (available at http://www.uni-kiel.de/ifw/pub/kap/2000/kap983.htm). Presented at the Annual Conference of the Royal Economic Society, Durham, April 9–11 2001.

USEFUL RESOURCES

André Haynes
Strategic Change and Quality Human Resources Group
Lloyds TSB Bank plc
1st Floor
71 Lombard Street
London EC3P 3BS

Business Link
Your local Business Link may be contacted through their national website:
www.businesslink.gov.uk/bdotg/action/home

Charter Mark
Full information on the award may be found at:
www.chartermark.gov.uk/

EFQM
General information on the wider application of the model:
www.efqm.org/

Investors in People Award
The award and its place in schools:
www.iipuk.co.uk/IIP/Internet/Investorsin People/Schools/default.htm

Lloyds TSB Quality in Education Program
Information on the adaptation of EFQM for specific use in schools plus CD-Rom 'Quality in Education'.

N.A.H.T.
School Self Evaluation – Primary Leadership Paper No. 1 (September 2000); www.naht.org.uk

The Numbers Game: Using Assessment data in Primary Schools
Hedger & Jesson, Shropshire County Council

OfSTED
Inspecting Schools: Handbook for Inspecting Nursery and Primary Schools: www.ofsted.gov.uk/

Scottish HMI. 'How good is our school?' is now available as a CD-Rom. This contains a wide-ranging set of performance indicators for school self-evaluation. See: www.hmie.gov.uk/documents/publication/cd/frames.htm

West Sussex. West Sussex have a comprehensive series of self evaluation materials available.

Index